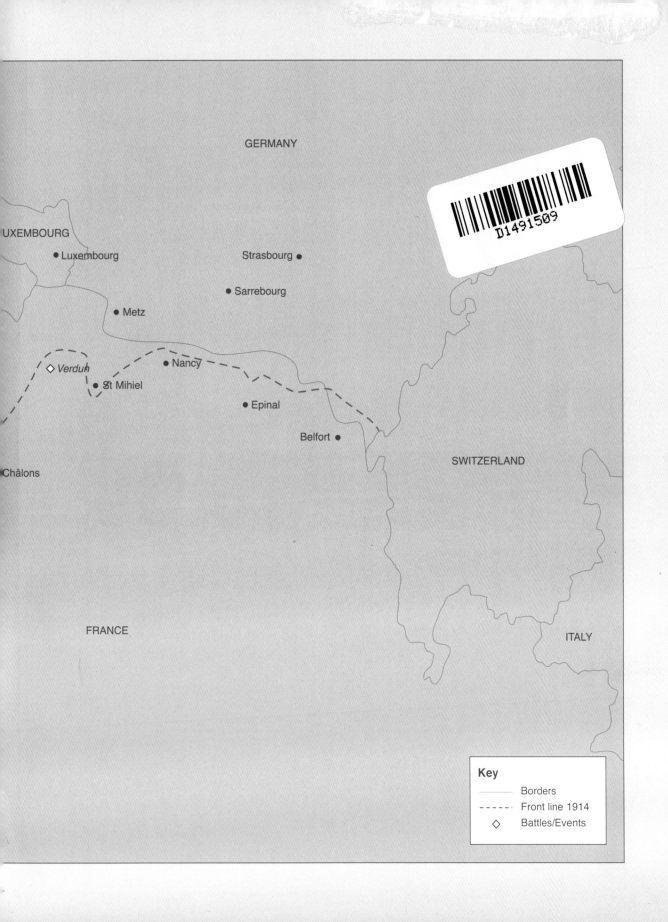

GERMANY

LUXEMBOURG

• Luxembourg

Strasbourg •

• Sarrebourg

• Metz

◇ Verdun

• Nancy

• St Mihiel

• Epinal

Belfort •

SWITZERLAND

Châlons

FRANCE

ITALY

Key

————— Borders

- - - - - Front line 1914

◇ Battles/Events

THE WESTERN FRONT
1914–1916

THE HISTORY OF WORLD WAR I

THE WESTERN FRONT
1914–1916

FROM THE SCHLIEFFEN PLAN TO VERDUN AND THE SOMME

MICHAEL S. NEIBERG

FOREWORD BY DENNIS SHOWALTER

amber
BOOKS

To John and Susan Lockley, for all of their support.

This edition first published in 2008
Reprinted in 2012

Published by
Amber Books Ltd
Bradley's Close
74–77 White Lion Street
London N1 9PF
United Kingdom
www.amberbooks.co.uk

ISBN: 978-1-906626-12-9

Ser ... Commissioning Editor: Charles Catton ...rd, UK
Pictur ... Bewsher, Terry Forshaw and Susannah Jayes
Design: Jerry Williams
... Aubrey
Indexer: Alison Worthington

For editorial or pi...ure enquiries please contact editorial@amberbooks.co.uk

Printed in Dubai

MAP SYMBOLS KEY

Infantry	Cavalry

XXXXX	XXXX	XXX	XX
Army Group	Army	Corps	Division

X	III	II	I
Brigade	Regiment/ Group	Battalion	Company/ Battery/ Squadron

ALLIED FORCES

BL Belgium
FR France
GR Greece
IT Italy
RO Romania
RU Russia
SE Serbia
US United States

BRITISH EMPIRE
AN ANZAC
AU Australia
BR British
CN Canada
IN India

CENTRAL POWERS

AH Austro-Hungary
BU Bulgaria
GE Germany
OT Ottoman Empire

OTHER NATIONALITIES

PO Poland

E.g.

GE

Contents

Foreword

World War I was limited in time and space, lasting only four years. Its outcome was determined in a single region—northern France and Flanders. Yet its unprecedented scale and cost created a spectrum of consequences, earning it another name: the Great War. That war was a Great Surprise. It was expected to be decisive and short. Instead it drew the entire world into an attritional death grapple whose outcome was uncertain until the end, and whose graves are scattered from Nova Scotia to Singapore. The Great War marked the end of European hegemony, the rise of the US and the Soviet Union as superpowers, and the emergence of the non-Western world on its terms. This conflict truly was the defining event of the twentieth century.

For all its impact, World War I remains shrouded in myth, mystery, and mourning. It exists as a series of disjointed images: old photographs and fragments of poems; devastated landscapes; anonymous soldiers scrambling over the top; above all, the endless cemeteries of the Western Front. *The History of World War I* returns that tragic conflict to the sphere of history. Based on a half-century of sophisticated research, incorporating state-of-the-art graphics, the six volumes of the series present the war on land, at sea, and in the air in a global context, and in human terms.

Dennis Showalter

A French cavalryman during a gas attack.

The Entente Cordiale

An 1898 Anglo-French conflict over control of the headwaters of the Nile nearly led to war between two traditional rivals. Although few could have predicted it, the incident led instead to the formation of the alliance that would see the two countries fight side by side for four terrible years.

The German High Seas Fleet was supposed to challenge the Royal Navy, but because it never reached anything close to parity it became instead a waste of money and was dismissed as a 'luxury fleet'. It lost its only large encounter with its British rival and spent most of the war in port.

The Anglo-French alliance that formed the heart of the coalition that defeated imperial Germany in 1918 had its origins not in Paris nor in London, but at the oasis of Fashoda at the headwaters of the Nile River in modern-day Sudan. There, in 1898, a French expedition from Senegal under the command of Captain Jean-Baptiste Marchand arrived to stake France's claim to Sudan. Under the terms of the 1884–85 Berlin Conference agreement the region belonged to the British sphere of influence, but the French hoped to exploit a clause in the agreement that required a colonial power to exercise effective control over a region or lose its claim to it. Britain's recent wars with rebellious Sudanese tribes led Marchand and his superiors to the conclusion that a march of more than 3200km (2000 miles) from Senegal to Sudan might be worth the risks involved if it allowed France to claim effective control over Sudan and add it to the growing French African empire.

Marchand's force was small, containing just seven officers and 120 Senegalese soldiers, but the British understood well enough the provocation they represented. The British dispatched their own force under the command of Horatio Kitchener, who had recently become a great hero in Britain after his defeat of Islamist Sudanese forces at the Battle of Omdurman. Three months after Marchand staked a French claim to Fashoda, Kitchener arrived there and demanded that Marchand leave British territory at once. Over champagne that Marchand's porters had lugged through jungle and gin that Kitchener's river boats had supplied, the two men politely discussed the

situation, but Marchand refused to leave without orders to that effect from his government.

The incident at Fashoda was simply the latest act in the long-running drama between France and Britain for control of imperial possessions. France had lost North America and India to the British as a consequence of the Seven Years War, but the French sensed an advantage over the British as a result of their growing power in Africa. Fashoda would allow France to create a contiguous empire through the middle of Africa, cutting British possessions in Egypt away from her colonies south of the Sahara. Britain saw Sudan in equally grandiose terms as the key to forming a unified 'Cairo to the Cape' chain of colonies with the Nile River serving as its backbone. Fashoda thus became important in its own right and as another symbol of the long-running rivalry between the world's two greatest imperial powers.

In London and Paris, government officials and members of the general public demanded war to settle the issue. The French shouted that they had suffered enough at the hands of the British, who had out-manoeuvred France for control of Egypt and the French-built Suez Canal in the 1880s. The British, for their part, saw in Fashoda an attempt by the French to threaten their control of the canal and the Red Sea, and thus also British communications to the core of the empire in India. As tensions mounted, the Royal Navy began to mobilize and the French Army to move units closer to port cities in the event that they might need to be transferred overseas quickly. War seemed a real possibility.

Paul Cambon, France's ambassador in London, led the small group of cooler heads that sought to avoid war. Cambon saw Fashoda as a distraction from the larger Continental issues central to French security. He argued that a war between France and Britain for control of a relatively insignificant place like Sudan

Few would have predicted that the clash between the British and French at Fashoda in 1898 would lead to an alliance between the two powers. At the time, war between the two nations seemed a real possibility. Cooler heads quickly prevailed, however, leading to a tectonic shift in the European alliance system.

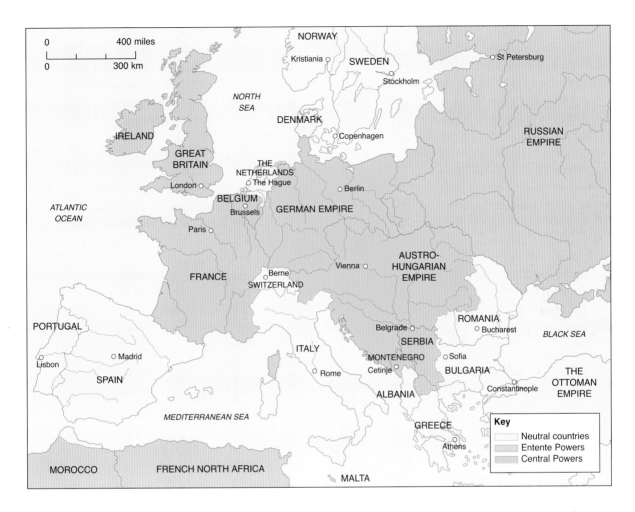

The redrawing of post-war Europe resulted in many new states, especially in Eastern Europe. The borders for almost all of them were the result of compromises based on national identity, economic viability and strategic realities.

would not be in either's best interests. Given France's naval inferiority, he doubted that France would win the war, and thus had plenty of motivation to find a way to avoid it. Perhaps most importantly, he understood that Anglo-French tensions in Africa played into the hands of Germany, a nation that Cambon saw as the biggest threat to European peace. He hoped to find a way to bind Britain, which had its own suspicions about German intentions, to France in some sort of diplomatic understanding. Tensions in Africa worked against this grand plan, while at the same time they encouraged German aggressiveness, and even opened up the possibility of Germany and Britain signing an alliance at France's expense.

Cambon thus worked out a deal that required France to withdraw from Fashoda in exchange for British recognition of a French sphere of influence in Morocco. The deal, Cambon knew, was far too good for the British to refuse because it gave them the Sudan they coveted without asking them to surrender any territory elsewhere. As Britain had no interests in Morocco, the agreement did not ask the British to do anything except recognize the reality of French influence there. French promises not to fortify its commercial bases in Morocco or put warships in ports near Gibraltar further sweetened the deal. Cambon was criticized by many of his fellow Frenchmen for giving away too much to the British, but he knew that the deal would pay enormous dividends in the future. Germany, not Britain, was France's most important rival for influence in Morocco; the deal bound Britain to support French claims there over the objections of Germany, thus placing a small but significant roadblock in the way of an Anglo-German agreement. Cambon had found a way to avoid war and tie the anti-German parties in France and Britain together.

As the dust settled on the Fashoda crisis, the British and French reached the conclusion that Cambon had anticipated. People on both sides of the Channel came to the view that Germany posed the greatest threat to their joint interests, and that Britain and France had more to gain by working together than continuing as rivals. France needed maritime help in the event of hostilities with Germany and the British needed a Continental ally with a powerful army to deter German expansionism. In the wake of Britain's costly war in South Africa (1899–1902) the British also needed time to rebuild their military and allies to help them diplomatically. An agreement with France could resolve many outstanding colonial issues and reduce the possibility of another large colonial war.

An Anglo-French agreement would also prove to be valuable to Britain on the high seas. In the same year as Fashoda, Germany passed a naval bill that called for the construction of 19 battleships, eight large cruisers, and 42 small cruisers. Believing the British to be economically strapped and strategically vulnerable after the South African War, the Germans passed another naval bill in 1900 that called for the construction of 38 battleships, 20 large cruisers, and 38 light cruisers within 20 years. The obvious target of this massive increase in naval construction was the British Home Fleet, which then had 32 battleships.

Dreadnoughts

The original Dreadnoughts displaced almost 22,000 tonnes (as opposed to the 15,000 tonnes displaced by most battleships of the time), featured 28cm (11in) nickel-steel alloy armour, ten 12in guns for destroying other large surface ships, 24 smaller guns to defend against torpedo boats, and an amazing cruising speed of 40km/h (21 knots). Simply put, the Dreadnought-class battleships were a revolution in naval warfare that made all other ships in the water obsolete. The British knew that other naval powers would soon follow suit and build similar ships, but they also knew that the French and Russian fleets of Dreadnoughts would serve as complements, not as rivals, to their own efforts. Germany, the British knew, would never be able to keep pace.

These two German appropriation bills proved to be money ill spent, as the British met the German challenge easily and had little trouble winning the ensuing naval arms race. The German threat to Britain at sea, moreover, inclined the British to talk more seriously with France, the country most threatened by Germany on land.

In 1904 British and French discussions led to a series of formal agreements known as the Entente Cordiale. Their official terms did little more than reinforce the realities in the two empires. The French reaffirmed their recognition of Egypt as a British zone of influence and the British reaffirmed their recognition of France's dominance in Morocco. A variety of other minor colonial questions, including the neutrality of Siam and the right of free passage through the Suez Canal, were also settled. The Entente fell far short of being an alliance; neither state

HMS *Dreadnought* instantly made all other ships at sea obsolete. Her appearance led to a naval arms race that impacted upon all of the great naval powers. Britain devoted enormous resources to winning that arms race, and as a result was clearly the dominant maritime power in 1914.

committed itself to come to the military aid of the other, nor did the Entente contain any provisions for joint military planning or coordination. Few contemporaries saw it as a landmark event in European diplomacy. Nevertheless, the agreement broke the ice that had existed between the two powers for centuries. The way was now cleared for a future of cooperation instead of competition.

GERMANY, RUSSIA AND THE EUROPEAN ALLIANCE SYSTEM

The Entente Cordiale did not mention Germany and it did not interfere with any diplomatic or economic agreement either side had with Germany. Still, the implications for Germany were clear. Britain and France would thereafter avoid the kinds of colonial conflicts that had kept them from acting together in diplomatic affairs. The Entente was therefore bad news for the Germans. A cartoon from a German newspaper showed a smug John Bull and a contemptuous Marianne (symbol of the French Republic, and depicted as a street tramp) walking arm in arm past an obviously miffed Kaiser Wilhelm II.

The Entente became more important as global events bound Britain and France together more closely. France brokered a deal between Britain and Russia (to whom France had been allied since 1894) that ended Anglo-Russian imperial rivalries in Central Asia. Britain, which had the world's largest navy, and Russia, which had the world's largest army, could now both focus energies on the shared threat they saw in German expansion. France, which saw the same threat, felt more confident that it would have diplomatic, and maybe even military, support in the event of German aggression.

That support was not long in coming. German diplomats assumed that the Entente Cordiale could not possibly be as strong as the paper on which it was

Britannia and Marianne, the symbol of the French Republic, shake hands. The Entente Cordiale between the two traditional foes changed the power dynamic of Europe. The entry of Russia into this alliance system at once ended most imperial rivalries and terrified German military planners.

printed. They therefore decided to put it to the test. In 1905 an increasingly bellicose Kaiser Wilhelm II tried to pry Morocco away from France on the expectation that the British would not risk a confrontation for France's sake and thus prove themselves fickle allies. Instead, the British, fearful that the Germans sought to use links to the Moroccans to build Atlantic ports for their growing fleet, defended France's claims, as did Russia. In a further show of solidarity, the French and British began joint staff talks in 1906 and increased the level of regular military visits between senior officers of the two armies and navies. Amid this environment of escalating European tensions, the British made two critical decisions, the building of HMS *Dreadnought* and the creation of a British Expeditionary Force (BEF).

Kaiser Wilhelm's childish envy of his cousin George V's fleet led him to undertake another massive shipbuilding programme in 1908. In the ensuing two years, the Germans came close to matching British naval expenditures, but the British replied with increases to their own appropriations, adding eight new Dreadnought-class battleships in 1909 and 1910. The British adopted a two-power standard that pledged the government to fund a navy equal in size to the next two largest navies in the world combined, regardless of whether those navies belonged to friendly or hostile states. The Germans could not keep up the pace, but the naval arms race between the two powers increased British suspicions about German grand designs. The British people also grew concerned about German intentions: German invasion schemes became common themes in British popular fiction. Wilhelm's threats and Germany's commitment to defence spending seemed to confirm British fears. As a result, all of the great powers increased their defence budgets, even in an age of generally liberal economic attitudes. Between 1909 and the outbreak of war in 1914, European defence spending rose by 50 per cent and the percentage of European GDP spent on defence rose from three and a half to five per cent.

Continental tensions rose further in 1911 when the Germans made another power play for Morocco. The Kaiser dispatched a powerful German warship to the Moroccan port of Agadir to back up demands for more German economic concessions in the region. The British, who had more annual trade with Germany than with France, agreed with the Germans in principle on the grounds of the general British belief in free trade, but most Britons saw the German dispatch of a warship for the threat it was. The Royal

Navy went on alert once again, and the British Chancellor of the Exchequer, the charismatic Welsh orator David Lloyd George, announced in a public speech that 'peace at that price [German control of Morocco] would be a humiliation intolerable for a great country like ours to endure'.

The great powers found a compromise solution that diffused the tension, but none of them came away happy. The Germans were convinced that Britain, Russia and France had agreed to encircle Germany and deny it the place in the world that it deserved. The British and French had learned once again the value of standing together against German aggression. The two soon agreed to a naval convention that gave France the responsibility for securing the Mediterranean Sea in the event of war (largely against Italy and Austria-Hungary, both of which possessed Dreadnought-class

Lord Kitchener had volunteered to fight with France in 1870 and had played a key role against France at Fashoda. In 1914 he was one of the few officials predicting a long, costly war. His face graced countless recruiting posters. In 1916 he died en route to Russia when a German U-boat sunk his ship.

battleships and were bound to Germany by alliance), while the British assumed responsibility for the North Sea. The generals of the two states also grew closer together, exchanging annual official visits and discussing ways to work together.

Despite these growing links, British officials were careful to guard their freedom of action. They repeatedly argued that nothing in the Entente Cordiale or any other Anglo-French agreement bound the British to go to war even if the Germans actually invaded France. In reality, however, the British had made too many commitments to France to back down in the event of a crisis. The Triple Alliance that Britain had agreed to with France and Russia had been a fundamental part of the larger British strategy of ensuring a balance of power on the Continent. A German attack on France would threaten that balance of power too much to allow the British to remain neutral. Although there were some signs of a thaw in Anglo-German relations after the Agadir crisis, German aggression on the Continent was simply too risky for the British to leave unchallenged.

For their part, the French worked to find ways to bind the British more closely to a joint defence of northern France and Belgium. Although neither government supported formal joint military planning, the basic outlines of joint defence had been worked out informally. France's war planning, covered in the following chapter, essentially left the Franco-Belgian frontier unguarded, and thereby created a natural area of deployment for the BEF. Some French generals, most notably the Ecole Supérieur de la Guerre commander General Ferdinand Foch, had formed close personal friendships with British generals and used those friendships to urge the British to send the BEF to Europe as soon as possible in the event of a major crisis. Foch and others concluded that even a small early British commitment to Continental operations would create a symbolic link between the

French and British war efforts that the British would have to honour no matter how long the war turned out to be. French officers argued that by the time a Royal Navy blockade took effect, the war on land would likely be over. Thus, in Foch's words the British fleet would not be worth a single bayonet. The rapid deployment of the BEF to the Continent, on the other hand, might form the critical margin of difference.

None of these discussions, however, committed Britain to any specific course of action when the July crisis, brought on by the assassination of Austrian Archduke Franz Ferdinand on 28 June 1914, began. British officials continued to stress that no public or secret agreement existed that bound the British to go to war. Prime Minister H.H. Asquith assured Parliament that Britain maintained absolute freedom in its policy. Strictly speaking, he was correct, but Britain had made many commitments to France and had based its entire Continental policy on the maintenance of the integrity of the borders of Western Europe. As officials such as British Foreign Secretary

Paul Cambon brokered the diplomatic deal that ended the Fashoda crisis. He helped to negotiate the Entente Cordiale in 1904 and remained France's ambassador to Great Britain for the duration of World War I. He worked hard to ensure British support for French interests throughout the war.

Kaiser Wilhelm II (1859–1941)

 Kaiser Wilhelm was a cousin of both King George V of Great Britain and Tsar Nicholas II of Russia. His bombastic and often unpredictable behaviour led many, including his grandmother Queen Victoria, to think that he was mentally unstable. Many people in Europe blamed his provocative foreign policy for two tense diplomatic crises in Morocco in the pre-war years. The Kaiser's schemes, however, backfired when they unexpectedly brought the British and French closer together. When the July crisis threatened to lead to war in 1914, he gave the Austrians the famous 'blank cheque' promise of support that led the Austro-Hungarian Empire to take a firm stance against Serbia. Nevertheless, there is some evidence that he tried to go to war with Russia exclusively, only to be told by his military advisers that the Schlieffen Plan did not allow for such a contingency.

As that episode reveals, the Kaiser's military knowledge was not as deep as he liked to believe. As the war went on, he became increasingly irrelevant to German military operations. By the middle of the war, Germany's senior commanders had largely stopped even informing him of many of their key decisions. In the last few days of the war, he realized that Germany was beaten and fled into exile in Holland. Despite pressure from the British and French governments to hand him over for trial as a war criminal, the Dutch refused. He died in Holland in 1941, just days before another German army invaded Russia.

Sir Edward Grey realized, Britain had tied its own security so closely to that of France that if France were threatened, Britain would have little choice but to commit to its defence with both the Royal Navy and the BEF.

AN ASSASSINATION IN SARAJEVO

It is important to recall that the July crisis primarily involved questions in Eastern Europe. Few Britons thought that the assassination of the archduke would lead to a general European war. If two Moroccan crises and the naval arms race had been settled without war, surely this crisis could be managed as well. British diplomats thus did not panic as a result of the assassination; Grey himself saw no reason to cancel a fishing trip. Instead, he and others planned to host a conference of the great powers once cooler heads began to prevail with an eye towards resolving the Balkan dispute peacefully.

Britain had plenty of good reasons to seek peace in 1914. British public opinion still retained significant ambivalence towards France, and the British business community relied heavily on its commercial ties to Germany. More importantly, Britain had its own crisis to deal with in the debates over Irish Home Rule. A bill promising Ireland semi-autonomy within the British Empire sat before Parliament that spring, pitting Liberals (who favoured the measure) against Unionists (who opposed it). In April, a contingent of Unionist Anglo-Irish British Army officers stationed at Curragh barracks in County Kildare announced that they would not obey orders to enforce Home Rule on Irish Protestants. The situation became tense enough to lead King George V to ask Parliament not to vote on the Home Rule bill for fear of it sparking a civil war in Ireland between Protestants (who had the support of the army) and Catholics (who would mostly benefit from Home Rule). The crisis led to the resignation of the secretary of state for war and the appointment of a new commander for the BEF just as the British Army needed stability to deal with the crisis in the Balkans. Tension in Ireland occupied much more British attention than the assassination of a little-known Austrian potentate.

The situation changed dramatically when Austria issued its ultimatum to Serbia on 20 July. The Austrians, with full German support, had written the ultimatum in such a way that they knew the Serbs could never accept it. They would then have the diplomatic cover they needed to declare war on Serbia and eliminate what they saw as the primary threat to their dominance in southeastern Europe. Diplomats and generals across the Continent immediately saw the danger. Russia, which shared political and religious links with Serbia, was unlikely to allow the Austrians to eliminate Serbia as a sovereign state. War between Austria and Serbia would thus mean war between Austria and Russia as well. Owing to the nature of the alliance system, such wars might drag in Germany and France. Italy and Britain, whose interests were less directly threatened, might be inclined to fight as well.

> 'The lamps are going out all over Europe; we shall not see them lit again in our lifetime.'
>
> Sir Edward Grey, British Foreign Secretary

THE PROBLEM OF BELGIUM

Germany's support for Austria's ultimatum, more than any other act, led the Continent to war in 1914. The Germans had concluded that their time was running out as the Russians completed a recovery from their disastrous defeat at the hands of Japan in 1904–05 and as the French moved from a two-year military obligation for young men to a three-year obligation. The Russian railway network, using French investment capital, would be complete in 1917, allowing for troops to be moved from the vast Russian interior to the front much more quickly. At the same time, the effects of the French three-year law would begin to take effect, vastly increasing the number of Frenchmen under arms. The Germans had therefore decided that their chances of winning a war in 1914

First cousins Kaiser Wilhelm II and King George V. Both were also related to Tsar Nicholas II. The personal relationships between the three sovereigns were cordial, but Wilhelm harboured a deep jealousy of the imperial power and Royal Navy of George V.

were better than they would be in the coming years. Even though they had scant faith in the military capability of their Austro-Hungarian allies, the Germans hoped to use the Austrian ultimatum to Serbia as the pretext for a war that they saw as in their best immediate interests.

German involvement in the Balkan crisis changed the strategic picture immeasurably. British and French generals had already divined the general outline of German war plans. Few of them expected the Germans to attack France's powerful line of border fortifications that guarded valleys and river crossings along the line Verdun–Toul–Epinal–Belfort. The only other logical avenue of approach was through Belgium, a prospect that worried the British more than the French. As early as 1908 British generals had begun designing likely scenarios of German invasions through Belgium. In almost all cases, they assumed these movements to have as their ultimate goal German control over Belgian ports, and therefore they represented in British eyes the first steps in broader German plans to invade southern England. The British general Sir Henry Wilson had even begun taking bicycling holidays in Belgium to familiarize himself with the terrain he expected one day to have to defend. Unbeknownst to Wilson, several German officers, most notably Erich Ludendorff, had also begun to vacation in Belgium.

Belgium presented a touchy political issue for British and French politicians. It was a neutral country not involved in either of the two major European alliance systems. Lying on a traditional invasion route and possessing cultural and linguistic ties to both France and Germany, it had achieved independence from the Netherlands in 1830. Nine years later, Britain helped to craft an agreement that kept Belgium politically neutral in order to avoid it being occupied by either France or Prussia (later Germany). Ironically, the British originally understood the neutrality scheme as a way to keep the French from dominating the Low Countries. Over time, the Belgians came to

Archduke Franz Ferdinand and his commoner wife Sophie. Neither was popular in the Viennese court, both because of their unconventional marriage and Franz Ferdinand's plans for reform of the empire. His assassination nevertheless gave Austria-Hungary the excuse it needed for war.

take great pride in what they saw as positive neutrality. Under this concept, the Belgians could possess an armed force and take active measures of self-defence, but they could not enter into any arrangements for collective security with another power. If attacked they could defend themselves and they could also call for help from the other guarantors of their neutrality according to the 1839 treaty. The Germans had inherited the Prussian signature to that treaty, and Belgian leaders assumed that Germany posed no greater threat than France or, for that matter, Britain.

Nevertheless, the Belgians could read a map, and as Franco-German tensions rose in the late nineteenth and early twentieth centuries, they understood the vulnerable position they occupied. From 1909 the Belgians began to take war planning more seriously and their new king, Albert I, took a much more

personal interest in security matters than had his predecessor, his avaricious uncle Leopold II. Still reluctant to enter into any agreements that might jeopardize their cherished neutrality, the Belgians rejected alliance overtures from the British in 1911, which were drafted by the young Winston Churchill. They also infuriated Kaiser Wilhelm by rebuffing his veiled offers to give Germany strategic parts of Belgium in exchange for parts of French Flanders that Germany would seize in a future Continental war.

Given the increasing bellicosity of the European security environment, the Belgians took steps to improve their armed forces in the years prior to the war. They introduced a conscription scheme that built an army of 180,000 men and they also invested heavily in a ring of powerful fortifications along the Meuse and Sambre rivers. They included the fortress complex at Liège, which was one of Europe's most powerful, and Namur, closer to the French border. They also heavily fortified the critical port city of Antwerp and the capital at Brussels. These defences were designed to repel invaders coming from any direction, although many Belgian officials, including the king, realized that they were inadequate to resist any one of the great powers without the assistance of the others. Thus the Belgians were caught in a trap: they needed help from one of the great powers to survive a war, but their own neutrality forbade them from planning for that contingency. The king, moreover, had limited constitutional powers over the military in peacetime and could do little more than demand more money from Parliament to improve Belgian defences.

Aware of the Belgian Army's shortcomings, King Albert helped to usher in reforms in 1913. A new conscription law increased the theoretical size of the army to 300,000 men, although it would take five years to reach that number. Orders for new artillery pieces (placed, ironically enough, with the German firm Krupp) were still being filled when the 1914 crisis began. Thus the army was critically short of heavy weapons. Nevertheless, the Belgians decided on a policy of engaging and fighting any army that violated its neutrality. Army war plans envisioned halting an enemy at the Meuse River fortification of Liège, then, if necessary, falling back to Antwerp. The plan allowed for the contingency of fighting Germany, France or even an amphibious attack from the British, but it involved a surrender of precious strategic space to any invader.

Few Britons were worried about the archduke's death. The great event of the day was a Liberal proposal to grant Home Rule to Ireland. Protestants, such as Irish Unionist Edward Carson, seen here, opposed the plan, but links between the British Army and opponents of Home Rule created tensions.

Crowds gather in Paris to greet troops heading to the front. The middle class and city dwellers welcomed the outbreak of the war with much greater enthusiasm than people in the countryside, who tended to view it with resignation rather than enthusiasm.

In 1914 the Belgian Army was inadequate to the tasks it had set for itself. It had 14,000 regular, professional soldiers and another 70,000 men in the fortress garrisons. The army was critically short of rifles and had severe command and control problems owing to the bilingual nature of Belgian society. All officers were expected to be able to give and receive orders in French, but many enlisted men spoke only Flemish. The Belgians had just 16 aeroplanes and although King Albert showed great interest in aviation, the air service only had enough resources to develop a limited photo-reconnaissance capability. The Germans therefore expected to make rather short work of the Belgian Army, which it held in barely disguised contempt.

Although military officials in Britain and France had already assumed that the Germans would violate Belgian neutrality, their own war planning had to be very careful to avoid even the appearance that they were planning to conduct any operations in Belgium. Under no circumstances could the British or the French plan to enter Belgium until it was absolutely clear that the Germans had already done so. Neither could the British nor French hold any joint staff talks with their Belgian counterparts. British and French politicians were sensitive to the question of Belgian neutrality, both in order to safeguard their own promises and to make certain that Germany would appear the aggressor in any war in Western Europe.

Outward support for Belgium might also prove to be unpopular among French and British public opinion. Brutal Belgian behaviour in the Congo had stood out even among the generally oppressive conditions existing inside European colonies. The disreputable King Leopold II had treated the Congo as his own personal diamond mine, using especially cruel methods to enrich himself. Publicity about the horrors in the Congo led to an international movement (led in large part by Britons) that eventually forced Leopold to transfer control of the Congo from his personal hands to the Belgian Government. Although the scandals over the Congo ebbed under Albert, many humanitarians in Britain and France saw little worth defending in a Belgium that used blood money gained from the Congo to build fortifications to support its commercial interests.

In the years before the war, British officials grew more concerned about the possibility of the Germans moving north of the primary Belgian fortifications and into northern France. The gap between Liège and Antwerp, they believed, was too weakly held. If the German Army got past the Liège and Namur lines, there would be nothing to prevent them from moving along the Belgian and French English Channel coastlines. Control of the coastline would be the realization of the worst British nightmares, placing a hostile fleet close to the south coast of England itself. German threats to Belgium, therefore, represented more than a threat to British guarantees of that country's neutrality. A neutral Belgium was absolutely central to the security of Britain itself.

Paul Cambon, the architect of the Fashoda compromise, was still France's ambassador in London when Austria-Hungary delivered its ultimatum to

The Imperial German Army

The Imperial German Army or *Reichsheer* had only been formed in the aftermath of the successful Franco–Prussian War of 1870–71 from the armies of the four kingdoms of Bavaria, Württemberg, Baden and Prussia (with its allied North German Federation of smaller states). Each of the armies remained as separate entities with their own war ministries, but all except Bavaria's forces were headed by the Kaiser and his military cabinet; and although Bavaria had its own General Staff, in practice it co-ordinated closely with the Kaiser's Prussian-dominated General Staff in planning and operational matters. The many Prussian successes during the wars of German unification meant there was a notable rivalry between the Prussian and non-Prussian contingents of the army.

Serbia. On 1 August, as war seemed inevitable, Cambon asked British Foreign Secretary Sir Edward Grey when his country would enter the war. Although Grey had already decided to resign if his Government did not support France, he hedged his bets with Cambon, telling the French ambassador that as it then stood, the crisis was an Eastern European one that did not directly affect the interests of Great Britain. Cambon, who believed that a German invasion of France was imminent, asked Grey what event might make the crisis of central interest to the British. Grey replied that a German violation of Belgian neutrality might be such an event. Even as he spoke the words, German diplomats were preparing to deliver an ultimatum to the Belgian government: allow German forces to pass through or be treated as an enemy of Germany and prepare to face a 'decision of arms' to settle the issue.

While the Belgian Army may not have been as outdated as this image suggests, it was small and poorly funded. Most of Belgium's defence spending went into fortifications capable of defending major river crossings in the hope that the country might maintain its neutrality.

The Schlieffen Plan

The war began with many soldiers and politicians believing that it would be like the Wars of German Unification in the 1860s and 1870s – bloody, but lasting just a few months. They had accordingly planned for offensive warfare and most had not expected to fight more than one large campaign.

Beginning in the 1890s when Franco-Russian relations began to grow warmer, German generals became haunted by the prospects of fighting a two-front war. Although they knew that they could take advantage of what strategists call interior lines by moving men between the French and Russian fronts along Germany's excellent east–west rail network, the generals understood that Germany would be at a severe disadvantage in a lengthy two-front war. They began strategic planning with this concern at the forefront and added to it two other guiding assumptions: that the Franco-Russian alliance meant that any war with France or Russia meant war

German reservists head to war. The German war plan made much greater use of reservists than did the French. This gave the Germans more men in front-line units, but demanded a gargantuan effort from men who had been out of the army for many months or years.

with both, and that one of the two would need to be defeated quickly in order for Germany to focus its military assets against the other.

After 1894, Count Alfred von Schlieffen, the chief of the German general staff, drew the logical conclusion that Germany could not count on a quick defeat of Russia. For Schlieffen (born in 1833) and officers of his generation, the Napoleonic experience in Russia presented an absolutely nightmarish vision of endless operations with tenuous supply lines deep into the interior of a barren and hostile country. From these beginnings, Schlieffen came to another conclusion: Germany's best chance to avoid a two-front war involved attacking France first. He believed that France's capital, Paris, was within Germany's reach, and that its capture would win the campaign. On the other hand, he was enough of a student of history to know that Napoleon had marched through Moscow without winning a war. Moreover, he assumed that the

The German General Staff

After the Napoleonic Wars, the Prussian Army reformed itself to encourage the recruitment and formal training of future staff officers on merit alone. This system proved very successful under von Moltke the elder, and was adopted by the Imperial German Army upon its formation in 1871. The best young officers were systematically trained in strategy, tactics, logistics and administration so that a brief command from a general would be enough for his orders to be carried out. Critics have argued that this encouraged over-rigid planning.

large, but slow-footed Russians were incapable of a rapid mobilization, whereas the French could use their excellent railway network to concentrate forces against the German border. France thus had to be beaten first.

The biggest impediment to a German invasion of France rested in the powerful French fortifications that covered the major river crossings and rail centres from Verdun to the Swiss border. To avoid them, German forces would need to move to their north, but the space between Verdun and the Belgian border provided too little room to move forces and supplies in the numbers the Germans would need. Schlieffen thus decided that the invasion of France would require an invasion of neutral Belgium, Holland and Luxembourg. In so deciding, he effectively tied the hands of future German diplomats, few of whom were privy to the details of war planning.

Schlieffen designed an operation that would function as a swinging gate, with the 'post' anchored in Alsace. The rightmost units of the German sweep would move along the English Channel through the Low Countries, swing north and west of Paris, then turn southeast, enveloping the French capital and

Count Alfred von Schlieffen bequeathed to the German Army an offensive war plan that called for an attack on France regardless of the diplomatic crisis leading to hostilities. His plan, which included an invasion of neutral Belgium, converted a Balkan crisis into a Continental war.

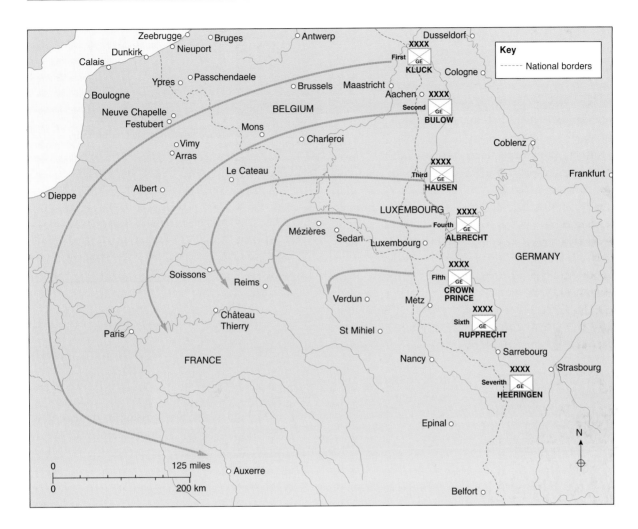

The Schlieffen Plan, modified by subsequent German commanders, demanded an almost impossible effort by German soldiers. They were to wheel around Paris and force the French out of the war in a mere six weeks. It took little account of the famous fog and friction of warfare.

trapping any French resistance inside a giant double pincer. The German right would act as the hammer, while the left (the 'post') would be the anvil. To ensure that his plan would have the forces needed to win this campaign in a mere six weeks, Schlieffen dedicated to it 1,750,000 men of the two million-man German Army he hoped to build. Once France had fallen, hundreds of thousands of these troops would be entrained and moved east by rail in time to defend the German eastern frontier against the now mobilized Russians.

The plan was far too risky and rigid, leaving little room for the fog and friction that always accompanies any large-scale human endeavour. It also presumed that Germany would have to make quick decisions,

perhaps even beginning military operations before war had been officially declared in order to give such a precarious plan the best chance of success. Consequently, the plan subsumed domestic politics, foreign policy and even grand strategy to the immediate operational need of the army to deploy into neutral nations as soon as possible. The details of the plan were closely guarded, and there is substantial evidence that even Kaiser Wilhelm failed to realize all of its implications. Rigging war games so that the

Kaiser's side always won did little to help him understand the military's many complexities.

Schlieffen retired in 1905, leaving the plan in the hands of a scion of one Germany's most legendary military families, Helmuth von Moltke (the younger). Moltke cancelled the invasion of Holland in order that Germany might have a neutral neighbour through which it could trade with the outside world. This change indicates that Moltke at least recognized the possibility that the plan might not work and that Germany might have to fight a two-front war after all.

The professionals of the British Expeditionary Force embark for France in 1914. The men were highly skilled soldiers, but their commanders had only worked out rudimentary arrangements with their French allies and had no shared war plan to implement.

Under Moltke's modifications, seven-eighths of the German Army would march west on the outbreak of war, whether the cause of the war was in the west, the east or even overseas, but Moltke placed fewer men on the extreme right wing of the advance in favour of assigning more men to the German left in Alsace and Lorraine. He appears to have been afraid of either a French breakthrough in the region or the impact on German morale if the French managed to take a symbolic city in the region such as Strasbourg or Metz.

The plan's call for an invasion of Belgium meant that it risked bringing the British into the war, but German soldiers showed little concern. If the war went as quickly as envisioned, then the entry into the war of the British would make little difference, as the Germans would be in Paris, sipping champagne and

Helmuth von Moltke (the younger) (1848–1916)

The chief of staff who replaced Schlieffen was the nephew of his namesake, the Helmuth von Moltke (the elder) who had designed Prussia's rapid victories in the wars of German unification (1864–71). The new chief of staff lacked Schlieffen's gambler's touch and made several modifications to the plans he inherited. Moltke had less confidence in himself and in the presumed superiority of the German Army over its French counterpart than his predecessor had. He is supposed to have reacted to his appointment by asking Wilhelm if he truly expected to win twice at the same lottery, an indication that he felt his job was more as a result of his famous name than his qualifications.

Moltke seen here with the Kaiser. Moltke always harboured doubts that the Kaiser had given him command of the German Army based more on his famous lineage than his abilities.

drafting one-sided peace terms long before the Royal Navy could put a blockade into effect. Moltke disregarded the small BEF, whose 100,000 men would make little difference in the face of nearly two million Germans. He assumed that the BEF would be swept up along with the Belgians by any advancing German forces. A disregard for the British Army ran rife through the German high command, with the Kaiser later dismissing the BEF as a 'contemptible little army'. Moltke himself once stated that if the BEF dared to deploy to the Continent he would send the Berlin police to arrest them. If, however, Moltke's plan did not work, then the vast resources of the British Empire, including the manpower of India, Canada, South Africa, Australia and New Zealand, might come into play. Even in his wildest imaginations, Moltke must have known that the Berlin police did not have enough handcuffs for that job.

Neither the Germans nor the Austrians were fully privy to their most important ally's war plans.

'It is my Royal and Imperial command that you concentrate your energies [and] … exterminate first the treacherous English and walk over General French's contemptible little army.'

Army order issued by Kaiser Wilhelm II, 19 August 1914

Consequently, while the Germans were planning to focus almost all of their energies on France, the Austrians were planning to move the vast majority of their forces south toward Serbia. If, as in fact happened, the Russians proved more adept at mobilizing than the Germans predicted, then no large-scale formations would be in a position to stop Russian forces from invading East Prussia, the traditional home of the German aristocracy, or the Hungarian breadbasket that would be critical to feeding soldiers and civilians alike if the British were able to put an effective blockade into place.

In late July when the Germans were considering their military options, Kaiser Wilhelm at first asked Moltke if the army could prepare for operations in the east only. Moltke informed him that such a deployment was not possible; every aspect of German war planning and resource allocation had been hardwired for years to attack France first. Changing strategic direction at such a late date and without any appropriate war

planning would cause tremendous confusion and traffic tie-ups. Wilhelm looked at Moltke and icily said 'Your uncle would have given me a different answer', although he had no choice but to accept Moltke's assessment of the likely outcome of any late changes.

THE GERMAN INVASION OF BELGIUM

The Schlieffen Plan as finally implemented divided the German Army into eight field armies. The German First Army would be the strongest, containing 320,000 men. It would sweep through the Belgian cities of Louvain and Brussels, cross into France near Lille and be on the Seine River northwest of Paris in just 37 days. Operating just to its south, the Second Army

The magazine rifle was supposed to be the main weapon of the war. Especially when fitted with a bayonet, it was supposed to be an expression of the individual soldier's élan. In the end, however, most soldiers would be killed by more impersonal weapons like machine guns and artillery pieces.

would clear the Belgian fortress cities of Liège, Namur and the French fortress at Maubeuge, arriving on the Oise River north of Paris shortly after the First Army had reached the Seine. The German Third Army would advance to Soissons, the Fourth to Reims and the Fifth to the Argonne Forest just west of Verdun. The left wing of the German Army, the Sixth and the Seventh Armies, would hold prepared defensive positions in Alsace and Lorraine. Only the German Eighth Army would deploy to the east to keep the Russians at bay until the surrender of France permitted German reinforcements and new call-ups to move east.

The ambition of the Schlieffen Plan is breathtaking. It demanded superhuman efforts from German soldiers, few of whom were in the hardened physical shape they would need to make long forced marches against active opposition. To increase the number of men in the field armies, the Germans planned for extensive use of reserve troops, whose training and physical fitness were both considerably inferior to those of first-line troops. German logistical preparations, moreover, were wholly inadequate to the task of keeping hundreds of thousands of men supplied. Most importantly, the Schlieffen Plan, by drawing the British and French empires into a conflict that did not involve their core interests, converted a Balkan crisis into a world war.

The Schlieffen Plan was only part of the war's early months. The French responded with their own plan, Plan XVII, which concentrated force in the centre. French troops advanced into the 'lost provinces' of Alsace and Lorraine with little gain and huge casualties.

FRENCH WAR PLANS

The French had guessed the general outlines of the German plan. They envisioned that the Germans would indeed avoid the powerful French fortifications and try to outflank the French by moving through Belgium. On taking command in 1911, French general Joseph Joffre discarded his predecessor's essentially defensive French war plan, known as Plan XVI. He had concluded that the French Army would need to be more aggressive and more offensively minded in the opening weeks and months of war for two reasons. First, the French Army, he believed, had a moral obligation to liberate the 'lost provinces' of Alsace and Lorraine, which the Germans had taken from France

German schoolchildren learn how to throw bombs during hand grenade training. Grenades were an integral part of trench warfare, allowing men to hit targets underground or around the blind curves of a trench system. Grenades could also be launched from a rifle or dropped out of an airplane.

in 1871. Although few Frenchmen in 1914 sought war to recover the provinces, once war began their reconquest became a war aim that Frenchmen of all political stripes could rally around. Second, Joffre believed that the French Army had to conduct an offensive in the early weeks of the war to prevent the German Army from deploying massive resources on the Eastern Front until the Russians were mobilized and ready to meet the challenge.

Joseph Joffre (1852–1931)

Chief of the French general staff, General Joseph Joffre was an engineer and a supposed expert in railways who had made a name for himself in a number of French colonial operations. He was also a moderate republican by political inclination, having once impressed anti-clerical French politicians by demanding to be served meat at a state dinner during Lent. He kept his opinions on the political issues of the day to himself, and was for a time nicknamed 'The Crab', able to move forward slowly, and incapable of rapid movements to either the left or the right. He was a safe compromise choice to command the French Army, even if he was far from the most experienced or brilliant of French generals.

While Joffre understood the outlines of German war planning, he underestimated the total number of German soldiers in the original attack on France, especially in its right wing, the German First and Second armies. Joffre assumed that the Germans did not have enough men to simultaneously defend East Prussia against the Russians, defend Alsace and Lorraine, and advance past the major Belgian fortification lines. If they did try all three operations at once, he assumed, they would create a critical weakness somewhere. His strategic thinking therefore revolved around concentrating his forces in such a way as to allow him to be ready to strike the weakness once he had determined it.

Although the French Government gave Joffre a remarkable degree of flexibility in deciding on matters of French strategy, it did hamstring him by forbidding the French Army to enter Belgium unless it was absolutely certain that the Germans had done so first. French diplomats wanted to be as clear as possible to

their British counterparts that the Germans, not the French, had been the first to violate the neutrality of Belgium. They were afraid that the British might remain neutral if French forces were the first to enter Belgium. Joffre foresaw that French troops would need to enter Belgium as early as possible, in an extreme case perhaps even before the Germans did so, but he hid this element of his thinking from French politicians, telling them that he was planning for nothing more than a concentration of forces near the Belgian border ostensibly to guard against German aggression.

Joffre's war plan, Plan XVII, was more cautious than the Schlieffen Plan and gave the French commander much more flexibility than his German counterpart. It envisioned two French armies, the First, based west of the Vosges Mountains near Epinal, and the elite Second, based around Nancy, liberating Alsace and Lorraine with swift attacks. They would erase the stain of the humiliation of 1871 and place direct and immediate pressure on the German homeland that would both disrupt any offensive the Germans planned against France and force the Germans to hold back troops that might otherwise

have been dispatched east against the Russians. Such an offensive would also allow Joffre to honour promises he had made to the Russians in 1912 that he would conduct a 'vigorous and determined' offensive with 1,300,000 men within 10 days of mobilization.

Joffre dedicated the French Third, Fourth and Fifth armies to deal with the German right wing's

The remnants of the Belgian Army retreating. Although small and poorly equipped, they regrouped and held parts of the line near the North Sea. Led by their king, Albert I, they remained in the line during the remainder of the war, hoping for a chance to liberate their occupied nation.

movement through Belgium. Assuming that the Germans would deploy more than one field army in the east, Joffre badly underestimated the number of German soldiers that would move west. Plan XVII placed the French Third Army just south of Verdun and the Fifth Army near Sedan. The French Fourth Army sat in reserve behind the Argonne Forest near Bar le Duc. The plan afforded Joffre the flexibility to see what the German Army was doing and then design the most appropriate response to it. If the Germans did not move into Belgium or were held up at the border, then Joffre could send the French Fourth Army into Lorraine to exploit French successes there. If the German Army did in fact move through Belgium, then the French Fourth and Fifth armies

would move north, entering Belgium from the south and smashing into the German flank, thereby disrupting the German advance before it ever got to France. The plan thus allowed Joffre's forces to enter Belgium, but only after it had become clear that the Germans were already there.

Plan XVII left few forces on the Franco-Belgian border itself. It also did not include any formal provisions for the BEF to deploy to the left of the French Fifth Army, although Joffre repeatedly said after

British forces deployed onto the left flank of the French Army in Belgium. There had been little serious coordination between the allies, generating confusion and a lack of proper military liaison. Near Mons the British ran headlong into the powerful German First Army.

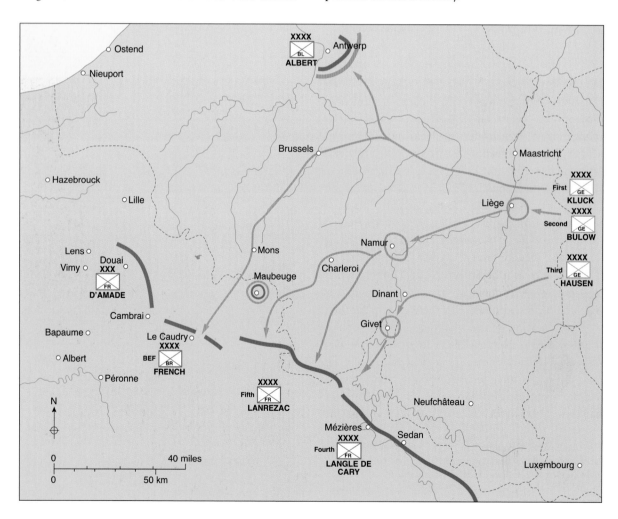

The Crown Princes

Both Prussia's Crown Prince Wilhelm (son of the Kaiser) and Bavaria's Crown Prince Rupprecht held senior army commands at the outbreak of the war, largely owing to their noble births. In the highly professional German system, most of their key decisions were made by their chiefs of staff. Over the course of the war, however, both men learned to lead capably. Wilhelm in particular shed his playboy image and played important roles at several critical battles, most notably at Verdun. He developed a much more accurate understanding of the nature of the war than his father, and in 1917 he had urged German diplomats to consider a compromise peace because he had concluded that Germany could not win. After the

war, he lived in Holland with his father until 1923. He then returned to Germany, but refused to support the Nazis. He died in 1951.

Rupprecht's career followed a similar path. By 1916 he had become one of the most highly regarded royal commanders in any army. In recognition of his accomplishments, he was promoted to field marshal in 1916 and spent most of the remainder of the war as an army group commander in Flanders. After the war, he lost his claim to the royal house of Bavaria and retired from politics. He opposed the rise of the Nazis and spent World War II living quietly in Florence. To punish him, the Nazis sent many of his relatives to political prisons. He died in 1955.

the war that he was fully confident the BEF would do just that. If and when the British did arrive, they would place more pressure on the German right either by reinforcing the French left or by deploying to the north of the German advance somewhere near Antwerp. Joffre therefore saw the danger of a German invasion through Belgium, but he believed that for political and military reasons the best way to defeat it was not to meet it head on. Rather, he presumed that he could disrupt it by striking its southern flank or by launching a successful invasion into Alsace and Lorraine.

In late July, as it became increasingly obvious that the Germans were mobilizing and preparing to invade Belgium, Joffre demanded that the French order their own mobilization. France's president, the nationalist Lorraine native Raymond Poincaré, and the recently appointed socialist premier, René Viviani, were on their way back from a pre-planned state visit to Russia and did not return to Paris until 29 July. The Austrians had cleverly issued their ultimatum to Serbia while the

German general Alexander von Kluck commanded the German First Army in the war's early months. His forces were supposed to move around Paris and encircle the French capital from the west, but they were unable to complete this very ambitious mission.

General Max von Bülow commanded the German Second Army, to Kluck's left. The demands of the march through Belgium caused a dangerous gap to develop between the two armies. After the allied victory on the Marne, he advocated withdrawing to defensible high ground along the Aisne River.

to withdraw 10km away from the frontiers. He hoped the Germans would read the gesture as one of conciliation; France, after all, had no vital interests at stake if Germany did not invade. He also wanted to avoid an accidental border conflict that the Germans could use to allege that the French had entered Germany or violated Belgian neutrality. Joffre was furious with the decision, warning the government that any delay in mobilization could cause France to lose its eastern provinces without a shot being fired in their defence. On 1 August, he told the government that every minute they delayed mobilization put the future of France in jeopardy. He even issued a thinly veiled threat that if they did not order mobilization soon, he could accept no responsibility for the defence of France and he might resign. At 3.30 that afternoon, the war minister, Adolphe Messimy, finally authorized the French Army's mobilization, as German forces, themselves already mobilized, were putting the finishing touches on their pre-emptive invasion of Belgium and Luxembourg.

French leaders were at sea, giving the Germans and Austrians an important advantage in time, and therefore in preparations for mobilization of their armies. On their return, Joffre gave Poincaré and Viviani reports showing that German forces had advanced in some places to within a few hundred metres of the Belgian and French frontiers. The Germans had also issued an outrageous demand that the French cede their fortresses of Toul and Epinal to German control as a gesture of their desire to avoid war. German press agents also falsely reported that French aircraft were routinely violating German airspace. Joffre correctly read these events as the first steps toward a German invasion of France and demanded that the government order the mobilization of the French Army. At the very least, he wanted furloughs cancelled, reservists activated and the French fleet sent to sea.

Instead, on 30 July Viviani, who had been in his job less than three weeks, told Joffre to order French forces

Franc tireurs

The issue of Belgian irregulars, known as *franc tireurs*, was particularly sensitive to Germans in 1914. The Germans had long memories of the French partisans who had threatened their supply lines and attacked isolated German soldiers in the 1870–71 war. Perhaps more importantly, *franc tireur* activity threatened to disrupt the careful timetables set by the Germans for their advance through Belgium, into France, and onto Paris. German officers, anxious that the guerrilla problem of 1870–71 not repeat itself, issued guidance that defined irregulars as war criminals and thereby subject to the most severe punishments.

Joffre immediately ordered a two-pronged advance into Alsace and Lorraine. He assumed that the main German force in the theatre, estimated by French intelligence officers to consist of six corps, would concentrate near Metz. Joffre therefore intended to send the French First and Second armies northeast through Lorraine, to attack the German left flank, while the French Third and Fourth armies moved east against the German right wing. A new army was quickly formed to protect the right flank of the French advance. If successful, the French double-pincer operation would trap thousands of German troops, encircle the German fortresses of Metz and Thionville and give France control of the coal and iron mines of the Briey basin. It would also liberate former French towns like Sarrebourg and Morhange.

French forces moved forward into Alsace and Lorraine on 14 August, as the Germans were then completing the encirclement of Liège in Belgium. At first, operations in the east seemed to go as planned. The French met little sustained resistance for the first

German soldiers in occupied Belgium. The Germans forcibly deported thousands of young Belgians to German factories and electrified the border with Holland to prevent Belgians from fleeing the country. They also forced war contributions from Belgian communities that far exceeded their occupation costs.

five days. Instead, the ethnically French residents of Alsace-Lorraine gave troops an ecstatic welcome, complete with wine, flowers and chocolates. A satisfied Joffre discounted the seriousness of the German movements through Belgium; he assumed that the Belgian fortifications and the arrival of the BEF, then concentrating near Amiens, would buy him time to complete the defeat of German forces in Alsace and Lorraine.

French intelligence had, however, underestimated the strength of the German positions badly. Instead of the six undersized corps they had reported to Joffre, the Germans in fact had eight full-strength corps, constituted as the Fifth and Sixth Armies, with 420,000 men between them. They had also concentrated reconnaissance aircraft in the region that gave them an excellent picture of the size and dispositions of French forces. Moreover, German units had intentionally withdrawn to carefully prepared mountain and forest positions that would be easier to defend. As French forces advanced into the forests, they lost contact with one another, creating dangerous gaps in the lines.

THE GERMANS IN BELGIUM

On 20 August, French forces unknowingly reached the main German line near Sarrebourg and Morhange. They advanced into a withering fire and, attired in bright red and blue uniforms, made particularly easy targets for concealed German riflemen and machine-gunners. One of the French corps, the elite XX Corps commanded by General Ferdinand Foch, had advanced, but those on his right and left had not, leaving XX Corps in a dangerously exposed position. Later in the day, the Germans took advantage of confusion in French lines and launched a determined counterattack that drove the French back and shattered the illusion of an easy liberation of the lost provinces. Second Army commander, General Edouard Noël de Castelnau, ordered his forces to retreat to the safety of a series of heights near Nancy known as the Grand Couronné. The retreat of the Second Army compelled its neighbouring units to do the same.

The German Army had carefully considered the problems posed by powerful French and Belgian fortifications. Their answers centred around modern steel artillery pieces which reduced even the strongest fortifications to rubble in astonishingly short periods of time.

By the time he gave the order on 24 August for French forces to withdraw, Joffre had come to realize the extent of the threat that the German advance through Belgium posed. The Germans had managed to advance further in Belgium than Joffre and his commanders had envisioned because of three key factors: first, they had placed their reserves into front-line units, giving their armies more men for manoeuvres and laying siege to the main Belgian forts than the French had anticipated; second, they had entered Belgium and Luxembourg even before the official issuance of the declaration of war, thus catching their enemies flat-footed; and third, they had brought into Belgium powerful artillery pieces specially designed to make short work of the powerful Belgian forts.

The German advance through Belgium was the responsibility of the First, Second and Third armies. The First Army, with the most ground to cover and expecting to have to execute a complicated turning movement to the west of Paris, was the largest, with 320,000 men commanded by General Alexander von Kluck, an aggressive and energetic combat leader with a reputation for independence of mind. The Second Army, with 260,000 men, was commanded by the more cautious General Karl

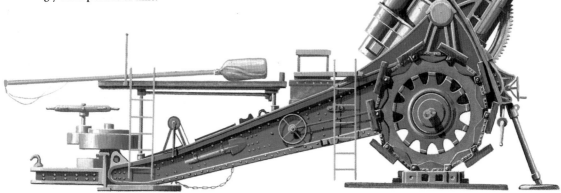

Liège

Belgian defence plans, and for that matter French plans as well, counted on the fortress complex at Liège providing a substantial obstacle to German movement through Belgium. Commanding the Meuse River railway crossings on the direct route to Brussels, Liège was vital to any German attempt to keep their men fed and supplied as they moved through Belgium into France. Liège boasted six large and six small forts built in 1891, but they looked more impressive on paper than they were in reality. Garrisoned by approximately 6000 largely second-rate troops and defended by obsolete artillery pieces, the forts were in poor condition. The rifle pits and trench lines outside the forts were also in bad shape, allowing the Germans to come much closer to the forts than they should have and approach them from the rear.

Operations against the forts were led by General Otto von Emmich's 60,000-strong force, which began crossing the Belgian border on the morning of 4 August. Liège itself fell on 7 August after the Belgian 3rd Division and 15th Brigade withdrew, and one by one the forts surrounding the city were battered into submission by the heavy German artillery fire. Only one fort, Fort Barchon, had to be assaulted by infantry on 10 August. The rest surrendered after being bombarded by shells that hit the forts from above and penetrated their concrete shell before the delayed fuse detonated. By 16 August all Belgian resistance in the area ceased.

The forts at Namur and Antwerp would later suffer similar punishment, with the German besiegers again victorious thanks to their heavy artillery.

von Bülow, and the Third, with 180,000 men was under the experienced General Max von Hausen.

The Germans had thought long and hard about how best to eliminate Belgium's powerful Liège fortifications quickly and expeditiously. In the years before the war German General Erich Ludendorff had taken frequent holidays in the region, carefully making calculations and recording observations on the terrain. By 12 August, Ludendorff, then a senior officer in the Second Army charged with taking Liège, was ready to deploy enormous 305mm and 420mm artillery pieces that were more than strong enough to pierce the concrete and metal defences of the Liège forts. By 16 August, the forts on which so much of the defence of Belgium had been predicated had fallen. Ludendorff himself pounded on the doors of the citadel with the hilt of his sword to demand the garrison's surrender. For his efforts, he received the prestigious *Pour le Mérite* medal, only the second awarded by Germany since the war's beginning. The German Second Army moved on to Namur, with powerful German artillery batteries levelling its forts in the amazingly short time of just two days.

THE BEF AND THE RETREAT FROM MONS

As a result of the shake up that followed the Curragh incident, the BEF received a new commander, Sir John French, on 30 July and Britain also received a new secretary of state for war, none other than the same Horatio Kitchener who had headed the British mission to eject the French from Fashoda in 1898. Kitchener was a legend, a veteran of successes around the British Empire, brought in to reassure the British people of the competence of their military leaders. He immediately recognized that the war would be long and require an army of hundreds of thousands of men. Britain, he knew, would need months, perhaps years, to create such a force. Alone among the great powers, Britain had avoided peacetime conscription and, as a result, its men had little experience of military discipline, firearms handling or any of the other important elements of war fighting. Kitchener set about to build a large, modern army and expressed doubts that the small BEF would do any good at all on the Continent.

On 6 August, the BEF began to assemble at its embarkation ports for its long-anticipated deployment to the Continent. In four days, 80,000 men, 30,000 horses, 315 small artillery pieces and 125 machine guns were brought together and dispatched to Rouen, Le Havre and Boulogne. Everywhere they went they were greeted with rapturous cheers from French civilians. By 11 August, the BEF was moving towards Amiens, a position that Kitchener thought was far enough behind the front lines to give French a chance to assess the situation and decide on his options. Intelligence estimates waiting at Amiens for French and his staff showed the Germans to be much more numerous than the BEF had at first thought. Kitchener advocated staying at Amiens, but French ordered an advance to the area around Mons and Maubeuge to place his forces on the left of the French Fifth Army. From London, Kitchener gave orders to French to cooperate with his French allies, but to keep his command separate from them. He then issued a notice to the men of the BEF warning them to avoid the temptations of French wine and women. Neither he nor French realized that the men would have little time for frivolity, as the BEF's route of march placed it directly in the path of the 300,000-man German First Army.

On 23 August, the BEF reached Mons at about the same time as the German First Army. Not yet realizing just how badly they were outnumbered, British II Corps set up along a 18m-wide (60ft) canal west of the town. It was commanded by Sir Horace Smith-Dorrien, who had only been in the job a few weeks and who had notoriously poor relations with Sir John French. Smith-Dorrien stretched his corps out along the entire 24km (15 mile) length of the canal and prepared to use its embankment as a main line of resistance. Sir Douglas Haig took I Corps to the east side of Mons, where he stretched his line along the Charleroi road to maintain contact with the French Fifth Army, whose leaders had already begun debating the wisdom of retreating and fighting another day when the odds might be more in their favour.

German troops advancing in open order. Because of their inexperience, the Germans often advanced in dense columns and lines, making them inviting targets for enemy guns. The weather was unusually warm for that time of the year and the heat and dust helped slow the German advance.

For his part, German First Army commander Alexander von Kluck appears not to have understood that he had 300,000 men (although they were widely scattered) opposite just 80,000 Britons. The Germans also possessed a two-to-one advantage in artillery pieces. The Germans thus attacked with some hesitancy using massed formations, playing into the strengths of the BEF – cool professionalism and superior marksmanship. German units began reporting that the British were in solid defensive positions and mistakenly believed that the high rate of British fire must have been due to large numbers of machine guns. British forces held on for six hours at Mons, then blew the bridges over the canal and retired

to a pre-established second-line position five kilometres (three miles) away. The tired Germans showed little desire to press the issue and thus failed to take advantage of their numerical superiority.

That night, the British liaison officer to the French Fifth Army reported that the French had decided to pull back, thus leaving the right flank of the BEF exposed. Although it was an easily defensible decision given the fall of Namur and the inferiority of Allied forces in the area, the British were furious, both at having to retreat and at not having been consulted on the decision in advance. Now with a more complete picture of the size and strength of the German forces opposite them, they had to conduct a fighting retreat

towards Maubeuge and then down the road from Bavai to Le Cateau almost 32km (20 miles) away.

Sir John French wanted to execute an even deeper retreat, get away from the French Fifth Army and regroup far behind the lines. The Germans had other ideas, advancing on Smith-Dorrien in force near Le Cateau, where II Corps had stopped to rest. With some of his units still arriving and Haig's I Corps engaged too heavily with another German force to retire safely, Smith-Dorrien took it upon himself to fight another holding battle against a superior German force. For 11 hours, Smith-Dorrien's corps, reinforced by the newly arrived British 4th Division, held off a German force three times its size.

Sir John French (1852–1925)

The new BEF commander, Field Marshal Sir John French was an unpopular choice inside the army. Hot tempered, frequently in debt and with a well earned reputation for seeking romantic liaisons with the wives of his brother officers, he had gotten the job based largely on his principled stand against the Curragh mutineers. Articulate, occasionally charming and comfortable around politicians, he seemed a safe choice for a Government unsure about the political reliability of many of its officers, even if King George V remarked 'I don't think he is particularly clever'. Even many of French's old friends (presumably those officers who were unmarried and had not loaned him any money) expressed thinly veiled astonishment that he had been chosen for such an important assignment. French also brought to France a serious distrust of his new allies and sought to do everything in his power to act as independently of the French Army as possible. Oddly enough, Sir John spoke very poor French.

Smith-Dorrien and his men fought until darkness fell, giving them a chance to slip away to safety. On 29 August, the French Fifth Army launched a surprise counteroffensive into the German flank near the village of Guise, then quickly slipped away, a deft move that bought the BEF some badly needed time. The II Corps had taken enormous casualties, losing more than 4000 men at Mons and 8000 more at Le Cateau, but its actions had saved the BEF from encirclement or annihilation and had permitted Haig's I Corps to get away to safety as well. Smith-Dorrien and Haig reunited and moved on to Noyon, where they finally found French, who had given II Corps up for dead. He was not pleased to see Smith-Dorrien, whom he unfairly accused of disobeying orders and placing the BEF in a dangerous position.

THE DESTRUCTION OF LOUVAIN

Further to the north, elements of the German Army had moved quickly on to Brussels. They arrived 24km (15 miles) east of the Belgian capital at the town of Louvain on 19 August. German advance guards moved through the town and into Brussels itself the next day, but the Germans kept an occupation force behind. The Belgian Government urged citizens not to

British soldiers during the retreat from Mons. Although they had been forced to execute a long fighting withdrawal, the BEF's morale and cohesion held together. As a result, the men of the BEF were still able to play crucial roles in the fighting of 1914.

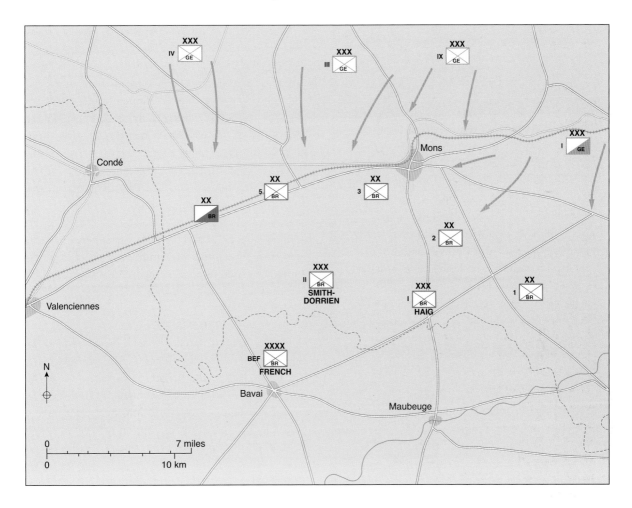

The BEF was nearly annihilated at Mons. It faced a much larger and much stronger opponent and had poor liaison with the French Fifth Army to its right. Nevertheless, it held its ground and was able to conduct an orderly retreat despite being significantly outnumbered by the German forces.

resist the occupation and thereby risk German reprisals. Rumours of atrocities committed by Belgian irregulars had already begun to spread through the German Army and had reached the German home front as well. The mood in Louvain was therefore tense, although there is no evidence to suggest that the Belgians had in fact organized guerrilla units anywhere near the city.

Such was the environment at dusk on the night of 25 August, when rifle fire broke out on the streets of Louvain. To this day, it remains unclear who did the shooting. Some attributed it to friendly fire among confused German units in the growing darkness and the fog of war. The Germans, however, placed the blame on unidentified *franc tireurs*, and broke into the homes of Belgians that they thought were harbouring

the shooters. Belgian men came in for harsh treatment, especially Catholic priests because German troops had heard rumours that priests were the central organizers of Belgian resistance cells.

German officers decided to make an example of Louvain, ordering a policy of *Schrecklichkeit* (frightfulness), which they had already employed in other parts of Belgium. The German commander ordered the removal of all of the town's 10,000 inhabitants. German forces set fire to key buildings in the town, burning the university, which dated to 1426,

The two corps of the BEF separated near Le Cateau. The II Corps, commanded by Sir Horace Smith-Dorrien, regrouped and fought a successful rearguard action. Holding off a force three times larger than his own, Smith-Dorrien's stand at Le Cateau severely disrupted German planning and timing.

to the ground. The flames engulfed the library and its precious and irreplaceable collection of 750 medieval manuscripts and 200,000 books, most of them in German. The Germans also torched the town hall, known as a jewel of Gothic architecture, and the church of St Pierre with its classic Flemish altarpieces. The Germans deliberately destroyed symbols of Belgian culture, but were careful to leave the Maison Américaine intact to avoid angering a powerful neutral nation. They also spared the cloth hall for use as a German army headquarters, thus belying arguments the Germans later advanced that the fires had been accidental.

For five days, Germans burned and looted Louvain. In the end, they destroyed more than 2000 buildings and killed 248 of the town's residents. They executed the burgomaster, the university rector and every member of the town's police force without a trial. They then deported thousands of civilians to work camps in Germany. The Germans tried to keep American and Swiss reporters away from Louvain, but correspondents saw and heard enough to publish reports that turned Louvain into shorthand for all of the worst elements of German brutality. For the Belgians themselves, Louvain was just the start of four years of occupation, humiliation and economic exploitation.

Other German atrocities followed, most committed with the full approval of the German chain of command. German officials never apologized or punished perpetrators, holding instead to the argument that cruelty was the only way to deal with what they claimed was a massive Belgian guerrilla campaign. Creative Allied and neutral propagandists unnecessarily embellished stories of German atrocities, just as German reporters embellished or invented tales of Belgian resistance. German atrocities motivated people in both neutral and Allied nations. The explicitly anti-Catholic nature of many of the

German atrocities inspired the French to commit to a tougher war, lest the same fate befall them.

By 24 August, the last organized units of the Belgian Army had gathered around the port city of Antwerp. Five Belgian infantry divisions sought safety among the city's fortifications and hoped to use them as a base from which to attack the German rear and lines of communications. In mid-September the Germans dispatched six divisions to force the surrender of Antwerp and end the threat. The force brought 170 heavy artillery pieces, including 210mm howitzers and a dozen of the 420mm guns that had turned Liège and Namur into piles of rubble. Awesome German artillery barrages began to fall on the city's defences at the end of the month as German armies pushed the Belgians further and further towards the river at their backs. The British saw German control of Antwerp as a dangerous, almost nightmarish, situation. The First Lord of the Admiralty, Winston Churchill, dispatched three brigades of Royal Marines, arriving himself with the men on 1 October. The next day, however, the Germans broke through the city's inner defences, making it impossible for the British and Belgians to

The Retreat from Mons

The retreat from Mons quickly developed into the stuff of legend. The two British corps undertook lines of march separated by 19km (12 miles) of forest and the Sambre River, but never allowed their retreat to dissolve into a rout. Confused and tired British soldiers began a fighting withdrawal in the rain, with only the 5000 men of the British cavalry to protect them and report on German movements. Fanciful reports began to spread that the retreat was protected by an 'Angel of Mons' or the ghosts of British archers from the nearby 1415 battlefield of Agincourt. In British eyes the retreat from Mons became the moment when the small BEF stopped the mighty German Army, holding up a force more than twice its size and disrupting the German drive on Paris.

hold on. They conducted a fighting retreat west towards Ostend, where they joined British forces in the small strip of Belgian territory not occupied by the Germans. That strip was based around the town of Ypres and the defensive line formed by the Yser River and canal.

THE FIRST BATTLE OF THE MARNE

By the end of August, all of the armies in Belgium and France were, in the words of one BEF veteran, 'dog tired, half-asleep, and dreaming at times'. Many men were walking wounded, barely strong enough to keep moving. Units were short of leaders, as junior officers and non-commissioned officers, leading their men from the front, had suffered especially high casualties. They were also short of ammunition, horses, food, spare parts and weapons. None of the pre-war estimates had come even close to guessing how fast modern armies could use up equipment.

The Germans pressed on, even if they were already dangerously behind schedule. The Kaiser sent congratulatory telegrams and medals to his senior officers, but most of them had already concluded that the original plan was failing. Belgian resistance and the heroic stand of the BEF at Mons and Le Cateau had destroyed the careful timing that the Schlieffen Plan had required. Moreover, their men had been marching and fighting for a month on limited supplies and lacked the strength to throw the final punches against Paris. Aware that the French capital lay beyond the reach of German forces, Alexander von Kluck, commanding the largest of the German armies, had already begun to formulate some new strategic ideas.

As he did so, Joffre began a massive reorganization of French forces. Always calm and always in control, he did not panic despite the seriousness of the new Allied position; he even kept to his normal daily schedule, which included an enormous lunch and a nap. He disbanded the Army of Alsace, which was no

General Joseph Joffre, nicknamed 'Papa', reviews French troops. Although the disastrous French war plan had been his design, he escaped immediate blame. He ruthlessly replaced commanders he thought were unsuited to the tasks of modern warfare and took firm hold of the crisis of 1914.

longer needed to protect the flank of a French advance into the lost provinces. He and his staff used their expertise in railways to move its men in 300 railway cars to a new position north of Paris near Montdidier. He added reinforcements to it to bring it to eight divisions, renamed it the Sixth Army, and gave it a new commander, General Michel Joseph Manoury.

Joffre formed another army, soon to be numbered the Ninth, under the command of Ferdinand Foch, whose aggressive attacks near Morhange had impressed Joffre despite their ultimate failure and despite a report from Foch's commander that he had willingly disregarded orders during the campaign. The Ninth Army deployed along the marshes of the Aisne River, closing the gap between the French Fifth Army to its left and the French Fourth Army to its right.

The BEF had positioned itself southeast of Paris and behind the French armies on its right and left. Sir John French argued that his men needed rest before they could once again go into the line. When pressed to say

when the BEF would rejoin the main Allied line, he told one of Joffre's officers on 29 August that the BEF needed a minimum of 10 days of rest. French proposed eight more days of retreating, placing the BEF well behind the Seine and leaving the French to their own devices. French also talked about moving the BEF to Le Havre, a dangerous move that could imperil the entire war effort. He wrote that his faith in Joffre and the French Army 'to carry the campaign to a successful conclusion is fast waning'.

French proposed to abandon the French Army in its hour of greatest need and put British forces in a position to either be rounded up by the Germans after they had beaten the French, be humiliatingly evacuated back to England or sit by idly while the French won a great victory alone. None of these options was acceptable to Kitchener. Nor was the BEF's positioning, because it left a dangerous gap of more than 64km (40 miles) between the French Fifth and Sixth armies just to the east of Paris. Kitchener read the report to an emergency session of the cabinet, informing the members that French's proposed actions risked losing the war.

Kitchener decided to act and act fast. Late on the night of 30/31 August, he hurried to No. 10 Downing Street and met with Prime Minister Herbert Asquith and a number of his senior advisers. He told them that

> ## 'My centre is giving way, my right is in retreat. Situation excellent. I shall attack.'
>
> Ferdinand Foch at the Battle of the Marne

he planned to go to France immediately to force Sir John French to move the BEF into position between the French Fifth and Sixth armies, thus covering the eastern approaches to Paris. Within an hour and a half of making his decision, Kitchener was on a special train to Dover, arriving in Paris on the morning of 1 September for a meeting at the British embassy.

Kitchener showed up at the meeting in his resplendent field marshal's uniform, underscoring his superiority in military rank, even though he was then serving in government as a civilian. John French took Kitchener's appearance in uniform, as well as his request to review the men of the BEF in the field, as a slight to his honour, adding a chill to an already tense room. The German Army was just 48km (30 miles)

German soldiers, exhausted from their gruelling march through Belgium, attack on the Marne. The German war plan had demanded far too much from them. By the time of the Marne they were tired and critically low on supplies.

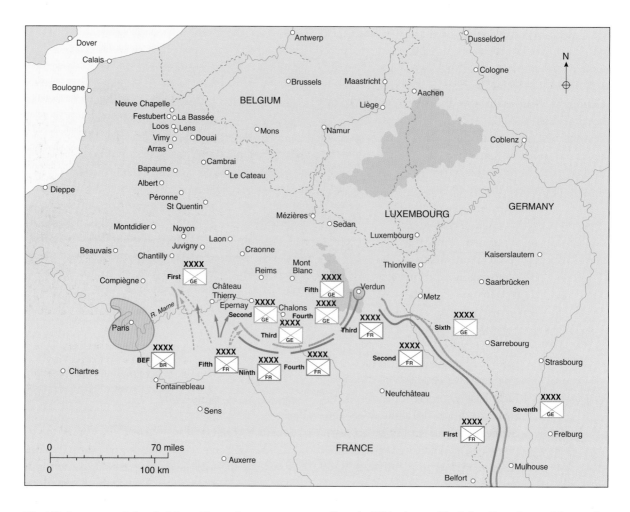

The Allied retreats ended at the Marne River, where a vigorous counterattack stopped the Germans from advancing on Paris. Then the largest battle ever fought, it put a dramatic end to all of the carefully crafted war plans of the pre-1914 years.

away and large elements of the French Government had already left the capital for Bordeaux, although most of the senior officials had stayed. Many of them were in the British embassy for this most important of meetings. Kitchener and French held a closed-door meeting ('we had rather a disagreeable time', French later noted) at which the former warned the latter not to retreat any further without written instructions from the cabinet. The two reached an angry compromise that the BEF could continue to move, but would do so east in order to affect a linkage with the

French Fifth Army. Sir John French would exercise caution as he did so, taking the utmost care to ensure that his flanks remained supported by French armies on either side.

The frenetic activity in the French and British lines existed on the German side as well. Kluck had determined that his First Army lacked the strength to execute the move around Paris called for in the Schlieffen Plan. A faster than anticipated Russian mobilization in the east had also led Moltke to remove five German divisions from the west for a rapid redeployment to East Prussia, further weakening the German right wing. Kluck's men had fought and marched over 480km (300 miles) in one month and, although they were within sight of the outskirts of Paris, they were also working on tenuous supply lines while the French could at the same time take advantage of the excellent rail and road network around the capital. As more men and more supplies reached the city, Germany's chances to win the campaign began to fade.

Although he gave up on taking Paris, Kluck did not think that all was lost. He had recently received intelligence reports indicating that the French Fifth Army was deployed north to south and moving generally east. It would therefore have a dangerously exposed left flank that the Germans could pour into, attacking the French formation at its weakest point. To use a well-worn analogy, armies are like opened dresser drawers, with their strongest parts facing forward. They are much easier to damage if smashed in at the sides. On 31 August, Kluck hastily ordered his forces to move southeast, breaking with the Schlieffen Plan, and directing his men east of Paris in the hopes of turning in the entire Allied left flank against itself.

Kluck had not, however, counted on the recently created French Sixth Army, which now sat poised to smash in his flank as he marched across its front. French aviators and radio signal interceptors picked up Kluck's turn and reported it to the military governor of Paris, the sharp-minded colonial veteran

German cavalry scouts known as Uhlans (note their distinctive Polish-style *czapka* hats) on the Marne. They largely failed in their mission to screen German forces and report on enemy formations and movements. Note the lances they carried into battle in 1914.

General Joseph Gallieni. Joffre initially wanted to wait until the BEF and French Fifth Army were in a better position to meet the German turn before ordering an offensive, but on 4 September, Gallieni sensed the chance for the smaller French Sixth Army to defeat the German First Army if it acted with speed and struck the flank with sufficient force. Gallieni had already taken the precaution of commandeering Paris's taxicabs and placing them outside railway stations to greet detraining troops from the provinces. With their meters running at full fare, the taxis drove new arrivals northeast along the N2 motorway, moving almost 6000 more men to the Sixth Army to reinforce it for a drive into the German flank.

While the Sixth Army attacked the German right, Joffre prepared the rest of the Allied line. On 5 September, Joffre sped 184km (115 miles) to BEF headquarters where he demanded that the BEF take its place in the line to cover the gap between the French Sixth and Fifth armies. He told the assembled British officers that he had given orders for the French Army

In 1914 the cuirassier stood as a paragon of military power. Since 1914 he has come to symbolize the backward-looking view of many European generals. All armies had to adapt uniforms and equipment to fight the new, more modern war that had developed.

to fight to the last man and that 'the lives of all French people, the soil of France, the future of Europe' as well as 'the honour of England' were at stake in the next few days. Would the BEF continue its retirement or turn and join the fight to save France? The BEF's commander began to stammer something in his bad French, turned to a French-speaking British officer and said softly, 'Damn it, I can't explain. Tell him we will do all we possibly can.'

On his return to his own headquarters later that afternoon, Joffre issued general orders for the eastern French armies, stretching all the way to Lorraine, to hold on the defensive while the Sixth, Fifth and Ninth armies attacked in conjunction with the BEF. 'Every effort must be made to attack', the orders read. 'A unit which finds it impossible to advance must, regardless of cost, hold its ground and be killed on the spot rather than fall back. In the present circumstances, no failure will be tolerated.'

Foch, whose Ninth Army stood in the centre of the Allied line, needed no encouragement. The Germans attacked him in force, driving back all four of his divisions. Foch stayed in his headquarters, even as the units around him began to retreat. He rallied them and ordered them to attack, knowing that if they continued to fall back they would expose the flanks of the French Fifth Army and thereby risk the integrity of the entire Allied line. One of Foch's more creative staff officers rewrote Foch's directive and transmitted it to French headquarters thus: 'My centre is giving way, my right is in retreat. Situation excellent. I shall attack.' Even though he probably never used those exact words, Foch was thrilled, and the directive made him famous throughout France.

Richard Hentsch (1869–1918)

Lieutenant-Colonel Hentsch was a staff officer attached to Moltke's headquarters. When the Battle of the Marne began Moltke was still attempting to direct operations from Luxembourg, over 300km (200 miles) from the First Army's HQ. Communication between the German commanders was either by wireless or by staff officers in motor cars. On 8 September Moltke complained about the 'lack of news from far-away armies' in a letter to his wife. Hentsch was sent to the front to ascertain the situation at first hand. Hentsch arrived at Bülow's Second Army HQ at 7pm, where he agreed with the latter's decision to withdraw behind the Marne. The following morning he visited First Army HQ and told Kuhl, Kluck's chief of staff, that First Army must withdraw.

First Army's war diary states that 'General Kuhl remarked to him [Hentsch] that the First Army was in the midst of an attack; a retreat was a very ticklish matter, as the troops were thoroughly mixed up and thoroughly exhausted.' Hentsch told Kuhl that nothing but retreat was now possible, and drew with a piece of coal on a map showing where the retreating armies should take up their new positions; he left without seeing Kluck personally. The decision to retreat – right or wrong – was a strategic disaster for Germany.

In early 1915 Moltke claimed that he 'did not give an order for the retreat of the First Army. Nor was an order given for the retreat of the Second Army.' An enquiry in April 1917 found that Hentsch's orders had been to coordinate a retreat *if one had already been started by First Army*. His staff officer colleagues also claimed that no retreat was authorised by Moltke.

However Ludendorff, in a general order issued to divisional staffs on 24 May 1917, stated that Hentsch acted in accordance with his instructions, but he added that 'historical research in later years' must determine whether a retreat was necessary. Hentsch died after a gall bladder operation in Romania in February 1918.

While the Allied centre held, Kluck met the unexpected flank attack of the French Sixth Army by ordering a complicated turn to the northwest. The move reoriented the German First Army to be better positioned to defend itself, but it simultaneously opened a gap of 48km (30 miles) between his own army and Bülow's Second Army to the east. Joffre instantly recognized that the gap exposed both the right flank of the German Second Army and the left flank of the German First Army if he could push forces forward into it. On 9 September, he urged the tired BEF and the worn-out French Fifth Army to approach the Marne River and get in between the two German field armies.

Meanwhile, Moltke, isolated in a headquarters 320km (200 miles) away in Luxembourg and unable to figure out what was happening from scattered field reports, sent a staff officer to the front with orders to achieve better coordination between Kluck and Bülow. Lieutenant-Colonel Richard Hentsch arrived at Bülow's headquarters as the French Fifth Army was starting to turn the German Second Army's flank. If it did so, nothing except its own fatigue could prevent the BEF from moving against the Second Army's rear and rolling it up. Bülow told Hentsch that he had no choice but to withdraw toward the Vesle and Aisne rivers to the north, even though such a move would

'The Miracle of the Marne' soon became the stuff of French legend, even though only a single brigade was moved to the front line by taxi. Once Paris was safe, Joffre 'invited' the French Government to return to the capital from Bordeaux, but kept a tight hold on the areas near the front line.

badly expose the left flank of the German First Army. Hentsch then raced to Kluck's headquarters and, on the authority Moltke had given him in Luxembourg, ordered the withdrawal of the First Army north as well.

Over the next three days (10–12 September) the Germans conducted a fighting withdrawal to the north, covering 64km (40 miles) of ground and destroying everything they could behind them in an effort to slow the Allied pursuit. Joffre pressed the French Army to pursue the Germans with utmost vigour, but the men were exhausted. The pre-war stocks of ammunition were empty, and the new German positions were well sited on high ground. The First Battle of the Marne was over. It was then the largest battle ever fought, with more than 1,200,000 men on each side and battle lines that stretched from Paris to the Vosges Mountains. Almost 250,000 men were killed, wounded or captured in this titanic battle for control of France. The war's opening shots had been fired and its first large battles fought, but neither side had achieved the quick victory it had sought.

CHAPTER 2

The Race to the Sea

As tired armies began to adjust to the possibilities of a long war, both sides began to dig in. Trenches offered protection from machine guns, artillery and the elements, but they also created an entirely new and largely unfamiliar form of warfare.

In the wake of the setback at the Marne, German senior officers accused Moltke of having lost his nerve at the worst possible moment. They alleged that he had been unable to exercise effective command over Kluck and Bülow, and was reduced to relying on the advice of a mere lieutenant-colonel. In fact, there is substantial evidence that Moltke did indeed suffer a nervous breakdown. On 14 September, the Kaiser removed him, putting the colder and more ruthless Erich von Falkenhayn in charge, although the decision was kept secret for several weeks in order to avoid having to announce that the German Army had suffered a defeat at the Battle of the Marne. Moltke served briefly as deputy chief of staff, but he was given no real responsibilities because it was obvious to all who knew him that he was a broken man. Convinced

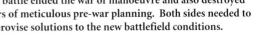

German troops advance during the First Battle of the Marne. The battle ended the war of manoeuvre and also destroyed years of meticulous pre-war planning. Both sides needed to improvise solutions to the new battlefield conditions.

that Germany would lose the war, he grew increasingly morose and died in June 1916 of a heart attack, thus making him the ideal scapegoat for German failures in 1914.

FALKENHAYN TAKES OVER

Moltke's successor, the 53-year-old Falkenhayn, brought energy, optimism and quick decision making to German headquarters. These qualities were much in demand because, unlike Joffre, Falkenhayn and his staff had to take into account events in two theatres. In the east, a quick Russian mobilization had allowed Russian forces to enter East Prussia in mid-August. On 20 August, much larger Russian forces had defeated the German Eighth Army at Gumbinnen, threatening the weakly held German line in the east. Fear of the Russians overrunning eastern Germany had led Moltke to order the transfer of two corps from France on 25 August and also to send most of the reinforcements that became available to the east.

The imposing heights above the Aisne River are seen in the background. The Germans logically chose these heights as a place to dig in once they chose to go on the defensive. British and French soldiers unsuccessfully tried to storm the heights in mid-September.

The Miracle of the Marne

The 'Miracle of the Marne' instantly became a part of the mythology of the war. French nationalists claimed that it proved the moral superiority of the French over the Germans. Some even claimed that Joan of Arc herself had contributed to the victory, inspiring the men from heaven. Whatever the cause of the victory, the French soldier had endured the rigours of battle and had answered his nation's call when needed. Joffre, Gallieni, Foch and many others were showered with medals and vaulted overnight into the most sacred ranks of the history of the French Army. The men and officers of the BEF shared in the glory as well, especially Haig, whose I Corps had conducted a courageous charge into the centre of the German line, filling in a dangerous gap in the Allied line. Thanks to the heroics of the British and French alike, Paris was safe, and the French Army, although battered, had escaped the noose Moltke had tried to tie around its neck.

By the time Falkenhayn took over from Moltke, the situation in the east had stabilized enough to allow the German general staff to focus its energies on the west. The first task involved straightening the German line and giving German troops some protection between themselves and pursuing Allied forces. Falkenhayn thus gave up on the idea of seizing Paris, accepting instead the temporary necessity of maintaining the integrity of his forces for the future. On 12 September, the German First and Second armies completed their withdrawal to the north bank of the Aisne River. Once on the north shore of the river, the Germans had time to destroy some of the bridges and began to set up defensive positions along the steep and formidable 32km-long (20-mile) ridge that ran parallel to the river, known as the Chemin des Dames.

Believing that he had his adversaries on the run, Joffre ordered an energetic pursuit of the retreating Germans across the Aisne. He hoped to catch them at their most tired and disorganized, and with substantial gaps still existing between units. The pitiful condition of German stragglers and prisoners of war seemed to suggest that the morale of the German Army might be cracking and that one more serious blow might destroy it. 'Victory', Joffre wrote in an order of the day on 10 September, 'depends on the legs of our infantry.' If the Allies could chase the Germans before the Germans could set up new lines of defence, they might complete the triumph of the Marne and win a great victory by chasing the Germans into the much more favourable plains east of the Chemin des Dames.

The spirits of Allied soldiers were willing, but their bodies were in no condition to conduct forced marches in the face of opposition from German rearguards. Rain, mud and fatigue slowed the Allied pursuit, which still had the aim of exploiting the gap that remained between the German First and Second armies. The rain also grounded French reconnaissance aircraft, further complicating efforts to determine the size and placement of German forces. In the haste, confusion and sheer exhaustion that characterized the situation, Joffre could not develop an accurate assessment of the enemy's position, although he sensed the urgency of moving faster than the Germans and striking them before they could reorganize.

The situation was little better for the Germans. For their part, German staff officers were not confident of their army's ability to resist another determined Allied charge. Recognizing that the Germans in the First and Second armies were too tired to reposition yet again and close the gap between them, the Germans moved the Seventh Army from Alsace and ordered it to fill in the gap along the Chemin des Dames. The BEF approached the last remaining gap in the German line just as German forces, made available by the recent surrender of the French fortress complex of Maubeuge, arrived. Maubeuge was one of the most powerful French fortresses and guarded the crossing

Cavalrymen near the Aisne. Their job was to probe for weaknesses on the enemy's flanks. The beginning of trench warfare, however, meant that there were no flanks to turn. Both sides therefore dug in and began to improvise.

of the Sambre River and two trunk railway lines along the Franco-Belgian border. It contained six forts and seven smaller works, known as *ouvrages*, with an impressive garrison of 50,000 men and hundreds of artillery pieces. It was a *fort d'arrêt* under Plan XVII, designed to slow any German advance into France through southern Belgium until Joffre could move into Belgium from the south. Stocked with food and ammunition for three months, it was to hold out as long as possible and await reinforcements in the event of a siege.

Maubeuge's situation became critical when the Belgian fortress at Namur, just 56km (35 miles) away, fell on 25 August. The same German Second Army that had reduced Liège and Namur arrived at Maubeuge on 28 August. Because of the crisis developing in other parts of the line, Joffre was forced to leave Maubeuge to its own devices. When the Germans cut the telegraph and telephone lines connecting it to the outside world, Maubeuge was completely isolated, with little idea of what was happening to the rest of the French Army. Between 2 and 7 September, the Germans pierced the northern and eastern defences of Maubeuge, taking one fort and four *ouvrages*. Maubeuge's commander, Brigadier-General Fornier, and his staff did not know of the furious Battle of the Marne then raging to their southwest. Nor did they know that the Germans were out of 210mm artillery shells and had

A French soldier from 1914. His bright blue and red uniform was unsuited to modern war, but it had become a symbol of French élan. The army had decided to replace it just months before the war. An enraged parliamentarian screamed 'But red trousers ARE France!'

> ## Limogé
>
> After the Marne Joffre conducted a ruthless overhaul of the command structure of the French Army. He replaced two army commanders as well as ten corps commanders and 38 divisional commanders. Many of them had been political favourites of one party or another; all had performed poorly in the war's opening weeks. Several generals, Joffre believed, were either too old to bear the strains of modern warfare or were manifestly out of their league. The French government, unsure about the wisdom of having 50 disgruntled generals near Paris in such tense times (and with no government in residence in the capital), reassigned them to the provincial city of Limoges, giving rise to the term *limogé*, a euphemism for being relieved of command. It was to become an oft-repeated and oft-heard term in France in the next four years. Joffre got a great deal of mileage out of just saying the word in the presence of a subordinate he felt needed motivation.

just 25 of the powerful 420mm shells remaining. Bülow was also demanding that the Germans bypass Maubeuge and send as many soldiers as possible to his Second Army on the Marne, where he determined that they would be of more immediate use to the German cause. Had Fornier known of these circumstances, he might have held out much longer than he did to disrupt German plans on the Marne, but all he saw was evidence that he had been abandoned by the French Army and could not long withstand Germany's presumably devastating artillery batteries. On 7 September, therefore, Fornier surrendered Maubeuge, along with its 50,000 soldiers and scores of powerful guns.

BATTLE OF THE AISNE
At the very limits of their endurance, the Allies went back on the offensive. On 13 September, lead elements of the BEF's 4th Division courageously crossed and

captured one of the last remaining bridges over the Aisne. Against heavy German fire, including 210mm artillery pieces carefully directed from the excellent observation posts along the Chemin des Dames, the men of the BEF set up a small bridgehead on the north shore of the Aisne. Despite the BEF's fatigue, Haig brought up his I Corps to support them the next day with an eye towards taking the 122m (400ft) heights of the Chemin des Dames Ridge. Haig was aware of the challenge of seizing what he modestly called a 'considerable' ridge, but he wanted to get over the ridge and into presumably open country before the Germans could convert the heights and its numerous caverns into an unassailable fortress.

Elements of the French Fifth and Sixth armies also crossed the Aisne, conducting attacks on 13 and 14 September. In one famous incident, a French infantry regiment to the BEF's right attacked while singing 'La Marseillaise' at the top of their voices. The infantry attacks, most of them uphill against stiff German

Troops prepare trenches near the Aisne. Soldiers quickly developed multi-layered trench systems that became very sophisticated and increasingly difficult to attack. Trench digging soon became a detailed science of its own.

resistance, failed to gain territory worth the human cost. The Germans had brought in machine guns and heavy artillery, allowing them to repel most Allied attacks with ease. On 14 September, elements of Haig's I Corps reached the crest of the Chemin des Dames Ridge, temporarily taking the town of Troyon and placing forces on the south embankment of the road itself. II Corps, however, made much less progress. Without significant support to their left, I Corps was driven back, although Haig reported to Sir John French that 'it will be harder to find an instance in our annals in which troops have [shown] a finer spirit, or fought with greater determination, at the close of such a trying period.'

The misery of tired, hungry and wet troops continued unabated. The weather turned colder and wetter, and hot food could not reach the men because the field kitchens could not keep up with the infantry. On 15 September, the Germans counterattacked with the aim of pushing the Allies back across the south bank of the Aisne. They largely succeeded, although localized fighting for control of the riverbanks continued in the region well into October. The next day, John French issued orders for his men to begin

German trenches tended to be more solidly designed and took better advantage of features in the terrain. The Germans had the luxury of choosing the ground to defend and had to plan for a much longer occupation. The Allies, by contrast, had to attack in order to win the war.

digging trenches to protect them from German artillery fire. Like most generals in 1914, he envisioned the trenches as a temporary expedient to give his men rest and protection until they were ready to attack again.

The British and French tended to see trenches as emergency measures designed to buy time until the resumption of the offensive. The Germans, however, were beginning to understand the value of trenches as defensive instruments. Built with right angles or in a zigzag pattern, they could allow well-placed machine guns to cover any and all possible avenues of enemy approach. Using the rapid-fire capacity of protected machine guns meant that fewer men were needed on the front lines. Thus thousands of tired German soldiers could be rotated off the line in order to give

them some badly needed rest. Especially in places like the Chemin des Dames Ridge, trenches could accentuate the natural advantages of high ground. Even from this early date, therefore, the German trench network tended to be more solidly constructed and more carefully sited than that of the Allies.

Above ground and below it, the fighting along the Aisne further contributed to the exhaustion of the two armies. Some British and French units had taken 30 per cent casualties on top of the losses they had already suffered in Belgium and on the Marne. Haig went to visit his wounded men in field hospitals and found the medical system completely and utterly overwhelmed. Nothing in pre-war planning had prepared the army medical staffs to have to deal with so many wounded men.

The fighting along the Aisne had demonstrated the difficulty of attacking against solidly placed enemy units. As on the Marne and in Belgium, local attacks tended to be too haphazard, going forward without much concern for the protection of flanks. Machine guns proved extremely difficult to locate and, even when spotted, were too small and too mobile to destroy with artillery. The fighting thus far also showed the difficulty of exploiting breakthroughs. By

> 'The Battle of the Aisne has once more demonstrated the splendid spirit, gallantry and devotion which animates the officers and men of His Majesty's Forces.'
>
> Sir John French's official dispatch

the time reinforcements could be organized and brought into the line, the enemy had normally brought in reserves to blunt any attempts at sustained breakthrough. Generations of operational thinking designed to create and turn exposed flanks had to be rethought.

The British official historian of the war, Sir James Edmonds, later wrote that the Battle of the Aisne proved to commanders that 'an entirely new strategic situation' existed in France. The soldiers hardly needed to be told. Most of them recognized even before their generals had that head-on attacks against enemy positions did not work. Moreover, no amount of élan or courage could compensate for the rapid fire of machine guns and the exhaustion that high-tempo operations brought. Generals and soldiers alike would need to find new ways to fight this new type of war.

THE RACE TO THE SEA

Falkenhayn, newly appointed and anxious to make a good name for himself, was among the first to craft a new set of solutions to match the new strategic situation. Believing that defensive operations could not win the war, he was loath to order a halt and an entrenchment all along the line. Instead, he wanted to show his commitment to restoring the momentum the Germans had had before the setback at the Marne. He had not entirely given up on the central idea contained in Schlieffen's grand plan, namely a strong

haymaker by the powerful right fist of the German Army that would send the Allied armies in front of him reeling. If he could move around the left flank of the Allied line and into its rear, he could still encircle his enemies and destroy them in a grand *Kesselschlacht*, or 'killing cauldron'. Falkenhayn also thought that resuming the offensive would provide a kind of moral tonic to German soldiers, inspiring them for what he felt might be one last push.

The two-front nightmare scenario that had haunted Schlieffen and Moltke haunted Falkenhayn as well. For the next two years his thinking would alternate between trying to seek the decisive campaign in the west or seeking it in the east. In September 1914, he was convinced that Germany had a better chance of winning the war in the west. Paris was still much closer than Moscow or St Petersburg and Falkenhayn thought that the Allied armies were close enough to expose themselves to the massive right hook he planned to unleash on them. The movements of the armies thus far had concentrated their main fighting formations between the Oise River and the Franco-

Erich von Falkenhayn (1861–1922)

A cool professional in the Prussian tradition, Falkenhayn had come to the Kaiser's attention as a result of his ruthless actions in China to protect German interests during the Boxer Rebellion. He had become a court favourite, and had done well in all the tasks assigned to him in the years before the war. At the time of Moltke's removal, he had been serving as the Prussian war minister, and he thus had a deep understanding of army administration. He was a ruthless general, advocating the bombardment of civilians from the air, unrestricted submarine warfare and the use of poison gas.

Cavalry's role changed in 1914, but horses did not disappear from the battlefield. They retained an important role in exploiting gaps in enemy lines, and, if conditions permitted, they could act like mobile infantry, using their speed to raid enemy lines of communication and cut off retreat.

The German 77mm field artillery piece, and its French 75mm counterpart, were designed to advance with attacking infantry. Their roles had to be readjusted for the realities of trench warfare, but both pieces remained the most common guns in their armies' respective arsenals.

German frontier. North of the Oise, both sides had only minimal forces deployed, even though the region contained the main railway lines the Germans used to bring supplies to the front. Thus there was room for operational manoeuvre of large units north of the Oise, meaning that an envelopment there might still be possible.

Further to the north, the critical English Channel ports lay virtually undefended. As late as 18 September, no organized Allied force larger than a battalion existed north of the Oise River. Even most of these units were made up of second-line Territorials rather than first-line combat troops. A German force, moreover, still sat outside the besieged Belgian fortress at Antwerp. If that city surrendered, those German troops would be free to move against the coastline, sweeping up the port cities before them. Without those ports, the BEF would have to extend its supply lines to Normandy or even Brittany, greatly complicating and slowing British operations.

The British especially worried about the Channel ports, often presenting German control of them in doomsday terms. British officials worried that the Germans could use ports like Nieuport, Dunkirk, Calais and Boulogne to stage an invasion of the British home islands; Falkenhayn later claimed that he had just a plan in mind, although there is scant evidence to suggest that he was doing much more than enjoying the delicious fantasy of it in 1914. Falkenhayn's hatred of the British was well known in military circles on both sides of the English Channel, making the British unwilling to take any avoidable risks. The Admiralty

also warned that if the Channel ports became German naval bases, then the German High Seas Fleet could outflank the Royal Navy in the southern portions of the North Sea, thus rendering all of the Royal Navy's pre-war strategic assumptions moot. Control of the northern French coastline also meant that the Germans could challenge the British for dominance in the English Channel. German battleships in the Channel might even be able to use their massive naval guns to bombard cities on the southern coast of England.

By the end of 1914 the so-called 'race to the sea' was over as the armies reached the North Sea in the north and the border of neutral Switzerland in the south. Two continuous parallel lines of trench systems thus developed. With no more flanks to turn, warfare became less mobile and more direct.

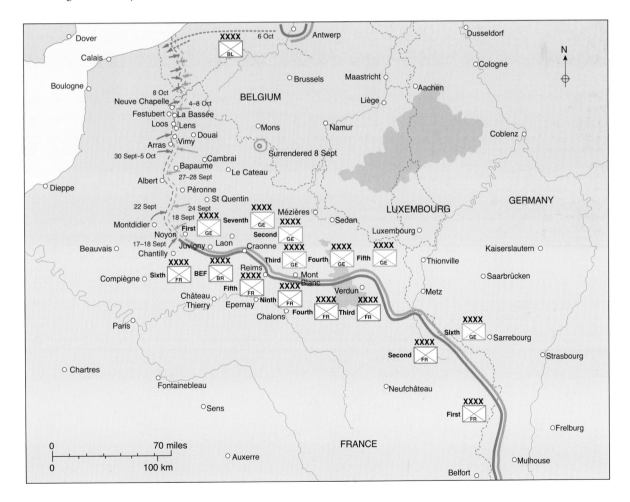

Falkenhayn, Joffre and French therefore all had reasons to try to stretch their lines west and north. Their plans were in fact mirror images of one another, with each hoping to turn the other's flank and threaten his enemy's lines of communications. Thus as Falkenhayn was preparing the Bavarians of the

German Sixth Army to move around the French left, Joffre was simultaneously preparing the French Second Army to move around the German right. Both had identified the still open ground around Noyon and Montdidier as the best place for their attack. On 18 September, the two forces met one another, drawing to a stalemate and ruining Falkenhayn's plans for a massive envelopment. Instead, both sides tried to swing around the other's flank once again, gradually extending their lines north in a twin effort to protect their own flank and turn that of their foe. By 25 September, both sides had reached the south bank of

Some of the aftermath of the First Battle of the Marne. Note the dead soldier by the side of the road on the left. Newspapers were reluctant to show photographs of the dead in the war's first few months, often using paintings instead to minimize the gore. By 1915 realistic images of the carnage of the battlefield had become much more common.

The Fall of Maubeuge

Not all French soldiers agreed with the decision to surrender Maubeuge. More than 1200 of them defied the order to surrender and made their way out of Maubeuge in two columns, marching across incomplete German lines in the north and arriving in Dunkirk with tales of Fornier's premature surrender. The fall of Maubeuge, combined with the fates of Namur and Liège, confirmed the beliefs of Joffre and others that forts were little more than death traps that had limited military utility in modern warfare. Those beliefs would have dramatic consequences in 1916 when the powerful French fortress complex at Verdun was threatened.

The ruins of Maubeuge seemed to prove to many German and French commanders that artillery had become far more powerful than forts.

the Somme River that would be the scene of such bitter fighting two years hence.

This movement became known as the 'race to the sea', though it was neither a race nor did it have the sea as its goal. It was instead a slow, deliberate series of flanking attempts from armies that were weakening their lines as they stretched themselves further and further north. The difficulty of moving men and supplies quickly along damaged rail and road networks meant that units never had the strength to complete the flanking movements they planned. Consequently most of the engagements were relatively small and indecisive, even if both sides sensed the urgency. Along the way, the Germans scouted and seized terrain, seeking ground particularly favourable to the defensive, especially high ground. They then dug in as they had around the Chemin des Dames, compelling the French and British forces opposite them to do the same. In most cases, the Germans occupied better defensive terrain, complicating all future efforts by the Allies to dislodge them.

THE CRISIS AT ARRAS

As both sides 'raced' north, they sought control of critical communications centres. One such centre was the town of Arras, against which Falkenhayn began to concentrate German forces on 1 October. The French Second Army was then already stretched over more than 100km (63 miles), had been engaged in active combat for weeks and was in no position to resist a determined German charge. Joffre sent in two infantry corps and a detachment of cavalry under the command of Louis Ernest Maud'huy. The detachment remained under the orders of Second Army commander General Edouard Noël de Castelnau.

Opposite Castelnau, Falkenhayn once again turned to the German Sixth Army, ordering it to take Arras. Its commander was the Bavarian Crown Prince Rupprecht, who had received his appointment owing to his royal blood, but had led well in the war's early months. He planned to make a large-scale diversion on Arras itself to draw French attention there, then wheel to the north of the city with his main force, swing around it to the north and west, then begin to roll up the French flank. As he did so, an opening in the French line appeared south of Arras as well, offering Rupprecht the chance to conduct a rare double envelopment.

Maud'huy feared that German forces might move both to his south and north, thus enveloping him and cutting him off from support. Maud'huy reported his concerns to Castelnau, who authorized him to prepare

to retreat, even if it meant abandoning Arras. Castelnau then informed Joffre of his decision and asked the French commander whether he thought Maud'huy ought to retreat to the northwest or southwest. Castelnau also indicated that he might have to retreat the rest of the Second Army to the south of the Somme River notwithstanding the attendant risk of leaving northern France unprotected. Joffre thought that Castelnau's proposals were an over-reaction to a situation that was serious, but not nearly as hopeless as Castelnau made it out to be. He told Castelnau that a retirement by the Second Army would put the entire French war effort at risk. It must therefore stay where it was at all costs. He also took Maud'huy's forces away from Castelnau's control, reforming them as the Tenth Army.

The crisis near Arras convinced Joffre that the defence of northern France needed its own dedicated commander. He therefore formed an Army Group North, encompassing the new French Tenth Army and Castelnau's Second Army. To command the new army

The town of Nieuport sat where the Western Front reached the North Sea. Desperate fighting raged around the town at the end of 1914. A combined French, British and Belgian force held off repeated attempts by the Germans to break through and threaten the ports along the English Channel.

group, he chose Ferdinand Foch, a fellow native of the Pyrenees whom Joffre had known for decades, and a man whose aggressive tactics and relentless confidence Joffre believed France badly needed. Joffre trusted Foch so much that in late September he had requested that the government name Foch his successor in the event of an accident, thus vaulting Foch over numerous more senior officers, including Castelnau and Gallieni. The government refused the request, naming Gallieni, Joffre's rival for the glory of the Marne success, instead. Although denied the succession, Foch was free to accept his new command. 'Go and see the situation,' Joffre told him, referring to the Somme and Arras, 'and do your best.'

Foch's first challenge involved convincing Castelnau, his commander at Morhange, not to retreat. Foch went immediately to Castelnau's headquarters for their first meeting with Foch as the senior officer. Castelnau once again made a pitch to retreat south of the Somme. Foch had anticipated the request and pulled out written orders to Castelnau that he hold his position at all costs. 'I take entire responsibility,' Foch told his new subordinate, 'and my decision is irrevocable.' Foch also gave orders to hold fast to Maud'huy, whose soldiers had dug in and were holding off the German attacks on their right flank. The Allies then received a bit of a blessing in disguise owing to the dire situation in Antwerp. On 6 October, anticipating the fall of the city at any moment, Falkenhayn decided to shift the German effort north and cancel all further attacks on Arras. On 9 October, the day Antwerp fell, Foch reported to Joffre that the situation around Arras was well in hand.

Antwerp's fall on 9 October radically changed the situation Foch faced in the north. The Belgian Army had escaped from the city and was making its way west. It had thus far slipped away from the Germans, but it needed help to make sure it could reassemble in safety. To cover its withdrawal and defend the Channel

Military Views on Trenches in 1914

Although pre-war plans and war games did not include trenches, the idea was not completely alien to generals in 1914. Several officers had seen trench warfare as observers in the Russo-Japanese War. They drew different conclusions about them, however. Some noted that the Japanese had managed to attack and break Russian trench lines, suggesting that powerful offensives were stronger than trench-based defences. Others saw how fundamentally trench warfare challenged prevailing ideas and assumptions. After his experience in Manchuria, Sir Ian Hamilton was asked what role cavalry played in trench warfare. He replied that the cavalry could do little more than help prepare rice for the infantry.

ports, the British dispatched a new force, soon to be called IV Corps, to the Belgian ports of Zeebrugge and Ostend. They were met by a detachment of French marines who protected the 50,000 remaining Belgians as they withdrew in the face of 60,000 German soldiers freed from the siege of Antwerp.

The Belgians hoped to set up a new line of defence in the small strip of Belgium not yet under German occupation. Joffre urged them to turn south in order that they might be in a position to cover the left flank of the French Army, then advancing towards the Lys River. Instead, King Albert took them west to the line of the Yser River and the town of Dixmude. Albert was desperate to hold on to the last remaining part of Belgium for symbolic purposes, even if doing so made questionable strategic sense. The Belgian king, and now commander-in-chief of its armed forces, wanted to use the Yser as a barrier behind which he could receive and integrate stragglers from the march from

Fighting in Flanders posed unique challenges. The high water tables and fragile drainage systems of the region made digging trenches difficult. The Germans responded by developing an elastic defensive system that stretched back many kilometres and made use of concrete blockhouses.

Antwerp, rebuild his threadbare units and restore his army's badly shaken morale. Foch ordered the French marines to go with him and help him hold the region around Dixmude at all costs.

THE BATTLES OF YPRES AND THE YSER

Even before the fall of Antwerp, the remnants of unoccupied Belgium were beginning to figure in the larger plans of both sides. They offered the last chance for a flanking movement before the race to the sea actually arrived at the finish line. Even more importantly, they blocked the way to the French coastline. Dunkirk, the closest large port to the front line, sat just 40km (25 miles) behind Dixmude. If the Germans could push through Belgium, they could sweep along the coast, then turn south and envelop the Allied armies of the north. Both sides soon saw the value in owning the town of Ypres, where most of the region's main roads converged. Low ridges outside the town made the dominance of the eastern and southern approaches vital as well. A canal running through the centre of Ypres also provided a last-ditch line of defence if it were needed.

Sir John French recognized the value of Ypres as early as late September. He saw it as the best place for the concentration of the BEF because it both protected access routes to the BEF's critical Channel ports and provided a logical area for the deployment of new British arrivals. Accordingly, he had proposed to Joffre that the BEF be placed there, at the extreme left of the Allied line. On the night of 1 October, the BEF began to disengage from the flanking movements of the race to the sea and moved north to its concentration area at St Omer in French Flanders. The confusion and continuing combat forced the BEF to take a circuitous route, with II Corps marching west to Compiègne, then taking a train to Abbeville, hiking to Béthune and taking another train to Ypres. I Corps followed, detraining near Hazebrouck and marching the rest of

the way to Ypres. By 19 October, almost all elements of the BEF were in and around Ypres, with its main combat strength along the ridges just a few miles east of the town. At the same time, the survivors of the Belgian Army had completed their assembly along the Yser River near Dixmude. French reinforcements began to arrive as well; Foch dispatched French cavalry divisions to patrol the region south of Ypres between the town and the La Bassée canal. Joffre quickly ordered several French divisions to Flanders as well.

By 12 October, the Allies had formed a 50km-long (31 mile) line from Nieuport on the coast south to La

The expert marksmen of the BEF form a skirmish line along a road during the race to the sea. The photograph was obviously posed or taken during a period of rest as the photographer must have been standing and therefore an easy target for any German snipers nearby.

Bassée. The line curved to the east and south of Ypres, forming a salient based on the ridges outside the town. The men defending this line included a mix of nationalities and types of combat arms. The Belgians had six tattered infantry and two worn cavalry divisions; the British had two full corps and a third arriving from Britain as well as two cavalry divisions; and the French had scratched together six infantry divisions, six cavalry divisions and three divisions of Territorials. Both King Albert and Sir John French refused Joffre's attempts to put all of the forces under French authority in order to ensure unity of command. Both men jealously sought to retain their independence of action. The mistrust between Sir John French and the French headquarters staff was especially high.

They did, however, agree to abide by the general strategic and operational guidelines laid down by Foch, the recently named commander of Army Group North. French had his suspicions about Joffre, but he came to respect Foch's optimism and determination. Despite the recent deaths of his only son and son-in-law on the same day in combat in Belgium, Foch had written to a friend that 'I shall work with all of the

An artist's depiction of the aftermath of fighting on the Yser River and canal in October 1914. King Albert I authorized the opening of sluice gates to flood the fields of Flanders in order to slow the German advance. The onset of winter weather forced both sides to stop the fighting.

energy of which I am capable, absolutely confident of the issue of the fight, with the mercy of God helping us.' In his first two and half days in Flanders, Foch travelled more than 800km (500 miles) and met with nearly every British, French and Belgian divisional commander in the region. He was well aware that both King Albert and Sir John French outranked him and that he could not therefore issue them direct orders even if they had agreed to serve under overall French direction. He also knew, however, that only the French Army had reserves in the area to help the tired Belgians and British. He used the authority Joffre bestowed upon him to direct those reserves to impart his strategic vision on the situation in Flanders.

First and foremost, Foch immediately redirected forces to protect the coastline, easing Sir John French's concerns somewhat. The Royal Navy had also moved a squadron of cruisers off the coast to provide additional fire support if needed. Still, Foch found Sir John French despondent and thought the British staff was contemplating retiring behind the lines to Dunkirk or even Calais. Foch took French aside and gave him a dramatic speech to bolster his confidence:

'The British Army has never drawn back in its history. You have the honour of England in your hands as I have that of France. The entire world has its eyes on us. Even should this act result in my own death, I give you my word as a soldier that I will not take one step back. I want you to give me your word [to do the same] and it is your duty to give it to me.'

French agreed to stand firm at Ypres, but it was not the last time Foch had to bolster the confidence of the British commander.

Allied soldiers would need all the courage they could muster, as the Germans had determined to take Ypres. No fewer than five new German corps were available for the attack, some of them relatively fresh after the Antwerp siege, others newly called up. More than 40,000 German reinforcements arrived opposite the beleaguered Belgians alone. Foch initially took the bold step of ordering an attack toward the Lys River on 13 October. He hoped that an Allied offensive, like his attack in the marshes during the Battle of the Marne, would disrupt German timing and throw the enemy onto the defensive. He even spoke of his plans for advancing deep into Belgium, freeing the French city of Lille and preparing the Allies for a drive on the ports of Ostend and Zeebrugge, to be followed by a drive on to Brussels.

These Allied advances produced some minor tactical successes, and they turned away an attack by German troops against the Yser River on 18 October. Such successes temporarily produced a false sense of optimism among Allied generals. As the German Army began to arrive in larger numbers and with heavy artillery batteries, however, it became increasingly obvious that no breakthrough of the enemy lines was going to happen. By 20 October, the steam had largely come out of the Allied attack, although Foch ordered more offensives over the next two days with the much more modest objective of seizing Roulers, unaware of the large numbers of German soldiers headed towards Ypres.

The Allied attack on Roulers ran headlong into a German offensive Falkenhayn launched on 20 October. The Germans launched two attacks, one against the Belgian Army around Dixmude, and the other against the British at Ypres. In the latter attack, the Germans captured the ridges around the towns of Passchendaele and Peolcappelle, denying the Allies the advantage of high ground and providing the Germans with excellent points of observation. They had even more success against Dixmude, crossing the Yser and threatening to break through the lines protecting the Channel ports. The commander of the French marines, the Breton Admiral Pierre Ronarc'h, told his commander that his men might have to abandon the town as they had been in trenches for 72 hours without reinforcements or supplies. His men, he reported, 'were at the limits of physical and morale resistance'. His commander, the new French Eighth Army Commander General Victor d'Urbal, replied, 'Dixmude must be held even if you only have one marine left. ... If attacked you may dig trenches. ... The only thing you must not do is retreat.'

The British thought the situation to be the most serious they had yet faced in the course of the war so far. Two divisions of Indian soldiers were then en route to the Western Front, but the BEF at Ypres was exhausted and there was no guarantee that the Indian

> 'I consider our situation very satisfactory. ... The Second Army is recovering its confidence. There is no more talk of a retreat, which, in any case I have expressly forbidden.'
>
> Foch to Joffre, 10 October 1914

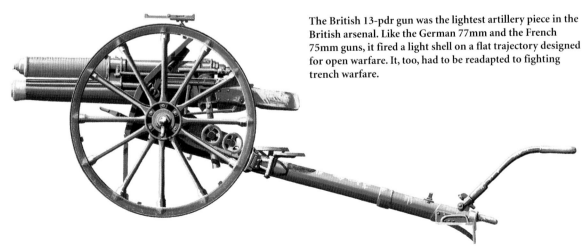

The British 13-pdr gun was the lightest artillery piece in the British arsenal. Like the German 77mm and the French 75mm guns, it fired a light shell on a flat trajectory designed for open warfare. It, too, had to be readapted to fighting trench warfare.

The Belgian town of Ypres was the scene of three major battles. Its magnificent cloth hall, like most other buildings in the town, was obliterated. It became a place of such intense connection to the British Army that Winston Churchill proposed having the British Government buy it from the Belgians.

reinforcements would arrive in time. The Indian Corps, 15,700 men strong, had left India on 27 August, but many British officers, including French, thought their weaponry and training not at all suited for modern warfare. French grew despondent again, turning to Foch and saying 'There is nothing left for me to do except to go up and be killed with the I Corps'. Foch responded, 'We must stand firm first. There will be time to die afterwards.'

The Allied line held, but only just. On 24 October, the Germans launched 15 separate attacks, threatening the integrity of the Allied line in numerous places. Young German draftees with minimal training and almost no combat experience conducted many of

these attacks. The inexperience of the Germans, combined with Foch's belated understanding of the need to assume the defensive, helped the Allies to hold on. So, too, did Albert's decision to open the sluice gates that kept the North Sea out of Flanders. He was loath to flood his own country intentionally and did so with the heaviest of hearts, but under his orders Belgian engineers snuck close enough to the German lines to hear their enemies talking, and, as high tide approached, opened the gates. The nearby Germans seem not to have recognized the importance of the gates and had left them undefended. Today the only official Belgian memorial to the battle is an equestrian statue of King Albert in military uniform standing by the spot where the engineers opened the sluice gates at Nieuport.

Over the next few days, the water levels in Flanders rose, providing a 32km-long (20 mile) and three-kilometre-wide (two mile) barrier of mud and mire behind which the Allies could regroup. The Germans were unable to move heavy equipment across the water and mud. Moreover, the inundations threatened to cut the German line in two, thus forcing Falkenhayn to order a withdrawal east of the Yser. Albert gave orders for the Belgian Army to form new defensive lines behind the inundations and posted marksmen behind the lines with directives to shoot any Belgian soldier they saw retreating. Foch then ordered attacks by the French 42nd Division south of the flooded regions that made some needed tactical gains and bought the Allies a bit of breathing room. The Germans still had important advantages; they were solidly in place on the Yser River and had many more men and artillery pieces in the sector than the Allies did. The region around Ypres, moreover, had not flooded as much as Dixmude had. Falkenhayn was so confident of imminent victory that he invited the Kaiser to come to Flanders and lead the triumphal entry of the German Army into Ypres. Foch heard of the Kaiser's arrival and told Sir John French 'The Kaiser wishes to enter Ypres. He shall not. I do not wish it'.

Around this time, one of the great German legends of the war was born. Desperate to break the British line, Falkenhayn sent in two reserve regiments filled with new draftees and volunteers. Some men were reported to be as young as 16. On 22 October, they attacked the British 1st Division near Bixschoote, approximately halfway between Dixmude and Ypres. They took enormous casualties, with one of the battalions losing 70 per cent of its men. Heavy losses were nothing especially novel for this phase of the war, but the youth of the soldiers in the reserve formations made their loss especially noteworthy. Also noteworthy was their singing of patriotic songs as they advanced. Some observers later claimed that they did so less out of a sense of patriotism than to be sure that their own inexperienced comrades would not accidentally fire on them, but whatever the reason, the event became one of the most memorable moments for Germans in 1914.

Reports of the young men singing as they went to their deaths quickly spread to both sides of the line. Adolf Hitler, then serving nearby with the Bavarians,

Antwerp

On 1 October, Churchill arrived in the city with three poorly equipped brigades of Royal Marines to help the five tattered divisions of the Belgian Army that had sought refuge there. A firm Allied presence in Antwerp would keep that port out of German hands and threaten the German lines of communication to northern France. At the very least, the Germans would need to commit troops to the siege of the city that would otherwise have either advanced on the coast or joined Falkenhayn's flanking movements. The British were anxious to maintain Antwerp as a thorn in the German side, but Joffre thought the city not worth saving. He wanted it abandoned so that the five divisions of the Belgian Army could join his own left wing and contribute to the defence of a more contiguous Allied line from the coast to the Alps. The Germans took Antwerp on 9 October.

Antwerp's importance had led the Belgians to invest heavily in its defence. The British and French disagreed on how to defend it in 1914.

wrote in *Mein Kampf* that the soldiers sang 'Deutschland, Deutschland über Alles', inspiring men all along the German lines. As Hitler's writings suggest, after the war the episode became a central tenet of ultra-nationalist German ideology, but it was not simply a fabrication of Nazi propagandists. British soldiers heard the singing as well, although some recorded that the song they heard was 'Die Wacht am Rhein'.

The charge of the young reservists, complete with the singing of patriotic songs, was custom made for a nation needing heroes. At the end of the battle, German Army headquarters issued a special communiqué on the incident. It soon became known in Germany as the *Kindermord*, or the slaughter of the innocents. Both a symbol of tragic (though at the same time heroic) loss and a source of much German propaganda, the *Kindermord* was one of the most enduring episodes of the war.

The Allies were still badly outnumbered, but the flooding around the Yser allowed them to focus their defensive efforts on Ypres. Foch even proposed two limited attacks on 26 October, one to rescue trapped French forces at Dixmude and another towards Courtrai. Once again, the Allied attack ran into a larger German attack and was quickly broken up. The Germans broke into the Allied line southeast of Ypres near Gheluvelt. That afternoon, hearing reports of panic in the British lines, I Corps commander Douglas Haig ran forward to find 'terror stricken men' running out of their trenches. They had been mistakenly placed in trenches on the forward slope of a hill rather than its reverse slope and were therefore dangerously exposed to German artillery and machine-gun fire. Haig reorganized the retreating men and formed a new defensive line that held.

Fortunately for Haig and the BEF, two divisions of Indian soldiers began to arrive, with the Lahore Division the first to reach Ypres, on 24 October. These

An aerial view of Ypres, called 'Wipers' by some British soldiers. This photograph shows the strategic importance of the town owing to the many roads that converged there. The destruction visible in the photograph is another grim testimony to the power of artillery.

Military Medicine in 1914

The French had introduced a limited number of motorized ambulances, but these were far too few to deal with the massive numbers of wounded men in 1914. The British system of horse-drawn ambulances failed entirely, forcing massive systemic changes. As it had been in the Franco-Prussian War, the German Army medical system was generally better trained and organized than that of their adversaries, but it too was soon overwhelmed by the demands made of it after months of combat of unanticipated ferocity. Doctors and nurses struggled throughout the war to deal not only with massive numbers of wounded, but with new physical and psychological conditions for which they had had little training.

forces provided much-needed relief to the men of the BEF. Of its 84 infantry battalions, 75 were down to one-third of the strength with which they had arrived in France in August. Kitchener considered removing French from command, but apparently could not find another officer in which he had any more confidence. He even approached Foch and Joffre about naming Sir Ian Hamilton to replace French, but the French generals thought it unwise to change commanders while such an intense battle still raged. Indications that the Germans were slowing their attacks gave Foch confidence that the crisis had passed and that he might be able to think about the Allies resuming the attack themselves. He soon began planning for a series of local attacks to begin on 6 November.

Falkenhayn once again beat him to the punch, launching yet another attack on 31 October. This time the Germans also attacked at night, chasing British cavalry units off the Messines Ridge to the south of

Ypres. John French had another of his moments of despondency, later remarking that 'during these two days [31 October and 1 November], nothing kept the British Empire from effective ruin and disappearance as a great power except a thin and irregular line held by exhausted soldiers'. Haig's men answered the call once again, counterattacking and holding off a furious German charge on 2 November. Foch rushed what few French reinforcements were available in the region into the line, stabilizing the situation somewhat, but at the same time underscoring just how precarious the Allied hold on Ypres was.

Falkenhayn made one last push, sending in the elite Prussian Guards on 11 November. They were supported by the heaviest concentration of artillery yet seen on the Western Front. Haig's I Corps sat in the direct line of the German attack. The Germans got to within six kilometres (four miles) of Ypres, but they were slow to exploit the openings they created. British soldiers, including cooks, clerks and orderlies hastily given rifles, fought them off, with the fighting becoming hand to hand along the critical Menin Road leading into Ypres. The Germans got inside Dixmude, but their efforts to gain Ypres failed once again. The

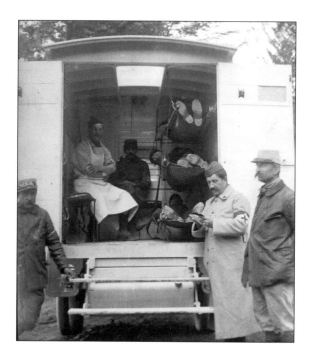

The medical staffs of 1914 were completely overwhelmed by the number of wounded they had to treat. The German medical system generally performed better than the French, although the French were at the forefront of creating mobile field hospitals like the one seen here.

Germans with abandoned 240mm French cannon after the First Battle of the Marne. The French had too few pieces of this size in 1914, but worked quickly to build more and more heavy guns throughout 1914 and 1915. Note the camouflage netting designed to hide the gun from enemy aviators.

Kaiser went back to Berlin, disappointed at his chance to lead his men into a town that had already acquired significant symbolic value to both sides.

Bad winter weather began in mid-November, adding to the misery of the tired men of four armies fighting there. Falkenhayn decided to end the campaign on 22 November, having failed to break through the Allied line and threaten the Channel ports. Both sides were spent, having used up all of their human and material resources. Joffre remembered what became known as the First Battle of Ypres as a 'severe trial' that had threatened the Channel ports. But if the Allies had succeeded in keeping the Germans from breaking through as they had intended, they had at the same time failed to break the German lines and recover western Belgium as they had hoped. 'Although we had succeeded in holding up the enemy in his attempt to reach the sea,' Joffre noted, 'I must admit that I hoped for more.'

Joffre's comments seem unmerited given how much the Belgians, French and British suffered. Both sides emerged from Ypres at the absolute limits of their efforts. Estimating casualty figures is a notoriously inaccurate process, but the generally accepted numbers for this battle are staggering. A century earlier, not far away from Ypres at another Belgian town, Waterloo, the British had suffered 15,000 casualties. It was then the largest battle ever fought by the British Army. By comparison, the British 7th Division alone at Ypres suffered 9865 casualties. It had less than one-third of the infantrymen that had arrived with it at Zeebrugge on 6 October. Five other British formations, including the Indian Corps, exceeded 5000 casualties each. Total estimated casualties for the BEF from 14 October to 22 November are 54,000, or more than three times British casualties at Waterloo. The old BEF was gone, doomed to become what one British journalist later called 'an heroic memory'. Ypres itself had already become known as 'the immortal salient', a symbol of British ability to fight against many times their numbers in the face of tremendous adversity.

Nor, of course, were the British the only ones to suffer at Ypres. In addition to the British casualties, one must add the estimated 50,000 casualties suffered by the French and 19,000 suffered by the Belgians to give a complete sense of what the defence of Ypres meant to the Allies. The Germans had suffered terribly at Ypres as well. Their casualty estimates vary considerably, but most experts accept a figure no lower than 80,000 and many think the true figure is closer to 134,000. The deaths of so many young Germans, highlighted by the legend of the

Ypres was at the centre of the last part of unoccupied Belgium. As such, this small town took on an enormous symbolic importance. The relatively flat nature of the ground meant that even modest ridges were strategically significant, as were the canals and roads that radiated from the town.

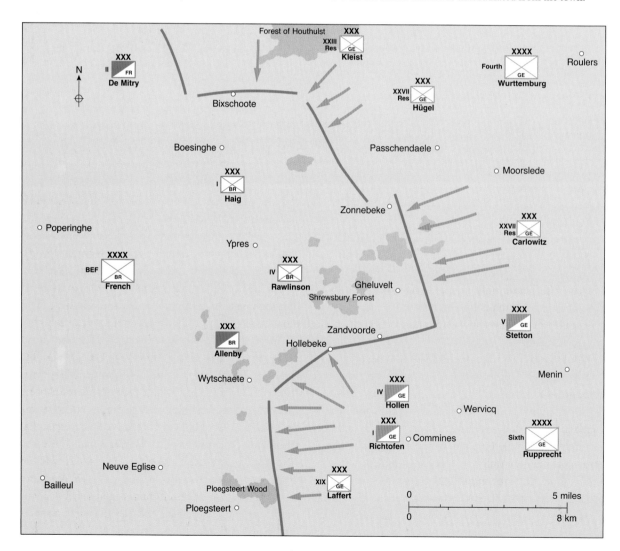

Kindermord, gave the battle a special poignancy in Germany as well as Britain. Some newly formed German regiments suffered casualty rates at 60 per cent or higher. In all cases, casualties had been particularly high among new recruits and among officers, who had held the responsibility of leading from the front. Armies would therefore need to find new leaders and devise new ways of fighting.

The campaign in Flanders encompassed two separate, but interrelated battles, the Battle of Yser and the Battle of Ypres. Whereas the Battle of Waterloo had essentially been decided in one dramatic day, the campaign in Flanders had lasted almost a month, with little opportunity for the men engaged to leave the line and rest. When it was over, the line around Ypres remained a salient jutting into German lines. The Germans controlled much of the high ground to the south and east, as well as the roads going south to the French town of Armentières. The British held a forest on the eastern edge of the salient called Polygon Wood and several of the smaller towns east of Ypres. This geography informed the basic military calculations of both the Allies and the Germans for the next three years amid constant desultory fighting and two more major campaigns.

The First Battle of Ypres ended the bloodiest year of combat that a violent Europe had ever seen. In less than four months, the BEF had reported almost 90,000 men dead, wounded or missing in action. The original BEF that had deployed to France had numbered only 80,000 men. France had seen more than a quarter of a million of its sons killed, and more than half of all of the men in the Belgian Army when the war began were casualties by Christmas.

None of the armies had anything to show for such losses except an uncertain future in a new kind of war.

Corporal Redpath of the elite Black Watch regiment won a DCM at the First Battle of Ypres for his role in holding up an attack by the Prussian Guards. His rapid and accurate fire helped to conceal the actual numerical weakness of British forces at Ypres and was symbolic of the professionalism of the men of the original BEF.

On an operational level, Ypres ended the mobile phase of combat in World War I and ushered in a war of positions. Men dug in to protect themselves all along the line, even in the soupy terrain of Flanders. By the end of 1914, no more flanks existed for armies to turn or exploit. The winter of 1914/15 gave soldiers time to consolidate their trench networks and reinforce them with concrete, steel, and whatever other materials were readily at hand.

In a very few isolated parts of the line on the Western Front, the year ended with informal truces at Christmas. Over the years, the significance of these truces has been blown far out of proportion as a way to celebrate the basic humanity of Europeans that seemed to be fading in 1914. The first year of the war had ended with the pre-war plans of both sides in ruins and hundreds of thousands of men dead and maimed. As 1915 began, all sides began to think about new strategies, operations and tactics to win the war and stop the suffering.

CHAPTER 3

Digging In

In 1915, any thoughts of a quick war began to dissipate. Massive offensives supported by enormous artillery barrages failed to break the stalemate on the Western Front. Armies reacted with even larger artillery pieces and introduced new weapons like poison gas, all to little effect.

There may have been Christmas truces on some parts of the Western Front, but not in Champagne, where a battle had been raging since the middle of December. Joffre had envisioned a grand offensive in the region aimed at attacking the southern shoulder of the enormous bump in the line (called a salient in military terms) that jutted toward Paris. At its extreme, the German front line created by the salient sat at Noyon, 112km (70 miles) from the capital. The losses of 1914 notwithstanding, Joffre knew he had to attack. The Germans controlled important French industrial sites, especially coal and iron ore mines that would be critical to winning any long war. The need to keep the pressure off the Russians also remained central to his thinking. If the

'Artillery conquers, infantry occupies' was the motto. Artillery, like the piece shown here in Champagne, was supposed to clear the way for the advance of the infantry. The reality, however, rarely corresponded to the theory.

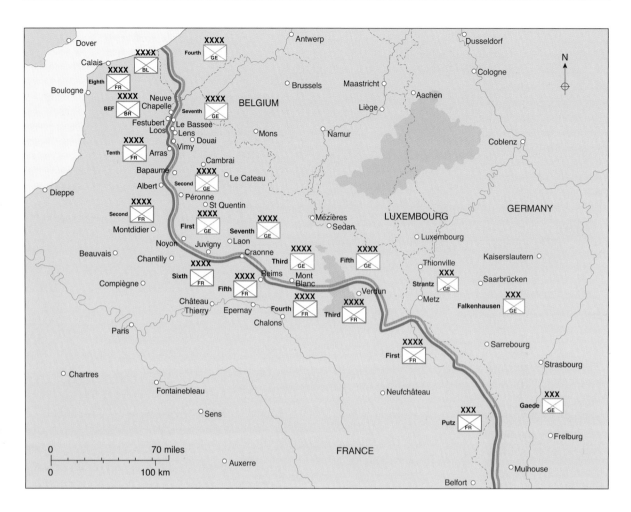

Russians were forced out of the war, he knew that the Germans would be free to focus all of their military energies against France.

THE FIRST BATTLE OF CHAMPAGNE

Joffre proposed advancing north through Champagne in order to break into the southern edge of the gigantic German salient. Joffre's order of the day of 17 December noted that the French had for three months stopped all German efforts to break French lines, but that the defensive alone was insufficient. The time had come to 'profit from German weakness' owing to Germany's losses in the war's early phases. The arrival of new French reinforcements, Joffre argued, would give the army the men it needed to resume the offensive. 'The hour for the attack has arrived,' he

The development of two strong parallel trench systems made the Allied requirement of attacking all the more difficult. The Germans, who had decided on a major offensive in the east in 1915, had the relative luxury of remaining on the defensive on the Western Front for much of 1915.

wrote, 'France counts more than ever on your heart, your energy, and your will to win at all costs. You have already vanquished the Germans on the Marne, the Yser, in Lorraine and in the Vosges. You will continue to vanquish [them] until the final triumph.' Once his offensive in Champagne succeeded, Joffre expected that the moment of that final triumph would not be too far away.

Joffre dedicated almost all of the guns in the French artillery reserve, 718 pieces in all, to this operation. They opened fire on 20 December 1914 on German positions well sited on high ground north of the road linking Reims and Valmy. These positions were much stronger than French intelligence had believed; in places they included three separate lines of barbed wire, timber revetments and concrete emplacements to buttress the trenches, and a system of buried telephone lines. Although the total number of French artillery pieces made it one of the largest such concentrations of the war thus far, more than two-thirds of the French guns were 75mm pieces, which proved to be of limited utility. In one case, a French corps fired 150 shells from each 75mm gun it had, but had not produced a single breach in the German barbed wire larger than three and a half metres by six metres.

French soldiers from XVII Corps attacked on either side of the village of Perthes-lès-Hurlus, soon to become one of the many in the region razed to the ground as a result of the fighting. Just to their east, men of the Colonial Corps (many of them Moroccans and Tunisians) had the responsibility of attacking a formation known as La Main ('The Hand') de Massiges because it featured five long, slender hills 'pointing' southwest like fingers. The tallest of the hills was 191m (627ft) high and featured some of the most intricate German trenches yet built. Most of the terrain between Perthes-lès-Hurlus and Massiges, by contrast, was open, gently rolling farmland, affording the Germans excellent observation of the French attack from their hilltop positions.

The French 75

Pre-war French doctrine had been based around the light, agile and rapid-firing 75mm field piece. It had been designed with the mobile offensive in mind, and could advance with attacking infantry in order to provide French soldiers with fire support on the move. The static warfare of the Western Front, however, demanded larger and heavier guns. The 75mm's agility came at a crucial price, as its shells were too light to penetrate the best trench defences. Moreover, its flat trajectory made it ill suited to strike targets underground or on the reverse slopes of hills. Because the doctrine of the pre-war French Army had never envisioned a war of positions, guns larger than 75mm were in relatively short supply. To complicate matters further, production of shells for the 75mm were at half of the minimum daily requirement Joffre had deemed necessary.

Without accurate and sufficient artillery support, the French attack was doomed. The artillery had been unable either to destroy the German barbed wire or silence enemy machine guns. As a result, French soldiers charged ahead into furious rifle and machine-gun fire, often having to stop to try to cut holes in the wire. The French managed to achieve some temporary gains, but they could rarely sustain them. Attacks from 20 to 30 December had gained only a few hundred metres amid heavy casualties. Sensing the desperation, Joffre fed more men from the French reserve corps into the battle, but these attacks failed as well, proving that mass alone could not break

The French 75mm artillery piece was an excellent gun, but not always adapted to the needs of trench warfare. Later in the war, the Americans took large numbers of them and invented a drink in its honour. The '75' was three parts Champagne, one part brandy.

French Colonial Troops

Like their British allies, the French relied heavily upon troops from their colonies to bulk up their armies on the Western Front and elsewhere, especially during the first year of the war. The majority of the French colonial troops came from northern and western Africa, such as Senegal, Ivory Coast, Gabon, Morocco and Algeria. The north Africans were generally known as 'Turcos'.

In all approximately 569,000 French colonials were mobilized to fight for France during World War I, of which about 58,000 were killed or missing by the war's end. They were primarily infantry formations, led by French officers, and the majority wore khaki rather than the blue uniforms of the metropolitan soldiers.

The Great Mosque of Paris was built after the war as a sign of France's thanks to the Muslim soldiers who fought against Germany.

were too weak to do enough damage to German positions to allow French soldiers to break through. Nor could breakthroughs themselves be sustained because of the difficulty of moving and supplying reserves through gaps in the enemy line.

Some French generals, including Ferdnand de Langle de Cary, whose Fourth Army conducted the Champagne attacks, argued that large-scale breakthroughs were unfeasible given the conditions imposed by modern warfare. He and others argued that the French should instead conduct smaller, more carefully designed offensives aimed at concentrating overwhelming force against specific points in the enemy line such as the Main de Massiges. Having secured these positions, French forces could then move on to another objective, always attacking carefully and methodically with prodigious quantities of artillery support. This strategy, which came to be known as *grignotage* (literally, nibbling), promised to spare French lives, but it also meant that there would be no quick liberation of France.

At the end of January, Joffre warned the French Government not to expect any sudden victories, but he was not converted to *grignotage* yet either. He

'As we approached the front the traditional brick-red trousers and kepis still worn by the second-line men gave way to the new uniform of silvery blue – the colour of early morning. There were soldiers everywhere.'

E. Alexander Parker, *Vive la France*

through well-defended enemy lines. Freezing rain and much colder temperatures arrived on 8 January 1915, putting a temporary halt to operations in the region.

These attacks mark the first real efforts by the Allies to break solid German trench lines. The high losses for such limited territorial gains stunned officers and politicians alike. In just over two weeks in Champagne the French had taken 30,000 casualties for negligible gains. The French high command concluded that it needed much heavier and more accurate artillery support. Many of the 75mm guns wore out because they had not been designed for so much use. As a result, the tubes warped and the shells fired from them often fell too short, sometimes hitting French troops by mistake. Even those shells that did find their marks

planned another offensive designed to sever the rail lines with which the Germans supplied their men in the Champagne region. Without the ability to supply their men, Joffre anticipated that the Germans would have no choice but to retreat to the next layer of lateral rail lines, thereby surrendering the Chemin des Dames

Ridge and making a new Allied offensive in the direction of the Argonne and Ardennes forests possible. Several subsequent Allied offensives followed similar lines of thinking, hoping to achieve great results by cutting the critical rail lines modern armies needed to keep them armed and supplied.

These rail lines, however, sat six kilometres (four miles) north of the positions the French had thus far failed to take, meaning that the French would need to achieve great success where they had already failed. To improve his chances at victory, Joffre requested that the British take over the defence of more of the Ypres sector with an eye toward moving the French Eighth Army south from Belgium to Champagne. The British

demurred, in part because they had their own plans for offensives in Flanders and Artois, and in part because they (correctly) sensed that the French were trying to subordinate British operations to their own. Even without reinforcement by the Eighth Army, by 12 February, de Langle's Fourth Army had concentrated 155,000 infantrymen and 861 artillery pieces for another attack in Champagne. Only 12 per cent of the artillery pieces were heavier than 75mm, but Joffre still anticipated a breakthrough, assembling 8000 cavalry

A trench along the Champagne front. This trench is relatively clean and dry, suggesting that it might be a second or third line trench. Most trench systems were abysmal places where men shared mud with lice, rats and unburied corpses.

to exploit any gaps the infantry created. They would use their speed to cut off German lines of retreat and reach critical railway junctures, holding them until reinforced by advancing French infantry.

One of the many unpleasantries of winter combat, a sudden snowstorm, struck French lines on the anticipated start date, 12 February. Snow made the movement of men and supplies difficult. It also grounded observation planes and blinded artillery observers, thus making indirect fire impossible. Consequently, the offensive had to be postponed for four days while the skies cleared. The Germans had already anticipated a resumption of the French attacks and had improved their defences in the area accordingly, turning many of the farmhouses of the region into veritable warrens of machine guns and

snipers' nests. The delay caused by the snowstorm allowed the Germans to complete their final defensive preparations and put reserve units on alert.

Nevertheless, the offensive went ahead as soon as weather permitted. On 16 February, four French corps attacked along a five-kilometre (eight-mile) front between Perthes-lès-Hurlus and Massiges. The French took some front-line German trenches, but failed to

Ferdinand Foch (1851–1929)

Foch was among the most aggressive and intelligent of World War I commanders. Before the war, while visiting England, Sir Henry Wilson had introduced him to senior British officials as the 'fellow who is going to command the allied armies when the big war comes on'. He had taught at the French War College that wars were won through superior morale and superior will. The fighting in 1914 and 1915 had led him to reject these ideas and develop more sophisticated notions of war. He also had a gift for working with allies, a trait that helped him become the obvious choice for the job of supreme Allied commander for the Western Front in 1918.

advance more than 1500m (1640 yards) in any one part of the line. French troops had managed to seize a critical German strongpoint, the ironically named Ferme de Beauséjour (Farm of the Pleasant Stay), which had traded hands two dozen times so far, on 27 February. Soldiers in the French lines came to call it Beauséjour le Mal Nommé (Beauséjour the Badly Named). Overlooking Beauséjour sat the 200m-high (656ft) Butte du Mesnil, which the Germans held, putting any French positions near Beauséjour le Mal Nommé under constant observation and German artillery shelling.

Knowing that his men could not sit for long in Beauséjour under the nose of the Germans, Joffre ordered the Fourth Army reserves forward for another major push. On 9 March, French forces launched what

Much of the Champagne region remained calm during the war, even as large battles that characterized the fighting of 1915 raged nearby. Many farmers stayed on their land and soldiers reported that in times of calm they could buy luxuries like foie gras and, of course, wine from the locals.

Joffre hoped would be a 'brutal' assault. This attack proceeded much like those of previous weeks, with small gains at high costs. Every French gain seemed to suggest to optimistic officers that the plan was working, but others described the gains as operationally meaningless and reported that French soldiers could not advance past the intense German machine-gun fire. By 17 March, de Langle had concluded that the offensive had failed and he requested that Joffre order it to be stopped. Joffre remained optimistic for three more days, but finally agreed to stop the attacks. France had taken 93,432

casualties to gain less than three square kilometres (one square mile) of obliterated French farmland, losses that were far too high to sustain for any length of time.

NEUVE CHAPELLE

By the time that the French offensive in Champagne had wound down, the British had decided to resume the offensive. They chose the region just to the south of the Lys River near the village of Neuve Chapelle. Fighting in the region during the race to the sea in 1914 had created a salient in the line that jutted west into British positions. The Germans could therefore pour artillery fire from the salient into the flanks of any British offensive to the north or the south of the town. The salient would have to be eliminated before any large-scale British offensive in the region could

A brigade headquarters attempting to camouflage itself on the British sector of the Western Front. Although it would be hard to miss from ground level, the camouflage is intended to deceive observation pilots.

take place. Douglas Haig's I Corps had recently been reorganized as the heart of a new British First Army and Haig set Neuve Chapelle as the first target for his new formation.

The geography of the Neuve Chapelle region promised large gains if the British could break through the German trench line. Neuve Chapelle lay less than 16km (10 miles) west of the French industrial city and railroad junction of Lille. To the northeast sat another critical railway juncture, Armentières, on the Franco-Belgian border. Between the two towns and Neuve Chapelle ran a major north-to-south trunk railway line that the Germans needed to supply their soldiers in the region. From the trunk line, the Germans used two light rail lines and the La Bassée Canal to move supplies west into Neuve Chapelle itself.

Haig wanted to cut these lines of communication. Doing so would make it impossible for the Germans to supply their troops west of Lille. They would, Haig assumed, respond to any rupture of their front lines by

The effects of a German artillery barrage. Throughout 1915 armies introduced larger artillery pieces that fired increasingly powerful shells. Men soon came to identify various types of shells by their sound.

retreating east of Lille and Armentières, thereby giving those two towns back to France. Control of Armentières would also provide access to southern Belgium, thus opening up a route into the Ypres sector for which the Germans had not prepared a defence. To achieve these aims, Haig laid out a three-stage plan. First, British troops would drive through German defences and eliminate the salient around Neuve Chapelle, thus neutralizing the ability of the Germans to fire into the flanks of advancing British units. Second, the British would advance east, creating their own salient jutting into German lines from which British gunners could cover the advance of British troops to the north and south of the salient. Third, British forces would continue to press east, cutting the light rail lines and the La Bassée Canal, thus putting

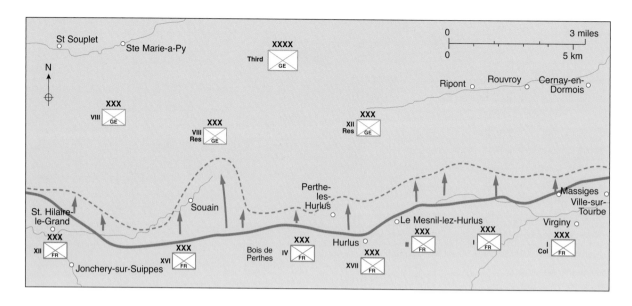

St Souplet
Ste Marie-a-Py

XXXX
Third | GE

Ripont Rouvroy Cernay-en-Dormois

N

0 .... 3 miles
0 .... 5 km

XXX
VIII | GE

XXX
VIII Res | GE

XXX
XII Res | GE

Souain

Perthe-les-Hurlus

St. Hilaire-le-Grand

Le Mesnil-lez-Hurlus

Massiges
Ville-sur-Tourbe

Virginy

XXX
XII | FR

XXX
XVI | FR

Jonchery-sur-Suippes

XXX
Bois de Perthes
IV | FR

Hurlus

XXX
XVII | FR

XXX
II | FR

XXX
I | FR

XXX
Col | FR

The meagre gains of the 1915 Battle of Champagne. The key action was fought at the Ferme de Navarin in the centre of this map. Even today the area remains littered with barbed wire and shell fragments, as well as enough unexploded ordnance to discourage farming in some areas.

pressure on the critical German supply lines. British forces would also capture a low ridge known as the Aubers Ridge that ran east to west between Neuve Chapelle and Lille. Although rarely rising much higher than 20m (66ft), control of it greatly facilitated observation and indirect fire of artillery.

To accomplish his goals, Haig assembled a multinational force. This consisted of IV Corps of the British Army, which included two divisions that had not been part of the original BEF: the 7th, which had already fought at Antwerp and Ypres, and the 8th, which had yet to fight a major battle. These two divisions had the responsibility of attacking the north shoulder of the German salient at Neuve Chapelle. Added to these forces were two Indian divisions and a Canadian division.

Haig had plenty of time to prepare the offensive in minute detail. Sir John French approved the plan on 15 February, but the British could not begin the attack until the ground began to dry. The British First Army had six divisions in the 21km (13-mile) frontage around Neuve Chapelle against just two German

divisions. To support them, Haig had concentrated an artillery barrage designed to, in Haig's own words, 'surprise the Germans, to carry them right off their legs'. He hoped that a surprise artillery attack of great intensity and power would shock the Germans in the front line and instil in them enough panic to make them break and run. British forces could then move into the breaches created and set up their forward lines. The British quietly moved 342 artillery pieces into the sector with the intention of unleashing a furious barrage with no notice, hopefully catching the Germans unaware. In terms of the intensity of fire per metre of enemy trench line, it was to be the most powerful barrage seen on the Western Front until 1917.

Its brevity, however, offset the intensity of the barrage. Owing to the low stocks of ammunition for most artillery pieces, the first phase of the artillery barrage would last just 35 minutes, enough time, Haig concluded, to eliminate most centres of opposition in the German front lines. The second phase of the barrage would then 'lift', or move forwards, and fire for 30 minutes on the village of Neuve Chapelle itself and likely areas near the village where the Germans might have concentrated reserves. Any other artillery firing had to be approved at Haig's headquarters in order to conserve precious ammunition.

At 7.30 in the morning of 10 March 1915, British gunners opened fire on the German front line. In just 35 minutes, the powerful British artillery outside Neuve Chapelle fired more shells than the entire British Army had fired in the three years of the South African War (1899–1902). The 18-pdr guns, the heart of the British artillery, fired more than 41,000 rounds in one day. In all the British guns fired 61,219 shells on the first day of the battle alone. The noise and power of the artillery was unlike anything men on both sides of the line had ever heard or seen. The ground trembled and the concussions from the shells threw up great chunks of earth. When the first phase of the barrage lifted at 8.05am, British troops left their trenches and moved into their front-line attack positions. The barrage seemed to have done its job, as British troops found the German positions only lightly held. At 8.30am they moved on to Neuve Chapelle and found it, too, lightly defended. By 9.00am advance parties from IV Corps held the main street of Neuve Chapelle and the Indian Corps had advanced in tandem, thus securing the southern approaches to the town.

Once troops were inside Neuve Chapelle itself, however, the British plan began to unravel. It proved to be more difficult than Haig suspected to maintain contact with his corps and division commanders, and to receive timely, accurate information on events in the front lines. Some battalions had no enemy troops in front of them, but had no orders directing their

World War I Artillery Techniques

World War I artillerists used a sophisticated technique known as indirect fire, whereby the gunners did not actually see the targets they were supposed to destroy. Instead they relied on information relayed to them by spotters, who could help the gunners to correct the accuracy of their shooting. All armies had begun the process of using aviators as their spotters, but systems of communication were still in their infancy. Eventually aviators worked out complex techniques for finding enemy target sets and relaying that information quickly to field commanders.

advance and thus sat motionless despite the lack of resistance. Other units needed artillery support to dislodge German defenders, but could not report their locations and correct the accuracy of the shelling in time to make a difference. Although the British had taken precautions to lay triple telephone lines, even many of these were cut during the heat of battle, leaving commanders without reliable means of contacting their men. Unable to coordinate the movement of his various units, and unwilling to risk sending them forward piecemeal without flank support, IV Corps commander General Sir Henry Rawlinson moved slowly. Rawlinson, who had

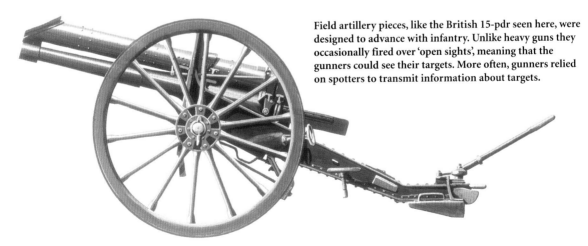

Field artillery pieces, like the British 15-pdr seen here, were designed to advance with infantry. Unlike heavy guns they occasionally fired over 'open sights', meaning that the gunners could see their targets. More often, gunners relied on spotters to transmit information about targets.

expressed doubts about the prospects of advancing as far east as Haig had envisioned, sought to consolidate and prepare to meet a German counterattack he believed might come at any hour. Thus as night began to fall, the British were well short of their objectives despite the lack of active German opposition.

On the night of 10/11 March the British held a line just east of Neuve Chapelle itself. As the French had done in Champagne, the British had managed to make a temporary break in the German lines, but had been unable to exploit it. The problems of commanding and controlling a large offensive were still too difficult for officers to solve. The art of designing artillery support on the fly for advancing units was also still in its infancy, making it almost impossible for units to advance beyond the effective range of their own field artillery pieces. Nevertheless, the British worked through the night, planning a coordinated six-battalion attack to be launched at daybreak against Aubers Ridge.

The Germans, too, were working during the night, strengthening their defences in front of the ridge. Perhaps more importantly, the Germans moved quickly to reinforce the sector. Within two hours of the start of the British offensive, the first orders had gone out for German reserves to move toward Aubers; they began to arrive in force late that afternoon. From the very start, the Germans envisioned not just containing the British, but launching a counterattack to recover the village of Neuve Chapelle and dislodge the British from the ground they had gained.

THE SECOND DAY

On the morning of 11 March, the British attacked again, but without success. They had not had time to repeat the careful planning that had characterized the attack of 10 March, thus the artillery preparation was much weaker and less accurate. Shrapnel shells especially proved to have only limited value in cutting German barbed wire. Thus some British battalions advanced against stiff German resistance based around carefully sited and concealed machine guns. German artillery barrages prevented the British from moving reserves to the front, thus isolating some units

from support and reinforcement. One British battalion commander even refused to honour a request from a neighbouring battalion for a supporting attack, saying that 'it is a mere waste of life, impossible to go 20 yards [18m] much less 200 yards [180m]'. Communications problems made it extremely difficult for Rawlinson and Haig to get an accurate picture of which beleaguered British units needed help the most. The British blamed 'misunderstandings', miscommunications and a thick mist that impeded artillery observation and indirect fire for the failure to break through on day two. Haig nevertheless ordered preparations for the offensive to be resumed the next morning.

The Germans, however, had their own plans. Having turned aside two days of British attacks and having accumulated six new battalions and dozens of large guns into the sector, they decided to attack. On the morning of 12 March, more than 10,000 German soldiers launched a counterattack aimed at retaking all of the ground they had lost over the preceding two days. German forces attacked at 12 separate places along the British front line, targeting the centre and both flanks simultaneously. Their attacks, however, proved to be little better organized than those of the British, resulting in heavy casualties to both sides. German artillery units missed many of their targets and, as the British had done on the second day of the battle, the Germans only succeeded in creating small gaps in the line that they could not exploit.

Around 3.00 in the afternoon, Haig received definitive reports that the German attack had gained ground, but had been contained. Acting on inaccurate information that the German failure had created a state of demoralization in the enemy's lines, Haig told Sir John French that the situation was 'promising', and requested that French release to him one cavalry

Lance-Corporal W. D. Fuller shown here in a painting depicting his heroic act. He won a Victoria Cross at the Battle of Neuve Chapelle for attacking Germans in a communication trench. He used a grenade in the attack, killing the senior German officer in the group. Although he was alone at the time of the attack, the remaining 50 men surrendered to him.

division and one cavalry brigade. Haig then ordered the Lahore Division forwards, but it had trouble moving against the Germans, who were not nearly as demoralized as Haig had believed. As dusk descended on the battlefield, the Indian Corps commander cancelled all attacks by his men and the battle ended.

When it was all over, the three-day Battle of Neuve Chapelle had done little to change the situation on the Western Front. The British had taken the village itself and had straightened out the front line, but even this small achievement had cost the British Army 11,600 men dead, wounded, and missing. German losses had

been similar, but the Germans still held the key lateral railway lines as well as Aubers Ridge and most of the light railway lines as well. Still, many British officers looked upon the operation as a great success because it had shown the feasibility of breaking the German lines and, they believed, they had learned several valuable lessons for the future, including the need for better communications between the infantry and the artillery and the need to increase the amount of artillery employed.

THE SECOND BATTLE OF YPRES AND THE INTRODUCTION OF GAS WARFARE

In the wake of Neuve Chapelle, the British assumed a generally defensive posture, refocusing their efforts to the north around Ypres. The British deployed 16 divisions in the salient, including the Canadian Division and the two Indian divisions. The French placed two divisions, the 45th Algerian and the 87th Territorial, to bolster the northern shoulder of the salient, although the British judged them as 'hardly first-class' units. Opposite them, the Germans had just 11 divisions, but the British and French took few chances. The high water tables of Belgium meant that digging in provided less protection than it did in other parts of the Western Front. The defences in the Ypres Salient therefore often relied on above ground breastworks and the fortified remains of farmhouses.

In March and early April 1915, the Germans appeared to show few signs of wanting to take the offensive in the near future. Daily artillery shelling increased in intensity, but not enough to cause the

The British hoped to break German positions near Neuve Chapelle and threaten the enemy lines of communication. Without the use of the region's rail lines and canals, the Germans could not supply their army in the area and would have to retreat to secure lines of communication.

British to take the situation too seriously. Most of the shelling was aimed at Ypres itself, with the intention of destroying any tall buildings the Allies might use for observation over the relatively flat region near the town. These buildings included the cathedral and the large Cloth Hall. On 15 April, however, the British received a report from French Second Army intelligence that had been prepared with information from what the French called 'a reliable agent'. It warned that intelligence received from German prisoners of war captured near Langemarck (the scene of the *Kindermord*) indicated that the Germans were planning an attack on Ypres in the coming days. It further warned that the Germans 'intend making use of tubes with asphyxiating gas'. When captured the German prisoner had in his possession 'a small sack

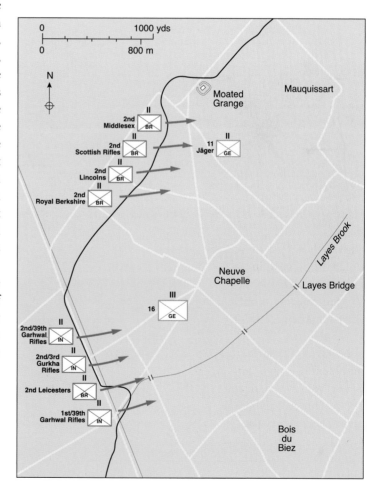

filled with a kind of gauze or cotton waste which would be dipped in some solution to counteract the effect of this gas'. The report also concluded that all indications pointed to a recent rise in German morale.

Neither the French nor the British took the information very seriously. There were few signs of an imminent German attack, and even the French general who passed the report to the British expressed doubt about its reliability, speculating that the soldier might have been part of a ruse to draw Allied attention to the Ypres sector while the Germans planned an offensive elsewhere. The British called the report 'circumstantial' and, when Royal Flying Corps

British positions near Neuve Chapelle in an obviously posed photograph. Note the communications trenches perpendicular to the front or 'fire' trench. The Germans were impressed by the speed of the British at 'digging in'.

sorties failed to find anything unusual behind German lines, they dismissed it. Some British commanders passed the report down their chains of command with the note 'for what it is worth', but few quite knew what to make of it.

The Allies had badly misread German intentions. Falkenhayn was indeed planning an offensive against Ypres and gas weapons sat at the heart of his plan. The German high command had decided on a massive spring offensive in the east to take advantage of the gains made there in 1914 and to provide some badly needed help to the Austro-Hungarians, who had not fared so well.

To give the offensive its best chance of success, Falkenhayn needed to shift eight divisions to the Eastern Front. He also wanted to blunt any Allied attempts to conduct offensives in the west that might disrupt German planning. He knew, however, that the Germans did not possess adequate resources (especially manpower) to conduct a large-scale offensive with any reasonable chance of success. The German high command therefore settled on a small attack near Ypres on the assumption that it would draw significant Allied attention and distract the British and French from German plans to attack in the east. The Germans planned to attack without a large artillery barrage in order to maintain secrecy; thus when the RFC pilots reported that they had detected nothing out of the ordinary they meant that they had seen no large artillery batteries and no masses of infantry reserves.

Even if they had spotted them, it is unlikely that the pilots would have known what to make of the 6000 small cylinders that the Germans had concentrated around Ypres. They contained the key to the offensive and the means by which Falkenhayn had planned to compensate for inferior German resources in the sector. Inside the cylinders was chlorine gas, a simple

compound to produce that caused irritation to the eyes in small doses, but in large doses could kill by suffocation. Poison gas had been banned by all combatant nations at the 1899 and 1907 Hague Conventions, but by 1915 these restrictions seemed quaint and outdated. They were certainly nothing to

> ## 'We soon found out at a terrible price that these gases were terrible poison. … The scene that followed was heartbreaking.'
>
> Sergeant-Major Ernest Shepherd,
> 1st Dorsets at the Second Battle of Ypres

get in the way of a man like Falkenhayn, who saw a chance to make military use out of Germany's large and sophisticated chemicals industry.

Sharing British opinions about their low quality, the Germans planned to use the gas on the Algerians and the French Territorials on the north shoulder of the Ypres salient. Because they would be releasing the gas from cylinders, however, they had to wait for favourable winds to blow south. The prevailing westerly winds would have the unfortunate effect of blowing the gas back on German lines, therefore the

The IEF

At the outbreak of the war, the British quickly dispatched the Lahore and Meerut divisions to the Western Front. Their soldiers were largely Gurkhas and Punjabis from the so-called 'martial race' Indians of the north. The British had relied upon such men in various campaigns in India and central Asia. Gurkhas and Punjabis had also remained loyal to the British during the Great Mutiny of 1857. The IEF's officers, however, were British, most of them trained at the British Staff College in Quetta in modern-day Pakistan. Later in 1915, the IEF was removed from the Western Front and sent to Mesopotamia.

Indian soldiers had a long tradition of military service in the British Empire. Nevertheless, the IEF's officers were exclusively British.

winds had to be exactly right. Favourable breezes finally arrived on the evening of 'a glorious spring day', 22 April, and Falkenhayn authorized the start of what became known as the Second Battle of Ypres. German gunners began 'a new and furious bombardment' of Ypres to distract Allied attention toward the town, and then engineers opened the 6000 cylinders of chlorine gas. From 5.00 to 5.10 that evening, the German artillery stopped so that the concussion of the shells would not redirect or dissipate the gas. The gunners then resumed their fire, using shrapnel in anticipation of targeting men in the open fleeing from the gas.

The ruins of the Château de Beury on the Neuve Chapelle front attest to the power of even light artillery. Many officers assumed that such destructive power must eventually prove decisive on the battlefield, but battles like Neuve Chapelle proved the limits of artillery support.

The gas seeped southwards along a 5km (three-mile) line from Bixschoote to just east of Langemarck. The French Territorials and Algerians noticed a greenish-yellow cloud coming towards them, though few of them had any idea of the danger it portended. The smell of chlorine was distinguishable more than 1829m (2000 yards) away, confirming the suspicions

of some officers that the unusual cloud was poison gas. At first the French troops just felt a tingling at the eyes and throat, but as the tingling grew stronger and breathing became more restricted, they began to defy orders to hold their ground and quickly moved out of the line. As men began choking and falling to the ground, the withdrawal turned into a panic, with some of the men's faces turning an unnatural purple as they struggled for air. The British official history understated the reaction of the British command that 'something very serious had happened'. The lack of knowledge about exactly what had just happened contributed to the sense of panic.

The gas had opened a six-kilometre (four-mile) gap in the Allied lines. Had Falkenhayn the reserves ready to exploit the gap, the situation might have become much more serious for the Allies than it did. But the attack on Ypres had not been designed with a breakthrough in mind. The inferiority of German

German soldiers fleeing their own gas cloud. At Second Ypres the Germans released gas from cylinders, which proved to be susceptible to the vagaries of winds. Armies soon began experimenting with other delivery methods for gas, including gas-filled artillery shells and an electric slingshot-type system.

numbers in the sector meant that reserves were not available, nor did German soldiers, poorly trained and equipped with only gauze pads for protection, show much desire to attack into the gas cloud.

The Germans released more gas during the next two days in an effort to rout the Canadians, who heroically stretched their line to fill in the gap. Canadian soldiers were advised to soak any available cloth in urine on the theory that the ammonium in urine would neutralize some of the worst effects of the chlorine. The Canadians, especially the 2nd Brigade commanded by Brigadier-General Arthur Currie, fought valiantly and held their positions against much stronger German forces. By this point, Falkenhayn was pleased with the preparations for the Gorlice-Tarnow offensive in the east and was coming to see a chance to take Ypres at the same time. Not one but two great victories seemed to be within reach. The Germans therefore redoubled their efforts on 28 April and came within 2286m (2500 yards) of Ypres.

As was his custom, Foch, still in command of Army Group North, ordered Allied counteroffensives to disrupt the Germans and throw off their momentum. By early May the British had given up more than half of the northern portion of the Ypres salient, but still held the town itself. From 8 to 24 May the Germans kept up the pressure as the British dug in along the Frezenburg Ridge to the northeast of Ypres. Successive gas attacks proved less successful as British soldiers learned ways of dealing with them. The British held Ypres, but the Germans had narrowed the salient considerably. They now sat close enough to the city's northern edge to shell any and all buildings inside it. The Germans had won a great victory, although it paled in comparison to the massive success in the east at Gorlice-Tarnow that it was in part designed to mask. German casualties at the Second Battle of Ypres are estimated at 35,000 compared to 53,000 British, 10,000 French and 6000 Canadian casualties.

Allied officers and politicians made much publicity use of what Sir John French called the 'cynical and barbarous disregard of the well-known usages of civilized war' that the German introduction of poison gas represented. Their moral outrage did not, however, keep Allied officers from demanding that their own governments respond in kind and develop chemical weapons for use against the

A German Uhlan, or cavalry scout. The gas attack at Second Ypres opened a hole in the British line that Uhlans and German light infantry could have exploited, but German reserves were too few in number to take advantage.

barbarous Germans who first deployed them in the field. Soon both the French and the British were hard at work to develop both respirators to protect their soldiers from German gas and gas weapons of their own. Chemical warfare rapidly became an element in the repertoires of all armies, and another of the horrors to be endured by the soldiers of the Great War.

SETTLING IN

The failure of the Allied armies to break the German front line in 1914 and early 1915 meant that trench warfare became a more permanent feature of the Western Front. In large part, the turn to trench warfare came as a result of the power of defensive weapons like machine guns and field artillery. Getting underground was the best way to protect oneself from machine guns and field artillery pieces, most of which fired on flat trajectories. By spring 1915 there were an estimated 760km (475 miles) of trenches on the Western Front, ranging from the English Channel to Switzerland. Adapting to such conditions required many physical and psychological adjustments for commanders and soldiers alike.

A soldier's experience in the trenches varied considerably depending on the nature of the terrain, the kind of trench system put in place and the attitudes of commanding officers in their sectors. Almost all systems, however, shared a few features in common. They were all dug with the lines at sharp angles to provide enfilading fields of fire against enemy attackers and to provide some protection against the concussions of artillery shells. These patterns also guarded against an enemy rifleman reaching the trench and firing across its length. They also formed a number of blind angles that would slow down any attacker moving across the trench line rather than through it.

The digging of proper trenches became a science of its own. First and foremost, military engineers had to take into account the nature of the terrain. Soggy terrain like Flanders proved to be the most difficult environment, as the trenches tended to fill with water on a regular basis. Tough, mountainous terrain also proved to be a challenge owing to the difficulty of cutting through rock. Chalky soil like that in Artois and Picardy, however, was ideal for the creation of deep trench networks that often reached depths of 6–9m (20–30ft) underground. Where possible, trenches were built on high ground, even if the rise was only a few metres.

Although no two trench systems were alike, understanding a typical trench network is easier to do

Poison gas clouds at Second Ypres. Gas was a particularly terrifying weapon to soldiers because of its novelty and the horrid ways it killed or incapacitated men. Heavier than air, it could seep into trenches or shell holes. It could also stay lethal for days.

The cloth hall at Ypres was the largest structure in the town and thus a target of German artillery. It was rebuilt after the war and today serves as the location of the In Flanders Field museum of the war.

if we trace the experiences of a newly arrived soldier to the front. He would have most likely arrived in the middle of the night so that enemy observers or snipers would not notice his arrival. Arriving in darkness, he would not have had the occasion to notice the sophistication of the network, focusing instead on the order to march as closely as possible to the soldier in front. One wrong turn in a complex trench system could spell disaster. If the soldier had arrived just before dawn, he might have had time for a quick bite to eat and maybe some tea or coffee before morning stand-to. An hour or so before daybreak, the newly arrived soldier would receive his first battalion orders, alerting him and his comrades to any unusual enemy

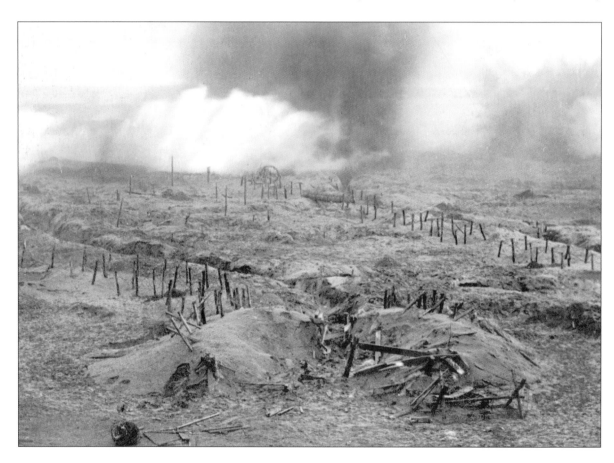

The Canadians

Upon the entry of the British into war in 1914, the Canadians began to raise volunteer units from among their militiamen. These men soon formed the backbone of one of the finest units on the Western Front, the Canadian Corps. At Second Ypres, the Canadians extended their line to the southwest, heroically closing parts of the gap that the gas attack had created. At the end of the day they even conducted a night-time counterattack that seized several important spots on the line and blunted the German momentum. Canadians won four Victoria Crosses during the battle for their active defence of the region around St Julien.

activity observed during the night. As dawn was the most likely time for an enemy attack, it was also the time when soldiers checked their weapons and lined up to defend in case that day was the day the enemy chose for an offensive. Allied soldiers were normally at a disadvantage at first light because their trenches most often faced east, into the rising sun.

As daylight arrived the soldier would have seen for the first time the architectural logic behind the design of trenches. Most trenches were dug to a depth of two metres (six feet), deep enough to allow the average soldier to stand in them at full height, with fire steps

German soldiers in their trenches near Ypres. Most armies tried to rotate men so that they spent no more than three days in a row in the trenches. They then served three days in training and three days in the rear before rotating back into the trenches.

one metre (four feet) deep to allow men to raise their rifles above the front wall, called a parapet. The parapet was protected with sandbags, often carefully placed with loopholes to permit the observation of enemy trenches and the placement of sniper's rifles. More sandbags, timber and any other material at hand could be used to buttress the mud of the trench walls. Trenches were kept as thin as possible, often no thicker than a few metres, to reduce the devastating effects of artillery. A back wall, or parados, was also protected with sandbags in the event that it had to be used as a defensive line. Most trench systems contained dugouts, which were dug either into or under trench walls. These spaces provided extra protection for communications equipment, command posts, first aid stations and ammunition storage.

If the morning stand-to passed uneventfully, the remainder of the day was likely to pass quietly. Front-line trenches, sometimes called 'fire trenches' had the responsibility of slowing or stopping any enemy attack. They were therefore based as much around observation as active resistance. Devices like trench periscopes helped soldiers to see across to the other side in relative safety and machine guns concealed behind sandbags or metal plates provided protection. Coils of barbed wire stretched out in front of the trench to offer further protection. During the day soldiers would take shifts observing any enemy movement, but if there was no active combat, life in the trenches could be quite dull.

The regular routine of trench life involved a dreary existence of bad food and squalid conditions. Men could not prepare hot food on the line because wisps of smoke from cooking fires would reveal their location. Food thus either arrived cold (and often quite stale) or was prepared in distant field kitchens and rushed

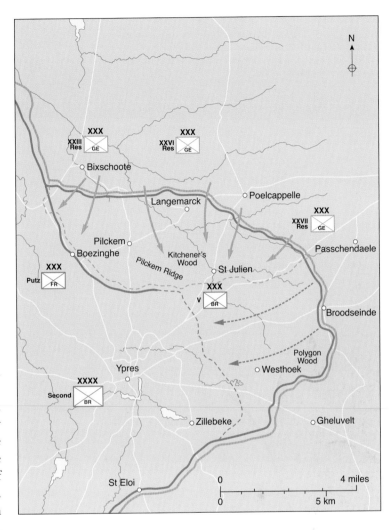

The bulging salient around Ypres was partly defined by the Messines Ridge to the south and the Passchendaele Ridge to the east. British positions in the salient were exposed to German guns on three sides, making the defence of Ypres that much more difficult.

forward. By the time it arrived, it too, was often cold and unpalatable. The absence of fresh fruit and vegetables was a particular problem with front-line food. Men passed their time cleaning muddy equipment, removing lice from their clothes and being inspected by officers for the symptoms of trench foot, a painful disorder caused by long periods of feet being immersed in water. Officers were judged on their success in combating trench foot, often using their own

A soldier modelling his gas mask. Most masks severely restricted breathing and made movement and vision difficult. The British introduced one of the best masks, known as the SBR (Small Box Respirator), but it, too, was clumsy and awkward to use.

money to buy dry socks for their men. In times of bad weather, rain, cold and snow could make life in the trenches especially unpleasant. Rats, attracted to the trenches by the nearby presence of decaying corpses, dead horses and the piles of human waste created by poor hygiene arrangements, posed another threat. Officers frequently offered bounties for rats killed, but men could only control the rat population temporarily. The only real relief from the drudgery of the trenches came in the form of daily alcohol rations, usually rum for the British, coarse brandy for the Germans and a rough red wine known as *pinard* for the French.

After the stand-down at dusk, men formed work parties to perform the regular maintenance that trench systems needed. Because of the danger involved, work on trenches had to occur at night and in near complete silence. Repairing the parapet, digging new trenches, laying new sandbag walls and placing new barbed wire were among the regular routines soldiers had to perform. Laying new belts of barbed wire proved to be

Gas Masks

In the wake of Second Ypres, a British lieutenant-colonel sent couriers to Paris with orders to buy materials for a primitive respirator. He then oversaw the production of more than 80,000 of them within a few days. The War Office quickly found ample supplies of hyposulphite, which, when attached to the respirators, neutralized many of the effects of chlorine gas. A Canadian medical officer designed the 'McPherson helmet', a flannel hood with a celluloid window and a respirator containing an effective mixture of hyposulphite, glycerine and bicarbonate of soda that served British soldiers well until the introduction of the more effective SBR (Small Box Respirator) in 1916.

especially dangerous in the war's early months. Iron stakes supporting the wire often had to be pounded into the ground, attracting a lot of attention from enemy snipers, even in the dark. The British eventually produced a corkscrew-shaped stake that could be turned into the ground to achieve the same effect in near silence. Despite their danger, these tasks were vital for maintaining the integrity of a trench and therefore its power to resist an enemy attack on it.

If life was generally dull in a trench, it could nevertheless be punctuated by moments of sheer terror. Random shelling from enemy artillery was a regular facet of existence, as was the occasional strafing from enemy airplanes. Gas masks had to be kept close at hand, especially because poison gas was heavier than air and could seep into the deepest recesses of trench dugouts or sit in a shell crater for days at a time. Most gas was designed to incapacitate more than to kill, and most gas casualties eventually recovered, but the process was painful. Many gas victims ended up blind or with diminished breathing capability for life. Soldiers might also be sent out into small outposts known as saps, which jutted out a few yards from the fire trench and served as forward listening and observation posts. A variety of field glasses and listening devices were invented to help soldiers conduct better reconnaissance of the enemy, who might be just a few yards away. Sappers also had the responsibility of locating snipers and giving the first indication of enemy gas attacks.

At night, small groups of men might be sent out into the region between the trenches, known even in French as no man's land. In some places no man's land was quite narrow; in others it might be hundreds of metres wide. In all cases the men who ventured there felt as exposed as a rabbit in a field with a hawk circling overhead. Often containing shell craters, putrefied bodies, and the destroyed remnants of buildings, no man's land was a horrifying place with

few natural or man-made defences. Nevertheless, it was important for armies to patrol there in order to gain information on any new developments in the enemy line and to prevent the enemy from making an easy reconnaissance of one's own line. Soldiers might also have to go into no man's land to recover equipment (or in a dire emergency, rations) from their dead comrades. Recovery of bodies was much more risky and usually frowned upon by officers unwilling to lose men shot while trying to bring in the dead for a decent burial. Most officers, however, permitted such acts if they were designed to recover the wounded, whose screams tormented men sitting in the relative safety of the trenches.

A German *Minenwerfer* crew in action. These portable artillery pieces came in several calibres and were useful in breaking up attacks and disrupting trench life in general, although experienced trench hands became used to dodging the shells. Note the basket-weave shell cases on the right.

The Shell Scandal

The day after the Battle of Neuve Chapelle ended Sir John French sent his report to Kitchener in London blaming 'want of ammunition' for the guns as the main reason for the British failure to exploit their initial successes. In a follow up report, French elaborated, telling Kitchener that 'the supply of gun ammunition … has fallen short of what I was led to expect and I was therefore compelled to abandon further offensive operations'. French and his staff drew the comfortable conclusion that if they had had enough ammunition for the guns they could have turned Neuve Chapelle into a great success. Feeling himself under criticism and anxious to protect his own reputation as a leader and a strategist, French shared his frustrations with the military correspondent of the London *Times*. The media soon began to report on what became known as the 'shell scandal', an alleged failure of the British War Office (and by implication Kitchener, the head of that office) to provide sufficient hardware to the men of the

Discarded shell casings. All armies had to find ways to increase shell production as quickly as effectively as possible to feed the voracious appetites of the front.

British Army. The scandal led to changes in the British economic effort, but it did not change the fundamental conclusion of British senior officers that the methods used at Neuve Chapelle were essentially sound.

Among the most terrifying trench experiences was the trench raid. These raids involved small groups of soldiers moving quickly through no man's land and into the enemy's trenches. The intent was to gain as much information on the state of the enemy's trenches as possible, seize documents, capture a few prisoners and return to one's own lines before the enemy could respond. Sophisticated trench raids were protected by artillery barrages called box barrages that isolated the area of a trench to be raided. Information taken from prisoners and captured documents often proved to be valuable; even something as mundane as the quality of food found in an enemy trench might give an indication of the state of the enemy's supply and even his morale. Trench raids could also help intelligence officers build accurate tables of the enemy's order of battle. Dangerous though raids were, most soldiers accepted their necessity, although they despised the trench raids some officers ordered on the theory that too long a period of calm in the trenches was bad for morale.

After a few days of such experiences in the fire trench, a soldier would likely receive orders to head back to the rear for rest or training in new methods. If he was lucky he might also expect to receive hot food and new clothes that were generally free of lice. As he came out of the line, he would leave by the same trench from which he had arrived over a few days earlier, but now he would be in a better position to understand the various kinds of trenches and their larger purposes. He would leave via a trench that ran perpendicular to the fire trench, called a communications trench, also dug in zigzag or crenellated patterns. As their name suggests, these trenches allowed men and supplies to be moved to and from the front lines. In times of active combat, these trenches would be further divided into trenches going to and coming from the fire trench in order to prevent massive traffic jams that might impede wounded men getting to aid stations and reinforcements from arriving in a timely manner.

Twenty-seven to forty-six metres (30–50 yards) down the communication trench, the soldier would arrive at a second line, called a support or cover trench. Its purpose was to provide additional firepower and to cover the retreat of men from the fire trench in the event of an enemy attack. Some trench systems used the fire trench for observation and the support trench as the main firing line. Covering trenches might also contain large manpower reserves for counterattacks or for keeping men relatively fresh. Thus an attacking army might work its way through an enemy's fire trench only to come up against much stronger positions in the cover trench.

Sophisticated trench networks might have as many as three more lines of trenches stretching back to rear areas. In some cases, the Germans built powerful redoubts shaped like ovals that provided all-around fire support and protection that covered all possible

avenues of Allied approach. Once outside the trench system, the soldier might see batteries of artillery pieces, carefully concealed from enemy aviation by camouflage netting or trees. These guns used indirect fire, being guided by aviators over the battlefield or by spotters in the fire trench.

The difficulties of attacking such defences were obvious enough to soldiers on all sides. Even if a breakthrough might be made on one part of one trench system, it would mean little to the overall effort. Larger breakthroughs, as at Neuve Chapelle, could not be maintained because of the extreme challenge of moving men and supplies across the charred terrain of no man's land.

Still, the Allies had to accept the reality of the military situation imposed by trench warfare because they still faced the need to dislodge the Germans and chase them from their occupation of Belgium and France. Much of the rest of the war was a search for methods to break the stalemate of trench war and return to the much more mobile open warfare that generals sought.

German soldiers at Christmas time, 1914. The formation of long trench lines across Europe and the rapid growth of sophisticated defences meant that few on either side could have had any illusion that they faced a long and difficult war.

CHAPTER 4

The Frustrations of 1915

By the end of 1915, the armies of all the combatants were starting to look much more modern and sophisticated than a year earlier. The difficulties involved in attacking strongly held trenches, however, remained. Thousands of soldiers paid the price.

Using contemporary estimates, by April 1915 the Allies had a superiority in numbers on the Western Front of 2,450,000 to 1,900,000. The Germans, however, had possession of most of the important pieces of high ground along the front line and, since they largely intended to remain on the defensive in the west in 1915, had redoubled their efforts to build an intensive network of trench defences. They added fields of barbed wire, reinforced lightly held areas with new draftees and poured tons of concrete. German defences had never been stronger.

Nevertheless, Russia's dire situation on the Eastern Front, combined with the abiding need to repel the invading Germans from France, compelled the Allies to devise a new offensive for spring 1915. Having

The high cost of attacks with densely packed infantry like the French *poilus* seen here became increasingly evident in 1915. The French responded with smaller 'penny packet' infantry formations and new tactics that presented smaller targets to enemy gunners.

The bolt-action magazine rifle was the standard arm of the infantry throughout the war. The French Lebel rifle, shown here, fired a light 8mm round. It was state of the art when introduced in 1886. By 1914 it was outdated, and was being replaced by newer models.

failed in Champagne, and just barely held on in Ypres, Joffre targeted the region of Artois, near Neuve Chapelle. He had in mind a combined Franco-British offensive that would unite the efforts of the two allies in a more systematic fashion than had theretofore been attained. At the end of March, Joffre told Sir John French that he envisioned 'an important attack' against German positions protecting the flat ground of the Douai Plain, through which many of the critical German lines of communication ran.

His plan involved a two-pronged attack on either side of the La Bassée Canal. To the south, a reinforced French Tenth Army would attack along a 16km (10 mile) front from Loos to Arras, aiming at the northern and southern shoulders of a German salient. In this regard, the offensive shared much in its original conception with the British attack on Neuve Chapelle. The most important obstacles in the way of French

forces were two commanding ridges, the 168m-high (551ft) Notre Dame de Lorette Ridge, named after the chapel that sat atop it, and Vimy Ridge, an even higher series of hills that gave the Germans excellent observation of French forces in the valley below. From the two ridges, the Germans could also pour artillery shells into many of the key French lines of communications. Joffre hoped that the Tenth Army could break the German positions atop the ridges. To their east sat an open plain that stretched across key German railway lines. If the French could take possession of the hills, they could disrupt all German activity in the salient and advance to the line Douai–Cambrai.

The British attack fell to Haig's First Army because the Second Army was still engaged in fighting around Ypres. The target was again Aubers Ridge, but this time the British would approach from the north. The tactics, however, would resemble those used at Neuve Chapelle in March. Ten British divisions, including two Indian divisions, would follow a brief but powerful bombardment by 600 artillery pieces. It would begin on the same day as the French infantry attack to the south of the canal, thus forcing German reinforcements to make decisions about which gaps to fill. The British offensive would cut the road connecting La Bassée to Lille and with it the German ability to move supplies to its forces in Artois.

AUBERS RIDGE

Both the British and French plans depended on artillery support, although the two armies planned to use their artillery in different ways. The British hoped to repeat their success in the first phase of Neuve Chapelle by firing a quick, but intensive artillery barrage. British industry had begun to produce more shells but the British were still constrained by limits on ammunition supply. The French, by contrast, had

The French Army in 1915

By the time of the 1915 Champagne offensive, the red and bright blue uniforms of 1914 were gone in favour of uniforms made of a duller bluish-grey called 'cigar smoke blue'. The fancy cloth hats were also gone in favour of steel helmets modelled on those worn by Parisian firemen. The old, cumbersome St Etienne machine gun had been discarded, with the lighter, more reliable Hotchkiss coming into use in large numbers. Grenades and better gas masks were also available in quantity.

The abysmal nature of the fighting in Champagne in 1915 is depicted in this painting. The battle disproved the French Army's newfound faith in heavy artillery to clear safe paths for the infantry.

proportion (almost one-fourth) so far of heavy guns. The guns fired more than 700,000 shells in all, which amounted to an estimated 18 shells per metre of German trench line. The French also used unprecedented numbers of high-explosive shells, which had enough power to do significant damage to German trenches. The French began a saturation bombardment of four days' duration. It began by targeting the suspected locations of German artillery pieces, ammunition dumps and assembly points. During the last four hours the gunners switched targets to the German barbed wire networks and the main German fire trenches. It was then the largest artillery barrage in the history of warfare.

The British barrage, by contrast, still contained too many light pieces. More than 90 per cent of the shells they fired, moreover, were shrapnel, extremely effective for hitting soldiers in open country, but almost worthless against well dug trenches. The paucity of British shells limited the barrage to a mere 45 minutes, or only slightly longer than the barrage at Neuve Chapelle had been. French and Haig hoped that the disparity in artillery might have the positive effect of pulling German attention south to the sector of the French attack, leaving the element of surprise intact for them in the north.

The enormous power of French artillery certainly opened up gaps in the German line. The mission of exploiting one of the largest fell to XXXIII Corps, then commanded by Henri Philippe Pétain, a morose 59-year-old general whose favourite maxim was *le feu tue*, 'firepower kills'. A firm believer in *grignotage* and the

concluded from the war's early battles that artillery bombardments had to be much longer and more powerful than those used thus far. 'The artillery conquers,' Foch and others began to repeat, 'and the infantry occupies.' The French had therefore dedicated much of their industrial production to heavier guns, which had begun to be made available that winter and spring.

The differences in artillery and its employment help to explain the differing fates of the twin Anglo-French attack when it began on 9 May. The French attack concentrated 1368 guns, with the heaviest

British and French soldiers interact. Relations between the two allies were generally good, despite tensions caused by different strategic outlooks, military doctrines and culture. The two allies fought with only a loosely coordinated strategy in 1915.

importance of massive artillery preparations, Pétain moved his men forwards and advanced more than three kilometres (two miles) on day one, reaching the slopes of Vimy Ridge. Several battalions even reached the crest of the ridge and began to move down the other side, but they were too few in number. Pétain tried to get reinforcements to the ridge and arrange supporting artillery, but he could not do either in time. German counterattacks drove the French forces off the ridge at midday, but the performance of his corps helped to continue Pétain's metamorphosis

from an officer on the verge of retirement to a rising star in the French Army.

Pétain's corps had made the most dramatic advances, and seemed to demonstrate the ability of powerful artillery to open passages in the enemy line. Most French units advanced 1500–2000m (1640–2187 yards), showing great courage and proving that they had learned many important lessons about modern warfare. Nevertheless, even successful offensives were tremendously costly, especially among junior officers and non-commissioned officers. When these leaders fell, units often proved unable to move forward. Moreover, in those places where artillery had been less effective, German resistance was too strong to overcome. One German redoubt known as the Labyrinth was only lightly damaged by the shelling and remained an important centre of German resistance. Despite the failure to take the ridges on day one, the French were generally pleased. Their men had been able to advance; indeed many of them had stood atop Vimy Ridge and looked down on the Douai Plain. French reserves had been stationed too far back to exploit the success, but the French optimistically believed that they could correct that mistake.

For their part, the staff of the British First Army was supremely confident of success because they believed that the Neuve Chapelle model on which they had based their attack on Aubers Ridge had been basically sound. As one officer noted before the attack 'this should be Neuve Chapelle all over again, and much more successful because we have learnt its lessons and

British troops advance through the debris following the Battle of Aubers Ridge. German defences in the region were much stronger than the British had guessed.

The Rolling Barrage

On 6 October 1915 the French introduced a form of what would become known as a rolling barrage. Under this technique, artillery shells preceded the infantry's advance by a few hundred metres, with the exact distance determined by the terrain and the strength of enemy positions. Infantry had to advance behind the barrage, far enough behind it to be safe but close enough to it to take advantage of its ability to protect them from enemy machine guns. Rolling barrages were innovative and offered an excellent means of closing the time gap between the artillery and infantry phases of an offensive. They did, however, require reliable communications and excellent observation, both of which were still in their development.

The New British Government

In May 1915, the British Government experienced a major shake-up, with the Liberal government of H.H. Asquith replaced by a coalition government that pledged itself to provide the army with more heavy guns and ample ammunition for them to fire. The chancellor of the exchequer, David Lloyd George, became the new minister of munitions. He began a massive reorganization of British industry to allow it to meet the needs of war. At the end of 1916, another major shake-up forced Asquith out of office and brought Lloyd George to No. 10 Downing Street as both Prime Minister and War Minister.

An artist's rendering of combat at Aubers Ridge. Because of the obvious danger, few photographers took pictures of battles. Some photographers posed soldiers in quiet moments and others created composite images out of several photographs.

shall know what to avoid this time'. Haig was so confident that he did not set final day-one goals, telling his men to advance as far forward as they could.

German troops opposite the British had been busy reinforcing their defences and welcoming a new division to their defence of Aubers Ridge. According to the British official history, the new German defences made attacking the region 'a very different proposition to that which had confronted the First Army at Neuve Chapelle'. More permanent German defences were almost impregnable to the light artillery the British planned to use in their brief 9 May bombardment, a circumstance that Sir James Edmonds, the principal author of the official history, later described as 'suspected', but 'not fully known'. It was to be a fatal oversight.

British artillery fire began around 5.00 that morning, and around 5.45am the infantry went over the top. They were supported for the first time by aeroplane observers equipped with wireless radio transmitters to help field artillery units target German

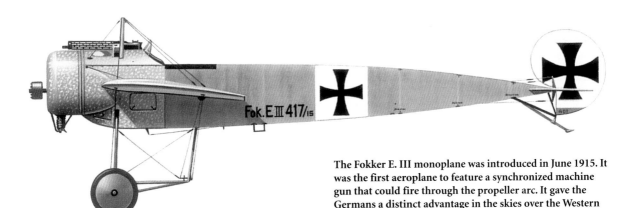

The Fokker E. III monoplane was introduced in June 1915. It was the first aeroplane to feature a synchronized machine gun that could fire through the propeller arc. It gave the Germans a distinct advantage in the skies over the Western Front into 1916.

reserves and enemy artillery batteries. Nevertheless, the British artillery had been so feeble that some German soldiers even dared to stand on their parapets to shoot at British infantry as they left their trenches. Undamaged German machine guns opened up a fierce enfilading fire as the British charge began, leaving hundreds of British soldiers dead or wounded just outside their own parapets. German barbed wire remained intact in most places, as did most of the carefully concealed machine guns.

The British attack had been an unmitigated disaster. Yet once again poor communications led Haig to order a late-afternoon attack in the mistaken belief that the first attack had made some local successes. The six battalions of the 1st Division took casualties of 60 per cent or more. The 1st Battalion of the Northamptonshire Regiment lost 17 officers and 543 other ranks in just one day. The 2nd Battalion of the Sussex Regiment lost 14 officers and 537 other ranks. Normal battalion sizes for that period of the war were around 800 to 1000 men. In all the 8th Division lost 4682 men. Nor did the British have much to show for the losses. Hundreds of men lay wounded in agony on the battlefield. British gunners tried to fire a hasty protection barrage in the hopes of giving the men a chance to get back to their own lines by nightfall, but few managed to do so. The Battle of Aubers Ridge shattered the confidence Haig had developed after Neuve Chapelle. On 11 May, he wrote that 'The defences in our front are so carefully and so strongly made, and mutual support with machine-

guns is so complete, that in order to demolish them a long methodical bombardment will be necessary by heavy artillery before Infantry are sent forward to attack'. In other words, there were no more surprises to be expected.

FESTUBERT

The ease with which the Germans repulsed the British effort at Aubers Ridge allowed the German Army to move two divisions from Aubers to Vimy, opposite the French. This shift worried Joffre, who demanded that the British resume the offensive as soon as possible. He also believed that the Germans were close to breaking because French intelligence estimated that they did not have enough manpower to prosecute a major offensive in the east and resist determined attacks in the west. He therefore urged the British not to give up

Notre Dame de Lorette Ridge

An imposing 168m-high (551ft) ridge overlooking Arras, Notre Dame de Lorette featured a chapel and pilgrimage site first built in 1727. Fierce fighting took place here between October 1914 and September 1915. After the war, the French built a basilica and a lantern tower on the ridge that watches over a cemetery containing 19,000 crosses and the remains of almost 23,000 unknown French dead. It is the largest military cemetery in France.

on their attacks, the losses at Aubers Ridge notwithstanding. Sir John French complied after Joffre and Foch put 'very considerable pressure' on him.

Kitchener still had his doubts about the possibility of breaking German lines. These concerns were reinforced by the failures of 9 May. Kitchener shared his worries in a letter to a colleague, the chief of the general staff (later chief of the imperial general staff), General Sir William 'Wully' Robertson. The French, Kitchener wrote, had 'an almost unlimited supply of ammunition', including the high-explosive rounds that the British so desperately needed, plus a much larger reserve of infantry. 'So,' concluded Kitchener, 'if they cannot get through, we may take it as proved that the lines cannot be forced.' Nevertheless, he gave reluctant approval to Sir John French to let the British First Army try again.

To fight what became known as the Battle of Festubert, the British decided to try the 'French method' of a longer artillery bombardment. They aimed at a three-day, around-the-clock artillery preparation using as many heavy guns and high-angle howitzers as they could find. The bombardment began on 12 May, with the infantry phase due to begin on 15 May. British artillery targeted a narrow front of 4572m (5000 yards). Lengthening the bombardment to three days theoretically allowed for careful observation of

French General Joseph Joffre and his British counterpart Field Marshal Sir John French. Joffre tried to assume strategic direction of the Allied armies, but a suspicious French fought to maintain his autonomy. Sir Douglas Haig, French's eventual replacement, is at the far right.

> 'The defences in our front are so carefully and so strongly made … that in order to demolish them a long methodical bombardment will be necessary.'
>
> Sir Douglas Haig

the damage the shelling was doing to German barbed wire and field defences. Thus gunners could take their time and be much more methodical in their fire, devoting special attention to the German wire and communication trenches in the hope of disrupting the enemy's ability to get reinforcements into the fire

trenches quickly. The British had also introduced better maps and reformed their methods of communication, allowing spotters and gunners to share information more quickly.

Nevertheless, the artillery still suffered from a number of problems. The rush to fill orders for artillery ammunition that the shell scandal had caused resulted in artillery shells that were, in Haig's judgment, 'very faulty'. Fuses were especially bad, with many howitzer shells failing to explode when and where desired. Faulty ammunition also caused a number of guns to burst or wear out prematurely. Where possible, the British fired high-explosive shells on the German wire and shrapnel on the communications trenches, but given the low ammunition stocks, such precision was not always possible.

As a result, several officers thought the artillery bombardment, although the heaviest the British had yet fired, insufficient. The commander of one of the Indian divisions reported to Haig on the night of 14 May that 'I do not consider sufficient damage has been done to ensure success of the assault tonight, nor from the artillery reports is it likely to be completed in time. As regards wire cutting, we have not yet begun, as the batteries detailed for it had to shift their positions.' Haig postponed the attack for 24 hours, aware that if the German wire remained intact, the British assault would go nowhere.

At the same time, the French were preparing for another attack on Vimy Ridge. Foch wanted it preceded by even heavier and more accurate artillery fire than that which had preceded the 9 May attacks. He also planned a slower and more deliberate

approach, envisioning the French Tenth Army taking as long as one week to capture the village of Souchez for use as a staging area for the final attack on Vimy. He also directed the Tenth Army to take care to eliminate German resistance from the villages of Carency and Neuville St Vaast, from which the Germans had been able to pour enfilading fire into French forces on 9 May. 'It was evident', Foch wrote, 'that these points of resistance must be captured before trying to advance to the ridge.' Heavy rains

The British Army relied heavily on Indian Army troops, such as these Gurkhas, to fill the manpower gap on the Western Front in 1915. As more and more of the New Armies units arrived on the Western Front, Indian Army soldiers were sent to fight in East Africa, Suez and Mesopotamia.

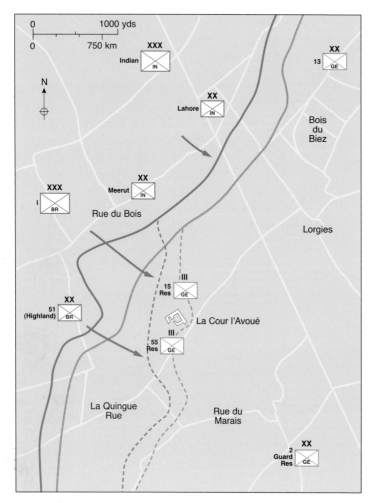

Festubert underscored the frustrations of trying to break enemy trench lines. Despite careful planning, the British gained little ground. The two Indian divisions of the IEF held the left of the British line.

them less willing to rush men forward at each alert.

The feints in turn supported the second method of support, the daring idea of attacking at night. The infantry attack went forward on the overcast and 'quite dark' night of 15 May. It was the first night attack of its size ever conducted by the British Army. Approaching in silence with bayonets at the ready, several British companies almost reached the German line before they were detected. Having achieved a remarkable degree of surprise, several British companies took their objectives in the German fire trenches without opposition. German troops had just enough time to fire flares to indicate that they were under attack before running down their communications trenches towards their support trenches.

Success once again seemed to be there for the taking. Haig ordered attacks conducted at 3.15 and 5.40 the next morning, both supported by 30-minute barrages from British field artillery batteries. Several British units experienced success, with the Scots Guards and the Royal Welsh Fusiliers assaulting the powerful German redoubt known as the Quadrilateral southwest of Aubers Ridge. But the British artillery had done only limited damage to the solid defences of the Quadrilateral and members of the Scots Guards who assaulted it 'were shot almost directly they rose'. British gains on day one had been as deep as 600m (1970ft) in places, but no breakthrough had yet been achieved.

Haig continued the attack for 10 more days. The objectives, in Sir John French's words, were to 'continue relentlessly to wear down the enemy by exhaustion and prevent him from detaching troops to

postponed French preparations, but Foch hoped to be ready to attack on or around 17 May to support the British, who were scheduled to attack on 15 May.

If British artillery could not fully support the attack on Festubert, British infantry had come up with two other ideas to give the attack its best chance of success. First, the British conducted a number of feints, firing a standard pre-attack barrage and having men yell at the tops of their lungs as if they were to go over the top. If German troops showed signs of rushing men forwards to meet the attack, the British would recall their men to their own fire trenches, then fire shrapnel at the Germans in the hopes of killing as many of them as possible. This tactic did not kill many enemy soldiers, but it did keep them off their guard and made

oppose the French'. Haig and his staff saw just enough indications of success to convince them to continue reinforcing the offensive. The German surrender of the Quadrilateral on 17 May following a particularly successful bombardment marked what Haig thought would be the final success. Unfortunately, the success of the artillery fire on the Quadrilateral was not repeated along the line, leaving many units dangerously exposed to German machine guns as they attacked.

The momentum of the British offensive had begun to slow down by 18 May. Tired units had to be taken out of the line, forcing French and Haig to conduct a massive reorganization. The new British line began at the village of Port Arthur, just south of Neuve Chapelle. It was guarded by the Lahore and Meerut divisions of the Indian Corps. Just to their south, inexperienced men of the 51st (Highland) Division sat opposite a German stronghold known as the Ferme Cour d'Avoué, a series of stone farm buildings that British artillery had partially reduced to rubble, but nevertheless proved to be an ideal place for the

Germans to hide machine guns and rifles. The remainder of the line was held by the Canadians, still recovering from their efforts at Ypres, who moved the line forward into an orchard known for the rest of the war as the Canadian Orchard. The line here formed a sharp right angle then gently moved south by southwest to the La Bassée Canal that divided the British and French areas of responsibility.

There the British line remained, with British units unable to move forward owing to shortages of artillery ammunition and heavy personnel losses. By 27 May, the British First Army had taken 16,648 casualties to move the line a few hundred metres in most places. British officers estimated German losses at less than 5000. At that rate, the British could not 'continue relentlessly to wear down the enemy by exhaustion' as Sir John French had ordered Haig to do. Indeed, such operations would likely wear down the British faster

The Battle of Festubert featured a daring night attack, but problems of coordination between artillery and infantry continued to hamper British efforts.

than they wore down the Germans. Accordingly, French told Haig that he thought it 'improbable' that the offensive would achieve much, especially in light of news that new Germans reinforcements were arriving in the sector. British guns, moreover, were to all intents and purposes out of ammunition. On 25 May, French ordered his units to assume the defensive, effectively ending the Battle of Festubert.

A German field hospital near Pinon in the region of the Aisne. The tents have been set up in the shadow of a ruined chateau, showing that they are still within range of the enemy's heavy guns.

The British official history called the results of Festubert 'tantalizing' because they had gained some limited successes even without requisite artillery support. British forces had reached their day-one objectives 'in some cases', but had not been able to follow them up as needed owing to the shell shortage. The British official history also noted that the offensive had been conducted largely to help the French, thus it accomplished its goals by merely attacking and drawing off German reserves toward Festubert instead of Vimy. Still, it reflected with a tinge of sadness that British were not yet 'in 1915 in a

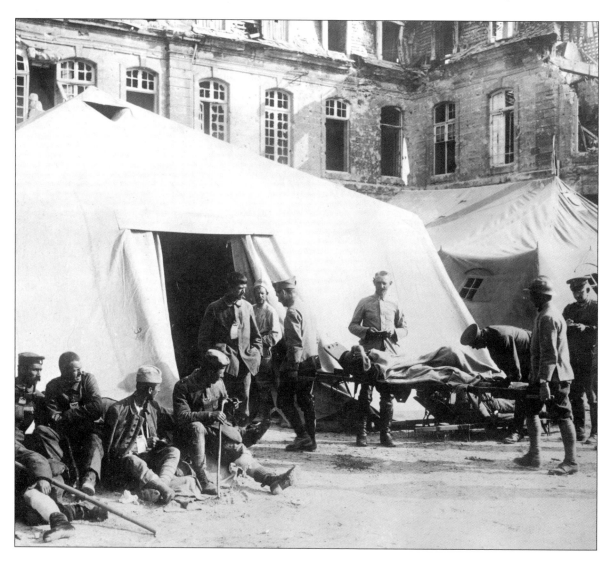

condition to make the effort that our French Allies expected of the British Empire in a life or death struggle'.

VIMY RIDGE

About 24km (15 miles) to the south, those French allies kept up their preparations for another attack on Vimy Ridge. In his memoirs, Foch explained why the ridge figured so prominently in French strategic thinking: 'The wide extent of the ground it commands, and the practicability of the terrain it dominates, as well as the impossibility for the enemy to make any addition to his defensive organizations, would give the occupation of the ridge an immense

French prisoners from the 1915 spring offensives. They represent the French Army in a period of transition. Some of the men are wearing the new steel 'casque Adrian' helmet, but many are still in their soft caps.

value and lead to the piercing of the enemy line.' What Foch called 'minutely prepared operations' seized the villages of Carency on 12 May and Ablain St Nazaire on the next day, although Souchez remained in German hands. Henri Barbusse described the damage to the village in his classic war memoir, *Under Fire*:

'The village has disappeared, and I have never seen a village disappear so completely. Ablain-Saint-Nazaire and Carency still retained some shape of a place, with their collapsed and truncated houses and their yards heaped high with plaster and tiles. Here, within the framework of slaughtered trees that surrounds us as a spectral background in the fog, there is no longer any shape. There is not even an end of wall, fence, or porch that remains standing; and it amazes one to discover that there are paving stones under the tangle of beams, stones and scrap-iron.'

By 10 June, all preliminary positions were in French hands, and the final attack on Vimy had been scheduled for 16 June. Joffre had ordered that the front to be attacked be shortened so that a greater concentration of artillery fire might be achieved. More than 30 per cent of the fire this time would be from heavy guns, whose targets would be primarily in the second German line, the logical place for the Germans to have assembled their reserves. Only at the last minute would the gunners switch targets to the

German firing line, so that French infantry would leave their trenches at the same time that French artillery saturated the German front line with shells. Despite having fired almost 500,000 shells (double the concentration that supported the 9 May attack), some French generals still feared that the damage done to German lines was not sufficient. Tenth Army Commander Victor d'Urbal ordered another barrage for the day of the assault, 16 June, which involved 63,557 more shells.

The pessimists were soon proved right. Despite the extra artillery support, French gains on 16 June were less than they had been on 9 May. Enough German gunners remained to fire shrapnel mercilessly into attacking French units, limiting French advances to a few hundred metres. No French units reached the crest of Vimy Ridge, and by mid-afternoon German counterattacks had recovered most of the ground the French had gained. D'Urbal originally ordered French attacks conducted around the clock, but Joffre intervened, recognizing the limited success of operations, and ordered that attacks only be conducted locally in areas where noticeable gains had already been made. These, too, failed to make substantial gains and on 18 June Foch intervened and ordered all attacks stopped.

The Artois campaign had failed to break German defenses and had brought with them heavy costs. The French had gained approximately 24 square kilometres (nine square miles), but had taken unsustainable casualties. More than 140,000 Frenchmen had been killed, wounded or taken prisoner. Contemporary estimates put the German casualties at just under 50,000. Thus the Allied offensive had cost them far heavier losses than they had inflicted. Moreover, the French had fired 2,155,862 rounds of artillery in the campaign, which represented a massive investment of industrial resources. Tactically, the offensives showed that even prodigious use of bombardments using heavy artillery shells failed to protect the infantry. Operationally they showed the difficulty of breaking German trench lines, which would only become stronger as the Germans had more time and resources to devote to them.

The heavy human losses for such little gain in the spring 1915 campaigns produced serious questions. Many French politicians, and a number of generals who were quickly making names for themselves like Pétain, began to criticize Joffre, whose status as a great French hero was being badly tarnished. By extension, Joffre's close allies, most notably Foch, were also coming in for increased criticism. In Britain, too, criticism of Sir John French and Kitchener was mounting. The need to break the German front line and liberate France and Belgium remained, but faith in the leaders of France and Britain to do the job was quickly fading. The Allies found themselves trapped into a corner that was partly of their own design: they could not abandon the offensive, but they had as yet found no way to use the offensive that did not produce minimal gains at unacceptable costs.

THE SECOND BATTLE OF CHAMPAGNE

'Only inaction is shameful!' Joffre declared as he prepared another offensive during the summer of 1915. The essential problems France and Britain had faced since the outset of the war remained: the

German occupation of France had to be ended and the Russians had to be given some breathing space to recover from a disastrous defeat. The Allies simply did not have the luxury Germany had of resting on the defensive. Once again, Joffre's grand strategic vision involved a double attack, with the British attacking in the north in Artois and the French trying again somewhere to their south. Joffre continued to believe that German attention on their offensive in the east

meant that their positions on the Western Front must be susceptible to a combined Allied offensive.

Accordingly, in June, Joffre asked Sir John French to extend the right wing of the British line 35km (22 miles) to the south. The British commander agreed, pulling the British line down to the Somme River. French reserves thus freed up could then be moved to reinforce an attack somewhere else on the line. Joffre had also 'invited' French to prepare an autumn attack on what Joffre thought was the favourable ground that sat three kilometres (two miles) south of the La Bassée Canal near the French mining towns of Loos and Lens. British commanders were not optimistic about the chances of success with the resources they then had on

The massive Battle of Champagne was supposed to prove that newer, heavier artillery pieces could clear the way for the infantry to advance. The failure of the offensive meant thousands of casualties for minimal gain.

The British Use of Poison Gas

The British saw in chlorine gas a way to compensate for their continued shortcomings in artillery. By early June the only British chemical firm capable of making chlorine gas was producing ten tons of it a day. By 10 July, cylinders of chlorine were appearing secretly in France as were large numbers of gas masks. Because so much of the German defences were underground in coal pits and the basements of coal miner's cottages, heavier-than-air chlorine gas could be especially valuable. Haig told his commanders that the gas 'is to be lavishly employed' and should be carried to the German lines by prevailing westerly winds, thus incapacitating most German soldiers. If secrecy could be maintained, Haig expected gas to be the weapon that would allow Britain to win the battle.

hand. At a mid-June conference of senior commanders, the British calculated that to seize Loos and Lens they would need no fewer than 36 divisions and 1150 heavy guns, resources they did not expect to have until spring 1916 at the earliest. In August 1915 the British had just 28 divisions on the Western Front.

Sir John French nevertheless directed Haig and his First Army to begin planning for an offensive in the area to be timed to support a much larger French effort elsewhere along the line. It is likely that French was feeling the weight of the criticism of his handling of the British Army in France. Even King George V had begun to have his doubts about French's suitability as commander. The heavy losses of 1915 had resulted in few gains, and French's increased use of his contacts in the press struck the king and many senior British as

Joffre held on to his job in 1915, although the high casualties of the year had begun to erode his support among members of parliament. He remained confident in public but could barely bring himself to visit field hospitals.

unseemly. The proposed summer/autumn offensive might be French's last chance to save his job.

Joffre set his eyes on Champagne as the only place where a quick and decisive French victory might be possible. He and his staff believed that German positions in Artois had shown themselves to be too strong to expect even minor gains there. A major offensive in Champagne therefore became the option Joffre ordered. His faith in heavy artillery gave him some reason to think that this time an attack in the region might work. By July 1915 France had more than 8000 artillery pieces, but almost half of them were heavy pieces. They included 13 guns of 190mm and 305mm, so large that they could only be moved by train.

Joffre had been correct in his assessment that the Germans were running short of manpower on the Western Front. In August 1915, the Germans had 102 infantry divisions facing 98 French divisions, 28 British divisions and six Belgian divisions. Although superior in overall numbers, the Allies still had just a 1.3:1 edge, far lower than the ratio normally sought for successful offensives. The Germans tried to compensate for their numerical inferiority by digging

Loos was an industrial town with several buildings that the Germans could use to set up defences. Although the buildings appear heavily damaged, the rubble can nevertheless be an excellent place to conceal riflemen, machine gunners, even light artillery pieces.

deeper and more powerful trenches. The Germans had also become much more sophisticated in their placement of machine guns and artillery positions to cover the most likely routes of an Allied attack with multiple guns.

As in 1914, the Germans held the high ground in Champagne and had dug three separate trench lines. The second line sat five kilometres (three miles) behind the first, with a third line as deep as 15km (nine miles) further back, although French aviators had been unable to confirm its existence. A French attack therefore unwittingly faced at least 20km (13 miles) of stubborn German defences before it could reach open ground. The German trenches were formidable positions, featuring reinforced concrete revetments and buried telephone lines. German forces in the region knew that they could expect few reinforcements and that digging in as solidly as possible offered the best chance at survival.

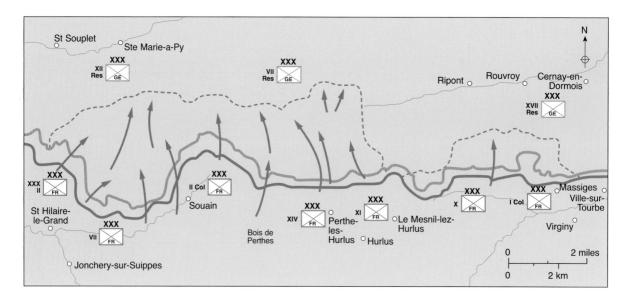

Given these obstacles, the British and French began minute preparations. The British accumulated 75,000 men for their attack in a sector where they estimated the Germans had no more than 11,000 men in the fire trenches. The British also assembled artillery that, although still short of ammunition, was four times as numerous as the German guns opposite them. Joffre agreed to have the French Tenth Army attack Vimy Ridge once again in order to draw German attention away from Loos.

The heart of the British plan involved introducing their 'accessory', the code name used in all correspondence for chlorine gas. The British also planned to use large numbers of 'candles', or smoke-generating machines. Favourable winds would blow dark clouds of smoke over German lines with the chlorine gas, thus neutralizing the ability of German observers to see the battlefield. In addition, heavy shelling over the chalky soil of Artois was expected to produce great white clouds of powder. Loos would mark the first time that the British had used either gas or smoke.

British gunners began firing their barrages on 21 September, as the French were putting the finishing touches to their preparations in Champagne. Joffre had assembled almost three-quarters of the French Army into the sector to exploit the anticipated success.

The battlefield at Champagne was dominated by high ground, especially to the east where a hand-shaped formation called the Main de Massiges gave the Germans excellent observation of the valley below. High ground was a frequent target of infantry and artillery operations.

More than 2000 heavy guns and 3000 field guns were massed in Champagne to provide the largest artillery barrage ever fired. On 22 September the French began a 75-hour around-the-clock bombardment that fired more than three million shells. It amounted to 3000 shells per hour on each 100 by 1000m (328 by 3280ft) portion of the German line.

At 9.00pm on 24 September, Haig received a final weather report indicating that the violent rainstorms of the past few days might let up. More importantly, the winds were expected to blow west to east the next day, offering the ideal conditions for the use of gas. Haig ordered British reserves forwards for an attack the next morning. Despite heavy rains in Champagne, Joffre did not worry as much about weather because the French had no gas shells to fire. He issued similar orders to his men, bringing his reserves forwards in final preparation for an attack. The next morning, 25 September, the French and British armies would advance at the same time, aiming for a joint rupture in the enemy line. Joffre's order of the day told his men that 'every chance of success exists'.

The British B.E.2c was first introduced to service in 1912. Its stability in flight made it an ideal plane for reconnaissance missions, but it was slow and therefore an easy target for enemy aviators. Nevertheless, it remained in service and was used against German bombers over the British Isles.

THE JOINT OFFENSIVES IN ARTOIS AND CHAMPAGNE

The day scheduled for the start of the joint Allied offensive, began with torrential downpours, a bad omen for an offensive already riddled with problems. Nevertheless, optimism reigned in the Allied lines. More powerful Allied artillery left many men with a greater degree of confidence in this attack, and, in Artois, the French and British armies would attack together, using the strength of two nations against enemy positions. Given the inferiority of numbers of German troops in the area (in some places the Allies outnumbered them more than three to one),

commanders expected a quick victory. In Champagne, Castelnau even predicted that the artillery had done its job so well that his men could attack with their rifles unloaded because bayonets would be the only weapon they would need.

At 5.15 that morning in Artois, Haig climbed a wooden observation tower to survey the 'desolate empty waste' that had become the area around Loos. He was also trying to get a clearer sense of the direction of the winds. If they were not favourable, then the British could not open their cylinders of chlorine gas, 5000 in all; without the gas, the entire British plan for the offensive would lie in ruins. The

The Terrain of Loos

Although naturally flat and chalky, the region had undergone a major transformation since the discovery of coal in the 1870s. Six large, iron-latticed pitheads rose 30m (100ft) or more above the ground. From a distance they resembled London's famous Tower Bridge and thus soon adopted that nickname. From their wheelhouses the Germans could observe almost any British movements and direct devastating artillery fire on to attacking troops. Made of iron and steel, they were difficult for British artillery to destroy; just

one of the Tower Bridges took gunners seven months to destroy. Being a mining region, the area around Loos also featured enormous slag dumps (called *crassiers* in French) that were ideal for observation. Two massive slag heaps known as the Double Crassier rose like mountains over Loos. When tunnelled into or hollowed out, the slag heaps formed nearly impregnable zones in which to hide artillery spotters or machine gunners. It was ground custom made for the defence.

air around Haig that cold fateful morning was still, and he knew that if it remained still, the gas would simply hang around the British trenches and do more harm to the British than to the Germans.

One of Haig's staff officers tried to postpone the offensive until the winds picked up, but senior officers were loath to cancel all the plans they had carefully put in place. The surprise of the gas, they knew, was its most potent characteristic. If orders to postpone failed to reach even a few of the chemical units, the Germans would undoubtedly find out about the British possession of gas and take counter measures. In any event, the French attacks in Champagne and on the British right flank at Vimy would go ahead as scheduled. The British could not sit in their trenches while the French attacked simply because the breeze was unfavourable. At 5.40am a slight breeze picked up,

Soldiers, like these men at Loos, marching in soft hats are a symbol of the war's early months. Armies soon learned the need for metal helmets, more as protection against flying debris than against bullets.

'gently rustling the leaves' of nearby poplar trees, leading British officers to conclude that the situation was as satisfactory as they could reasonably expect.

Ten minutes later, British artillery opened up a furious barrage, followed by the opening of the chlorine gas cylinders. The British had finally caught a piece of good luck. Owing to information taken from a prisoner seized during a trench raid, the Germans had gone on alert in expectation of a British attack, but they had expected it to come much earlier in the day. Consequently, they began the morning stand-to at 3.30am. A German regimental history described the scene: 'Everyone was at his post, bayonets fixed, hand grenades given out, and a reserve of ammunition put ready.' When, however, the expected attack did not materialize at first light (approximately 5.15am), the Germans stood down. They were thus relaxing after a period of intense concentration when the British attacked. Surprise was therefore complete even though the prisoner had given the Germans the correct day for the attack.

From his observation tower, Haig would have had quite a scene unfolding beneath him. Artillery shells were falling all over the battlefield, tossing up puffy white clouds of chalk dust while the candles spewed forth thick, billowing dark smoke. At the same time, the yellowish white gas that came out of the cylinders began slowly drifting and amassing. Through all of this smoke and haze, Haig must have seen dozens of green, white and red signal rockets, fired by panicky German units in their fire trenches in the hopes of eliciting artillery support in their sector. If, however,

he was looking carefully, Haig would also have noticed that the poplar leaves had stopped rustling and that the gas was not moving far from the British front line.

Thirty-five minutes later, the gas had still not made it to the German parapets. British troops thus had to advance through the gas and smoke. Training for such an assignment helped men overcome some of their fears, but no amount of training could simulate the task in front of them. They moved slowly through their own poison gas, encumbered by clumsy gas masks of unknown effectiveness with respirators made mostly of cotton gauze. In some places, German units fled to reserve trenches at the smell of chlorine, but others held their ground. In many areas the gas had arrived in such weak concentrations that it only

The growth of aviation led inevitably to countermeasures. These Germans have adapted a machine gun for anti-aircraft fire. By 1916 dedicated anti-aircraft crews with new types of weapons had begun to appear on the Western Front.

caused a stinging of the eyes by the time it reached German lines. In other places, German troops built fires, whose convections were strong enough to halt the gas's progress on a windless day.

British success was therefore inconsistent. Elements of the British 47th Division captured the Double Crassier and the town of Loos itself, breaking two German trench lines as they did so. In other places, gas blew back on advancing British troops, forcing them to retreat to the presumed safety of their own lines. In still others, British troops attacked with no protection from the gas at all. German troops were therefore able to fire into approaching British troops with impunity. On one part of the Loos front the slaughter had been so bad that German troops refused to fire on retreating British soldiers out of pity.

By noon the German first and second lines had been pierced in three places and, including the reserves, the British had a four-to-one superiority in manpower. Haig tried to reinforce these areas of success at Loos with his reserves, but on Sir John French's orders they had been held too far back to exploit gains in time. Haig could not get access to them because French had chosen a headquarters building that lacked a reliable military telephone line. Instead, French's headquarters relied on the local French telephone system, which was incompatible with the British military one. Thus the reserves sat motionless at a time when they were desperately needed. As Haig later complained, 'If there had been even one division in reserve close up we could have walked right through.' Haig and Sir John French soon began a furious dispute over the reserves issue at Loos, which further undermined the British Government's faith in French's leadership. The Government allowed him to hang on until December in order to avoid the potentially demoralizing impression of mismanagement at Loos, but Sir John French's days were numbered. On 17 December Haig, his former student, was promoted in his place.

Sergeant Piper Daniel Laidlaw von a VC at Loos for playing 'Blue Bonnets over the Border' while the men of his battalion advanced. He continued to play his pipes despite being wounded in the ankle and leg. Other members of the battalion suffered from poison gas at the battle.

Opposite Vimy Ridge, the French attacked with enthusiasm in spite of heavy rains, with bands playing 'La Marseillaise' as French troops went over the top shortly after noon. Bad weather and poor visibility limited the efforts of French troops to move forward, although they cleared the stubborn strongpoint of Souchez on the first day. Joffre ordered the French to advance methodically and carefully. In light of British failures to their north at Loos, Joffre knew that any French attack would have limited utility. He also wanted to conserve ammunition and reserves for his main strike in Champagne, launched on the same day (see below). Nevertheless, he did not want to give the British the impression that the French had abandoned them, so he directed that the Tenth Army launch limited supporting attacks. These attacks were aimed at the powerful German salient between Loos and

The Western Front wasn't all trenches. The battlefield at Loos was dominated by the pitworks of the region's coalmines. This one took on the name Tower Bridge and was a constant artillery target because of its use as an observation point.

Vimy, from which German gunners could fire shells into either the British or the French positions.

The French thus kept attacking, although Joffre sent only limited resources to help them do so. Nevertheless, the French managed to gain the summits of two of the three hills of the Vimy Ridge on 29 and 30 September. Joffre briefly saw new promise in the offensive and agreed to release more artillery and ammunition. Foch and Sir John French met and agreed to conduct two more simultaneous offensives on 2 October, but bad weather and poor roads made it too difficult for the Allies to get all the pieces in place before the Germans responded. Disagreements over exactly where and when to attack ensued, delaying the Allied attack until 13 October. In the meantime, the lead units of the French and British armies had to be relieved owing to their fatigue and new, less experienced units brought up in their place.

As a result, the Germans had time to regroup and reorganize. When the offensive resumed on 13 October, the results were, in the words of the British

The French St Etienne machine gun, introduced in 1907. In the hands of a skilled crew, it could fire as many as 500 8mm rounds per minute. Made with cheap materials, it rarely achieved that rate and was replaced by 1916 by the more reliable Hotchkiss.

official history 'useless slaughter of the infantry'. Combat continued until the end of the month, but the gains had been minimal. French and British losses are estimated at 50,000 men each; the German losses were approximately half that number. As the British were losing faith in Sir John French, so, too, were many Frenchmen losing faith in Joffre and his deputy, Foch. Although the debates were much more muted and private in Paris than in London, Joffre had shown little to gain for all of the resources given to him. His continued complaints about interference from politicians did not serve him well either.

Nor had Joffre's Champagne offensive achieved much more than his Artois offensive had. The fighting there was over much of the same ground as the winter offensive, ranging from the east bank of the Suippe

> 'We cannot win this war unless we kill or incapacitate more of our enemies than they do of us, and if this can only be done by our copying the enemy in his choice of weapons, we must not refuse to do so.'
>
> Lieutenant-General Ferguson, commander of British II Corps

River to the Main de Massiges, 30km (19 miles) due east. At 9.15am on 25 September, French artillery lifted to targets in the second German line, and French soldiers entered no man's land. The results were inconsistent. On the east, the Colonial Corps took the 'thumb' of the Main de Massiges, a 190m (623ft) rise. In the centre, French troops took a key German position

known as the Trou Bricot near Perthes. To the west, a force of Senegalese soldiers, commanded by the same Jean-Baptiste Marchand who had led the march across West Africa to Fashoda in 1898, took the Ferme de Navarin amid heavy fighting. Marchand himself was wounded and carried from the battlefield. These gains were serious enough to lead Falkenhayn to order all available German reserves to Champagne, not to Artois.

Joffre had sought to avoid the problem the British had faced of placing reserves too far in the rear to exploit opportunities as they presented themselves. Consequently, he had packed his reserves into support and communications trenches close to the front lines. There they had taken enormous casualties as they sat helpless in the face of heavy German artillery barrages. Thus neither the British, who had kept their reserves further back specifically to avoid German artillery fire, nor the French, who suffered when they packed reserves near the front, could exploit success. At the end of day one, the French had made enough local gains to lead Joffre and Foch to be optimistic and order the attack resumed on day two.

Good news seemed to pour into Joffre's headquarters. On day two, the French advanced the line six kilometres (four miles) in most places and had taken more than 15,000 prisoners. Continued poor weather prevented aerial reconnaissance and artillery

Sir Douglas Haig (1861–1928)

Sir Douglas Haig was a polished, professional cavalryman with a sizeable personal fortune and close connections to the royal family. He had led I Corps well in the war's opening months, making him the logical choice to replace Sir John French as BEF commander at the end of 1915. Haig handpicked men loyal to him for senior staff positions; few of them distinguished themselves. Haig also had acrimonious relationships with many in the British War Office and with British politicians like Prime Minister David Lloyd George. He remains a controversial figure.

The destruction at Loos proved the difficulty of attacking strongly defended enemy positions. Even when temporary breakthroughs could be achieved, the limits of supply and reserve systems meant that success could not be maintained.

targeting, but Joffre nevertheless saw enough positive signs to order the French to reorganize and prepare to attack again. The Germans were still in solid possession of the Butte de Mesnil, almost 200m (656ft) high and sitting just west of La Main de Massiges. The French would need to seize this and other German positions before a general advance could be made. The French thus pressed on, but they faced an insoluble dilemma. To exploit gains, they needed to pack reserves into tight spaces, but this method left their men terribly vulnerable to German artillery. Without aerial spotting, moreover, French gunners could not conduct the necessary counterbattery fire to silence the German guns.

Thus by 30 September, the French could feel some pride in gaining more terrain than any other offensive they had yet conducted. They could also point to 23,000 German prisoners of war, 120 German artillery pieces and hundreds of German machine guns captured. These successes had, however, come at a steep price in terms of artillery shells fired and, more importantly, men killed and wounded. The French thus ordered a pause from 30 September to 6 October while Joffre resupplied the French Army with more

artillery shells and men. They represented the last reserves Joffre expected to have in 1915, but he committed them anyway because they were the last great hope for a meaningful success before the onset of bad weather halted operations.

For the next eight days French forces put pressure on the Germans in Champagne, with German commanders constantly reporting that they were near collapse. Still, it proved much easier for the defender to shift forces along the line to fill in gaps than it did for the attacker to move men and *matériel* through no man's land and into the battle zone. As a result, the German line was pressured, but always held. Each passing day showed less and less promising results while at the same time French losses mounted. By 14 October, the diminishing returns of the offensive were obvious to all and Joffre cancelled it. Still, he was unwilling to consider it a failure. The French had taken the Main de Massiges, the Ferme de Navarin, and several other difficult positions, proving in Joffre's mind that his methods were working.

For the Allies, 1915 ended on the Western Front in little better position than it had started. The Germans continued to occupy much of the same terrain in December that they had held in January. Repeated major efforts to dislodge them had failed. Still, the Allies believed that they were making progress in learning how to conduct offensives. The problem of placing reserves and the difficulty of getting accurate information passed quickly up the chain of command remained, but many Allied commanders believed that they had figured out the way to break the stalemate of the Western Front using massive quantities of artillery and rushing reserves into the gaps in a timely manner.

On the other side, Falkenhayn thought that the Allies had nearly been able to break German lines. Lacking reserves of his own, he had opted to remain

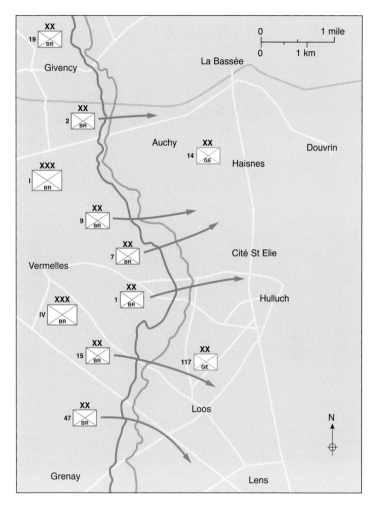

Loos sat at the centre of a lengthy salient (or bump) in the front line. Such salients were often difficult to attack, even though attacking armies could strike them from three sides, because defenders could easily move resources to threatened areas inside the salient.

on the defensive on the Western Front in 1915 in order to pursue victory in the east. The Germans had, indeed, won a massive victory in Poland, although that victory had not resulted in eliminating the Eastern Front. The essential German two-front dilemma remained, and Falkenhayn was not confident of Germany's capability to maintain two fronts in 1916. Clearly, staying on the defensive had come with some serious risks that Falkenhayn did not want to repeat in the coming year.

CHAPTER 5

Verdun

The war on the Western Front took a new and more murderous turn at Verdun. German general Erich von Falkenhayn introduced a new strategy and methods of warfare that would turn this border town into a killing zone unlike any in history.

The Battle of Verdun remains one of the most dramatic and bitterly fought battles in military history, but its origins are still shrouded in mystery and controversy. German general Erich von Falkenhayn gave one account of its origins in his post-war memoirs. He had, he claimed, written a memorandum on Christmas Eve 1915, which had been approved by the Kaiser, in which he outlined his views on German strategy for the coming year. He continued to assume, as had a generation of German officers before him, that Germany could not win a two-front war. As the British blockade cut further and deeper into the German supply situation, moreover, the constrictions of the two-front dilemma would become ever more acute.

German infantrymen amid the destruction of Verdun. Their commander had hoped to kill Frenchmen faster than the French could kill Germans, but both sides soon found that the battle took on a life of its own and killed men of both armies equally.

German soldiers enter the 'meat grinder' of Verdun. The battle became an iconic symbol to men on both sides, forcing the opposing armies to fight for it even after it had lost all strategic value.

Falkenhayn had also come to believe that the war would be won or lost on the Western Front for two reasons. First, major victories in the east had weakened the Russians and given Germany thousands of square kilometres of territory, but titanic losses notwithstanding, the Russians were showing few signs of imminent collapse. The need to occupy, pacify and Germanize the newly acquired lands of the east also required an investment of men and resources that could not be used on either fighting front. Second, Allied power in the autumn 1915 battle in Champagne had frightened Falkenhayn into believing that the Allies had the strength to pierce German lines.

Although the Germans had solid defensive lines in place across the Western Front, the loss of even one of them would be catastrophic. They had held so far, but there was no guarantee that German troops would be able to hold off Allied attacks that were sure to be more powerful in 1916 than they had been in 1915.

BLEED FRANCE WHITE

Like most senior German officials, Falkenhayn had more hatred and contempt for the British than he had for the French. In his eyes, it had been the British whose powerful navy had interfered with German plans for a profitable worldwide empire. That same British fleet now conducted a blockade that was slowly but surely depriving the German Army and the home front of needed supplies. Like his Kaiser, Falkenhayn wanted to defeat the British so that Germany could write post-war terms that would shift the maritime and colonial balances of power. The French, however, stood in the way of achieving those goals. Some means had to be found to force the French Army, what Falkenhayn called 'England's best sword', out of the war. Without France, he concluded, the much smaller

British would have no choice but to sue for peace. Germany could then insist on almost any peace terms it desired. This threat to the British Empire helps to explain the high rates of volunteerism among men in the various parts of the empire, few of whom had any desire to become German.

Falkenhayn's final set of conclusions was tactical. His analysis of the first year and a half of the war had led him to the belief that Germany did not have the strength to take the French capital. As numerous battles in 1914 and 1915 had shown, the defensive had become so much stronger than the offensive that the Germans would be unable to muster enough men and guns to break Allied lines and threaten Paris. The Germans would have to find another way to defeat France.

From these presumptions, Falkenhayn determined that the only way to win the war was to defeat France through attrition. The tactical realities of the Western Front meant that the Germans needed to find a way to convince the French to do the attacking on unfavourable terms. Then the German Army could kill Frenchmen faster than the French could kill Germans. In his words, 'Just behind the French lines

The Christmas Memorandum

No vestige of Falkenhayn's Christmas memorandum survived the war. Falkenhayn quoted it in his memoirs and claimed that the Kaiser had both seen it and approved its conclusions. It is possible, therefore, that Falkenhayn invented the memorandum after the war to justify his actions in beginning one of the bloodiest battles ever fought, although the absence of the memorandum does not itself prove the charge of some historians that it never existed. Regardless, Falkenhayn's thinking seems to have been shared by many senior German officers, including one who used similar imagery, writing 'We must apply a suction pump to the body of France, and gradually but steadily drain the strength from its half-open veins.'

on the Western Front there are objectives which the French command must defend to the last man. If it so defends them the French Army will be exhausted by its bloody losses in the inevitable combat, regardless of whether or not we win the objectives immediately.' The real object, Falkenhayn chillingly wrote, would not be territory, but to 'bleed France white'.

Falkenhayn's great challenge, then, was to find a place that France would have to defend, to the last man if necessary. He chose Verdun, an austere French city with both military and symbolic value. Militarily, Verdun sat astride the Meuse River, guarding the eastern approaches to Champagne and Paris, which sits 200km (125 miles) to the west. The city lies just west of a series of dominating hills known as the Heights of the Meuse,

The Austrian Skoda 305mm howitzer, whose shells were capable of inflicting tremendous damage to the forts of Verdun. It fired a high-trajectory shell that weighed 385kg (850lb) and had a maximum range of 11,800m (12,905 yards). Heavy guns like these killed untold thousands of men on the Western Front.

Evidence of the impact of German shelling in Verdun. Many small villages outside the towns were pounded to rubble and never rebuilt. They are today the *villages détruits* (destroyed villages) of the Meuse River valley.

which had been a barrier to the invasion of France for centuries. To the northwest, the Argonne Forest screens Verdun, giving it a strong natural defensive position.

To complement Verdun's natural defences, armies had been building fortifications in the region for centuries. The very name 'Verdun' means fort in a Gallo-Roman dialect once spoken in the Meuse region. Over the centuries fort after fort had been built there, including the massive eighteenth-century Citadelle that protected the city centre. The modern fortifications of the region dated to the period of Louis XIV's great military engineer Vauban. After the Franco-Prussian War, the French

government reinvested in the forts of Verdun, making the region one of the most heavily defended in the world.

The newer forts and *ouvrages* were a far cry from the elegant star-shaped forts of Vauban's era. Built to withstand modern artillery, most of their key components were deep underground in dank, damp corridors and galleries. The largest forts held command posts, communications centres, dormitories and ammunition storage. They also held reserves of food and water cisterns designed to allow a garrison to survive for long periods of time if besieged. The only parts of the fort that reached visibly above ground were gun turrets for artillery pieces and a few carefully concealed apertures for machine guns and observers. Atop the forts sat as much as several metres of earth designed to absorb the concussions of enemy artillery fire. In short, they were extremely unpleasant, even terrifying, places; moreover, as the experience of Belgium had already shown, modern artillery was stronger than modern fortifications if the guns were given time to do their methodical work. The key to the Verdun defences was supposed to be the trench networks outside the ring of fortresses. French trenches in the region were designed to keep the German artillery as far away from the main forts as possible to impede their observation and thus their accuracy. At

A famous image of French soldiers attacking at Verdun. Unlike their comrades in 1914, they are wearing metal helmets (modelled on those worn by firefighters) and their uniforms are made of a greyish blue. The French Army also modernized its weapons, doctrine and training.

the end of 1914, fighting in the region had died down and the two sides had dug in, producing a salient that began near the town of Varennes northwest of Verdun. From there it arced east to Maucourt, turned due south around the Fort of Etain (which the Germans had taken in 1914) before heading south to St Mihiel.

Falkenhayn depended on the French to make a full commitment to Verdun. The lines of communication around the salient were almost custom built for Falkenhayn's needs. Because the Germans held the exterior line around Verdun they could bring men and supplies into the area from the west, north and east. The French, by contrast, could only supply Verdun by one reliable narrow-gauge railway line and one two-

The Importance of Verdun

Verdun's symbolic value convinced Falkenhayn that France would fight for it to the last man. French (or more accurately, Gallo-French) forces had been defending Verdun since the AD 450 invasion by Attila that left the area 'like a field ravaged by wild beasts'. Charlemagne himself had chosen Verdun as the place to sign the agreement that divided his holdings into three bequests, two of which formed the mythic beginnings of France and Germany. Since then, the region had been the scene of numerous battles and sieges, most recently in 1792 and 1870, when an estimated 25,000 German shells struck the city.

lane highway running north into the city from Souilly and Bar le Duc. Both were within the range of German artillery. If the Germans could cut this slender umbilical cord, the French would only be able to move men or supplies into Verdun or its fortifications with great difficulty. The geography of the salient also meant that German gunners could fire into it from three sides while hiding their artillery batteries in the numerous large and small forests in the region.

Falkenhayn did not initially share his plan for attrition warfare at Verdun with the man he entrusted with leading the battle. He had chosen the crown

Verdun sat inside one of the great salients of the Western Front. French positions inside the salient were thus exposed on three sides. The salient also meant that the French could resupply their men from only one direction, the southwest, while the Germans had many more options.

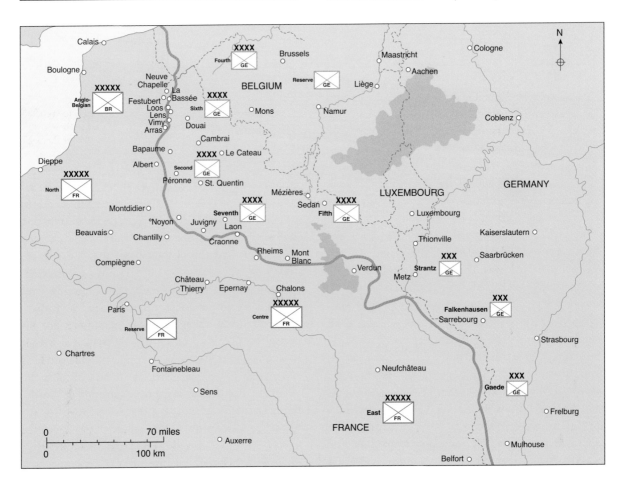

prince's army as the main fighting force at Verdun, perhaps as part of an effort to flatter the Kaiser by naming his son as the commander of the operation. Over the war's first few months, the crown prince had achieved a modest reputation for military acumen, and his chief of staff, a long-standing veteran general, had transformed the crown prince's army into one of the best in the German order of battle. The crown prince understood his assignment to be the capture of Verdun, not the fighting of a bloody slogging match whose only goal was the killing of men at an unprecedented pace. Falkenhayn thus deceived his most important subordinate about his real intentions, hoping to be able to flatter and dupe the crown prince into fighting the battle his way.

Unaware of the true goal of the offensive, the crown prince's army used the forests well, assembling a massive artillery concentration right under the nose of the French garrisons. In all, the Germans had 1400 guns, of which 850 were of heavy or 'super heavy' calibre. They included the same 305mm and 420mm guns that the Germans had used to pummel Liège and

The famous 'horizon' or 'cigar smoke' blue of the new French Army uniforms is shown in this colour photograph. French soldiers were known as *poilus* (hairy ones) due to their grubby and unshaven appearance, which also comes through in this photograph.

Namur. More than 160 German aircraft flew overhead to provide observation for the gunners and, equally as importantly, to blind French gunners by dominating the skies. The bombardment Falkenhayn planned would thus be not only the most powerful ever fired, but it would also be one of the most accurate. In addition, the Germans planned to fire poison gas and tear gas at suspected locations of French artillery batteries. Unlike the gas released by cylinder, this gas would be placed in artillery shells, meaning that it would not be as dependent upon favourable winds as that used at Second Ypres and Loos. Finally, the Germans had a new weapon in store for use in the forests around Verdun, flamethrowers, 96 of which would be used for clearing trenches and for setting the forests on fire. On 20 February 1916, German infantrymen began making probes along the line,

Verdun was often a battle of small units, as companies and platoons became isolated from support. Eventually both armies made a virtue of this necessity, devolving command to lower and lower levels.

looking for weak spots in the French trench network, but the French saw nothing to indicate that German goals were any more ambitious. At the same time, however, Crown Prince Wilhelm was promising his men that they would witness the signing of a pro-German peace treaty on Verdun's Place d'Armes.

THE FIRST ATTACKS

German gunners unleashed the full weight of their astonishing barrage on the cold, icy morning of 21 February. For nine hours, the German guns fired more than one million shells, aiming at every conceivable target set along a 10km (six-mile) arc of the front line

between the Meuse River and the village of Ornes. The German fire was concentrated in a pie-shaped wedge, formed on the west by the river and the east by a line connecting Fort Vaux to Verdun. Falkenhayn's orders directed the Germans to 'concentrate an all-powerful artillery, cut with gun-fire the main railway connecting Verdun with France, crush the French defenses, isolating their occupants with heavy artillery barrages, then rush the town with huge masses of men, irrespective of losses, crushing the last vestiges of resistance'.

The French had made inadequate preparations to meet such an assault. They had fewer than 270 artillery pieces, most of them either 75mm field guns or the outdated Rimailho guns, whose short range made them unable to target German artillery batteries. French gunners, moreover, had fewer than 60 shells per gun on average, compared to the 3000 shells per battery that the Germans had amassed. Even many of the French guns that did have ammunition sat silent during the opening phases of the battle because their commanders had received no orders to fire: the German shelling had destroyed the French communications system. Signal flares were of little use, so thick and so intense were the clouds of smoke the shelling and fires produced.

The French had been caught badly by surprise at Verdun. They needn't have been. All of the signs of a major German attack had been there, and many of them had been noticed and reported to senior officers. One French officer, who was also a member of the Chamber of Deputies, had seen the risks and had put his career on the line to prevent Verdun from being

Germany's tremendous edge in heavy artillery pieces gave it a critical advantage in the first few weeks of Verdun. The French responded by rushing more heavy guns to the sector and assigning two commanders, Henri Philippe Pétain and Robert Nivelle, who reorganized French gunnery and made it much more effective.

attacked. He had tried to warn those responsible for the defence of France about how dire the situation was, but his warnings went unheeded. It was a mistake for which France, and Germany, would pay dearly.

FRANCE'S DESPERATE DEFENCE OF VERDUN
Joffre, like Falkenhayn, had spent the Christmas holiday thinking about strategy for 1916. In the first few weeks of December he had hosted a high-level meeting of French, British, Italian and Russian officers. They discussed ways of defeating Germany in the coming year and analyzed their failures in the year just past. They concluded that they needed better coordination of all of their efforts so that the Germans, Ottomans and Austro-Hungarians would need to respond to pressures on all parts of their lines simultaneously. The Germans, especially, would need to make critical choices about which parts of their far-flung war effort to reinforce and prioritize. Joffre presumed that they would have to leave themselves weak somewhere and that constant, coordinated

French colonial soldiers made up the *force noire* that the French Army hoped to use to counterbalance Germany's larger population. Senegalese soldiers were among the fiercest – and most feared – soldiers on the Western Front. They rarely took prisoners and fought with great élan. The Germans were terrified of them and accused the French of war crimes for using Africans in a 'white man's war'.

pressure by all of the Allied armies would make sure that they broke.

As the conferees sat in the luxury of Joffre's headquarters château at Chantilly, they discussed the implementation of Joffre's grand vision. The Russians reported that they were still recovering from the horrendous bloodletting of the previous year and were in no position to attack. The new commander of the British Army, Sir Douglas Haig, was eager to attack, but needed some time to integrate the new battalions of British volunteers then joining the army. France, too, needed time to bring larger, more powerful artillery pieces into service. By mid-summer, they agreed, all of these conditions could be met. By then the Russians would have replaced their losses, the

British Army would have grown to three field armies and the French would be ready to conduct an attack with unprecedented artillery support. The meeting concluded with an agreement that the Allies would begin a major joint offensive around 15 July.

British and French officers then sat down to plan their part of the great offensive. Joffre envisioned their largest effort yet, to take place on either side of the Somme River that marked the general dividing line between the British and French areas of responsibility on the Western Front. The French Army would take the lead, attacking south of the river with 40 divisions advancing across a wide front that had been thoroughly saturated beforehand by heavy artillery. The British would use similar methods north of the river and commit 25 divisions. The tactics and methods would resemble those used thus far, relying on artillery and trusting in a slow, methodical advance of the kind advocated by French *grignotage* theorists. The French commander of this operation, Ferdinand Foch, wrote that 'we must give up the idea of an assault undertaken with more or less deep and dense masses, the reserves following closely on the heels of the first line. … This method has never succeeded.' In other words, the massing of reserves as in Champagne must be avoided. 'We see that the power of organization is stronger than the bravery of troops', he concluded. 'We can launch infantry only against obstacles which we have with entire certainty prepared for this action.' In other words, the battle would be won with artillery conquering and the infantry occupying.

With eyes firmly set on a methodical, coalition battle on the Somme, Joffre was deaf to the warnings

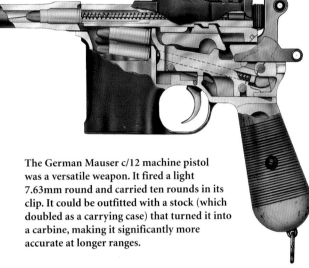

The German Mauser c/12 machine pistol was a versatile weapon. It fired a light 7.63mm round and carried ten rounds in its clip. It could be outfitted with a stock (which doubled as a carrying case) that turned it into a carbine, making it significantly more accurate at longer ranges.

The Death of Driant

Driant became an instant hero in France and a figure so legendary that he transcended even the barrier of the Western Front. The German soldier who later found his body was a baron who still had a modicum of the ancient notion of chivalry about him. He sent Driant's personal effects to his wife in Germany, who in turn sent them via an emissary in Switzerland to Driant's widow along with a letter of condolence.

The death of Lieutenant-Colonel Emile Driant in the Bois des Caures at the start of Verdun gave the battle its first martyr.

of one French officer that Verdun lay vulnerable to an attack. That officer, Lieutenant-Colonel Emile Driant, was no ordinary battalion commander. He was a member of the Chamber of Deputies from Nancy and the son-in-law of his former commanding officer, the notorious General Georges Boulanger, who had once threatened a coup against the French Republic before being exiled and committing suicide on his mistress's grave. Driant was the author of a number of works on the role of fortresses in modern war. Convinced that the French Army had passed him up for promotion because of his links to Boulanger, he had resigned his commission, written a number of novels under a pseudonym and decided to run for election to the Chamber of Deputies. From his seat in the Chamber, he had been a vocal critic of the army's failures to prepare for war in the pre-war years. Although he was in his 60s in 1914, he immediately left the Chamber of Deputies (France had more elected officials fight and die in the war than any other country) and refused a number of chances to take a cushy desk job. Instead, he rejoined his old regiment and went to the front, fighting with distinction at the Battle of the Marne.

Despite his relatively low rank, Driant was not the sort of officer Joffre could easily ignore. Joffre knew exactly who he was and knew how deep his connections in the army and the government ran. In

1916, Driant was the senior ranking officer in a two and a half square kilometre (one square mile) grove of chestnut, oak and beech trees known as the Bois des Caures. It sat north of Fort Douaumont on the outside arc of the pie-shaped wedge the Germans were planning to target with their massive artillery bombardment. Driant had been increasingly concerned that Joffre and the French Army headquarters had not taken the defence of Verdun seriously. He had complained through his chain of command that he had neither the men nor the hardware to defend the region against an attack he believed to be imminent. The trenches around Verdun, he pleaded, needed more men, more concrete and more artillery support. Because French intelligence had not detected any indications of Falkenhayn's planning, the French Army disregarded Driant's warnings.

Joffre had another important reason for wanting to marginalize a disruptive subordinate like Driant. He knew that Driant was right. Joffre was among those senior French officers who had concluded that forts were death traps, unable to withstand the power of modern heavy artillery. The only way to defend Verdun (or any other place for that matter) was to defend it from a distance, in the trenches outside the city's belt of fortifications. As a result, Joffre believed that the heavy guns in Verdun's fortifications could be better used elsewhere and had ordered them moved to Champagne in time to be fired in his 1915 offensive there. Joffre had also rotated most of the region's best infantry units out of the region and replaced them with smaller numbers of Territorials, men who were

> '[T]he forces of France will bleed to death – as there can be no question of voluntary withdrawal – whether we reach our objective or not'
>
> Erich von Falkenhayn

deemed unfit for offensive warfare because of their age or physical condition. Verdun itself was administratively its own region, the Fortified Region of Verdun, and commanded by an officer of indifferent ability, General Frédéric Herr. Focused on resuming the offensive in the summer, Joffre did not want Verdun to become an issue for discussion inside the army.

Frustrated at the lack of response from the army, in August 1915 Driant wrote a letter to his friend Paul Deschanel, president of the Chamber of Deputies and future president of France. He warned Deschanel that although the troops at Verdun were working as hard as possible to secure the region, the army was not providing the men and resources necessary. The fancy army maps that Joffre showed the government, he warned, indicated an intricate defensive line around the Verdun perimeter, but his own observations of the front line showed that the trench networks were nowhere near as strong as they appeared on paper. Several sections were desperately short of barbed wire despite repeated requests. Driant begged Deschanel to warn Minister of War Joseph Gallieni of the problems at Verdun and Joffre's unwillingness to do anything about them.

Gallieni needed little convincing. He had already lost faith in Joffre as a commander and was anxious to know more about Driant's concerns. Gallieni and Deschanel sent a delegation to Verdun in December 1915, at the same time that Joffre was hosting his conference at Chantilly. The delegation's report confirmed all of Driant's concerns and recommended a major reinvestment of resources into the area. Gallieni gave the report to Joffre. The normally reserved and controlled Joffre flew into a furious rage, accusing Driant of subverting the normal military chain of command and trying to 'disturb profoundly the spirit of discipline in the Army'. As to Verdun, he told Gallieni that 'I consider nothing justifies the fear

German soldiers in a trench they have recently captured from the French. The powerful artillery barrages that characterized Verdun obliterated most trenches and field defences. Men sought shelter wherever they could including shell holes, the ruins of fortifications, and in what remained of the region's once dense forests.

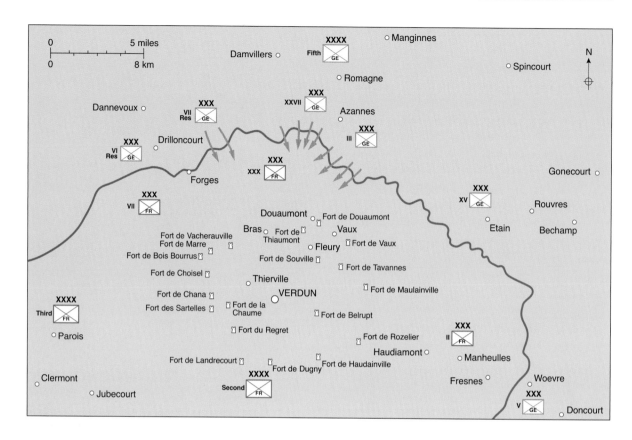

The map shows positions and movements around Verdun. Labels include:

Manginnes • Damvillers • Fifth XXXX GE • Spincourt • Romagne • Dannevoux • VII Res XXX GE • XXVII XXX GE • Azannes • III XXX GE • Drilloncourt • VI Res XXX GE • XXX FR • Forges • Gonecourt • XXX FR • XV XXX GE • Rouvres • Douaumont • Fort de Douaumont • Vaux • Etain • Bechamp • Bras • Fort de Thiaumont • Fort de Vaux • Fort de Vacherauville • Fort de Marre • Fleury • Fort de Bois Bourrus • Fort de Souville • Fort de Tavannes • Fort de Choisel • Thierville • Fort de Maulainville • Fort de Chana • VERDUN • Third XXXX FR • Fort des Sartelles • Fort de la Chaume • Fort de Belrupt • Parois • Fort du Regret • Fort de Rozelier • II XXX FR • Haudiamont • Manheulles • Clermont • Fort de Landrecourt • Fort de Dugny • Fort de Haudainville • Jubecourt • Second XXXX FR • Fresnes • Woevre • V XXX GE • Doncourt

Scale: 0 – 5 miles / 0 – 8 km. N (north) arrow.

The initial German attack at Verdun, launched on 21 February 1916, was spearheaded by the three corps of the German Fifth Army commanded by Crown Prince Wilhelm. They fell upon the outnumbered French defenders of XXX Corps, pushing them back from their prepared positions.

which, in the name of the Government, you express in your dispatch'. In short, Joffre would do nothing for Verdun except perhaps consider a court martial for Driant.

The German artillery barrage that began on 21 February confirmed all of Driant's fears, although not even Driant could have predicted the power and magnitude of the German offensive. He was in his concrete command post, an underground bunker named R2, in the Bois des Caures when it began. By one later estimate, a rectangle of the Bois des Caures 1000 by 500m was hit by 80,000 German shells. Of the 1300 men in Driant's battalion, only 350 survived the barrage. Many of the survivors were half-crazed; one soldier had to be dug out of his bunker when it

collapsed on top of him. He emerged yelling and screaming and went running off into the woods, never to be seen again. The woods themselves were unrecognizable, having been smashed into sticks in a few short hours. Bits of uniform and human flesh hung from the branches in what would become a familiar scene in and around Verdun.

Driant organized his defenders as well as he could. Repeated efforts to contact brigade headquarters and arrange for artillery support all failed. Driant and his remaining men fought off a succession of German attacks, throwing off German timing and buying a few precious hours for General Herr to get a handle on the situation and contact Joffre. Along the line, the situation was much the same. The powerful German artillery had done tremendous damage, but enough Frenchmen survived to slow the German advance through the outer French defence lines. Both sides began firing phosgene and chlorine gas, and the Germans brought up their flamethrowers. The novelty of these devices more than their power accounted for their early impacts. French soldiers later learned to shoot at the tanks, which contained oxygen and often exploded when pierced.

In the face of such overwhelming German power, Driant knew that he could only hold out for a few hours. He began to burn his papers and destroy whatever equipment his men could not carry. When the Germans began to advance in superior numbers, he divided his few soldiers into three columns and ordered them to fall back, but most never made it. As they left the shelter of their bunkers and trenches, a furious German enfilading fire struck them from several directions. Driant himself was hit in the temple, dying shortly after uttering the words 'Oh! Là, mon Dieu'.

More than 10,000 Frenchmen became casualties on the first day, but French resistance had slowed up the Germans and thrown off the careful timing of Falkenhayn's plan. On 23 and 24 February, the Germans kept up a steady pressure on the right bank of the Meuse inside the wedge. They also kept up a constant and brutal artillery barrage from both banks of the river. The right bank batteries focused primarily on the French forts; two batteries of super heavies from

> ## The Forts of Verdun
>
> Fort Douaumont, the largest of the Verdun forts, covered three hectares (seven acres) and could hold a garrison of 500 to 800 men. In all, there were nine forts on the right (east) bank of the Meuse and 10 more on the left bank. A number of smaller works, called *ouvrages*, existed to provide extra fire support. They also provided secure places in which to store men and munitions. The strength of the Verdun forts lends credence to the theory that Falkenhayn's plan for attrition was genuine.

the Bois de Tilly targeted Fort Vaux while no fewer than five batteries targeted Fort Douaumont. The German batteries on the left bank of the river aimed to cut the road that led west out of Verdun itself.

On 24 February, the Germans broke through the French first line, the semicircular arc on the outside of the wedge. The second trench line, the one whose inadequacy had concerned Driant so much, fell soon thereafter. As no third line had yet been constructed, there were no more man-made defences between the Germans and Verdun, less than eight kilometres (five miles) away, except the under-garrisoned and under-strength forts. The Germans had achieved the long-desired and long-anticipated breakthrough of the enemy lines. The French responded by rushing any reinforcements they could find into the sector to fight a desperate battle in open country. They included the 37th Division, made up mostly of Senegalese soldiers who had a reputation for not taking prisoners. The mere sight of them on the battlefield terrified many German soldiers.

Fighting in open country took its toll on both sides. The French, with no bunkers or trenches to protect them, were exposed to German shelling and took

Verdun's network of forts was among the strongest in the world. Several large forts guarded key terrain features and smaller forts, called *ouvrages*, covered strategic points of approach. *Ouvrages* could also be used to spot and correct artillery fire or observe enemy movements.

enormous casualties from artillery and machine guns. The Germans, however, were ahead of the pre-registration of their artillery and could no longer count on massive, pre-planned barrages. Nevertheless, they at least had artillery support; most of the French guns had gone silent, their crews dead or their guns out of shells. The two largest French guns at Verdun,

French soldiers at rest near Fort Vaux, one of the two most powerful of the Verdun forts. In the background, vehicles are moving along the road to the railway station at Bar-le-Duc, the only sizeable artery connecting Verdun to the outside world. It became known as *la voie sacrée*, the 'sacred way'.

240mm pieces that would count as medium guns to the Germans opposite them, were destroyed by their own crews in a moment of panic to prevent them falling into enemy hands. French morale began to drop as it appeared that the infantry had been left to their own devices, with no help from the artillery or the air service.

By nightfall on the 24th, French resistance in the Verdun sector was on the verge of collapse. The Germans, however, appear not to have realized just how much of an advantage they possessed. One French corps was completely out of reserves and in another

corps, brigade commanders were refusing to send their battered men back into the battle. Ambulances were taking hours to remove men to hospitals, always a demoralizing situation for soldiers, and ammunition stocks were almost empty. Herr and his staff had begun to consider ordering the demolition of all the French forts on the right bank of the Meuse (including Douaumont and Vaux) and defending the left bank only. Even if he had wanted to take such a desperate measure, however, it is extremely unlikely that his troops could have carried it out, as Herr's staff had no idea where their units were or how many men they had left. Herr himself began to panic and the officers around him proved unable to manage the crisis. Only the isolated pockets of French resistance in the face of overwhelming enemy power stopped the Germans from walking into Verdun that night.

By some accounts Falkenhayn did not want Verdun. His grand plan counted not on taking the city, but making the French fight for it. What he really needed at Verdun was a long, bloody slaughterhouse, as long as he could manage the battle so that Frenchmen died faster than Germans did. If his men cut the roads to Verdun or took the city itself, he might lose his chance

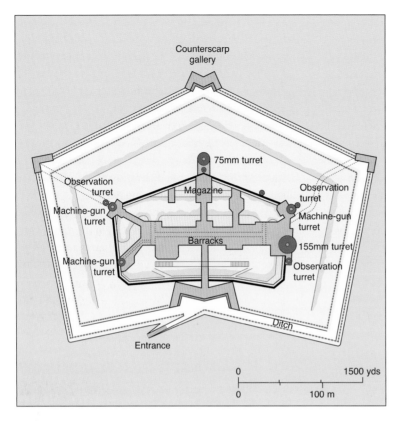

Counterscarp gallery

75mm turret

Observation turret

Machine-gun turret

Magazine

Observation turret

Machine-gun turret

Barracks

155mm turret

Machine-gun turret

Observation turret

Ditch

Entrance

0 — 1500 yds
0 — 100 m

A bird's-eye diagram and cross section drawing of Verdun's most powerful fort, Douaumont. Most of its key features were hidden underground and it used terrain very effectively. It was a cornerstone of France's frontier defences and its loss was a tremendous blow to French morale.

to fight his gory battle of attrition. Whatever the reason, the Germans moved slowly and cautiously on the 24th and may therefore have missed their best chance to take Verdun. Falkenhayn might also have missed his last chance to maintain firm control over the battle, as events would soon overtake him. Verdun had already become a battle like no other in history.

THE FALL OF DOUAUMONT

Fort Douaumont sat directly in the German line of advance. It had been designed to resist the full power of an attacking army, with walls of steel and concrete custom built to withstand even the massive 420mm 'Big Bertha' guns of the German Army. Indeed, it had survived three days of intensive bombardment in

better shape than anyone had any right to expect. With a battalion of infantry and a full complement of artillery pieces and ammunition, the fort would have the ability to hold out during a long and protracted siege. By 25 February, the Germans had advanced their front line to just north of the fort but had not yet brought up any supporting artillery. Douaumont should have been in a solid position to defend itself, even without the artillery pieces that Joffre had removed.

Douaumont was not, however, prepared to defend itself from the kind of attack it was about to face. A small company of German soldiers had gone beyond their orders for the day and had advanced close enough to scout the defences around Douaumont. They noticed that only one of the fort's machine guns seemed to be firing, and that the dry moat around the fort seemed to be completely undefended. The small party of Germans climbed down into the 7m-deep (24ft) moat, approaching Douaumont from the northeast. Still no rifle or machine-gun fire challenged them. A sergeant Kunze had his men form a human pyramid that he then climbed to gain access to the fort through an empty machine-gun aperture. Once inside, he realized that he had entered the main northeastern gallery of Fort Douaumont without firing a shot.

Kunze urged his men to follow him into the fort whose strength they had so feared. Only two did so at first, the rest fearing either the French response or the response of their own officers for exceeding orders. The three Germans advanced slowly and quietly through dim tunnels wondering where the French garrison was. They found four French soldiers in the turret of a 155mm gun and stunned them, taking away their pistols and rendering the most powerful gun Joffre had allowed the fort to keep utterly harmless. The Germans found 20 more Frenchmen in a meeting room, made them prisoners as well, and locked them in a barracks room. When no more French soldiers appeared to challenge Kunze, he sat down at a table in the officers' mess with eggs and wine; having had no rations for days, he helped himself to a snack.

Unbeknownst to him, Kunze had isolated not just the fort's largest remaining gun, but rendered almost half of the fort's garrison on that day out of action. On the morning of the attack, Fort Douaumont's once mighty garrison of 800 men had been reduced to just 57 Territorials with no officers at all. French units were in the vicinity and could easily have moved into the fort to take it back but none did. No units ever received

orders to that effect, probably because at that time General Herr was still planning to demolish the fort and everything else on the right bank of the Meuse. Given that plan, there was no reason to reinforce the garrison. While Kunze continued his meal, other German soldiers had crept closer to the now curiously silent fort. Some Germans began to wonder if they had been victims of a great trick. Surely the French would not give up Fort Douaumont without a tremendous fight – perhaps the fort had been rigged for demolition already and would blow up at any second.

The fort, of course, had not been rigged, and by late afternoon it was entirely in German hands. By nightfall an entire German battalion had taken refuge inside and another had set up a rudimentary line of defence outside. Europe's most powerful fort now stood in the way of the French Army, not the German. One group of French soldiers had barricaded themselves inside one of the fort's galleries and still

A group of visitors (note the neck ties) visit the trenches outside Fort Douaumont. All forts needed trenches to defend the approaches and to prevent the enemy from placing artillery too close. Note also the zigzag nature of the trenches, designed in part to prevent one enemy machine gun from firing up and down its length.

refused to come out. A delay ensued until the Germans found one of their own who had been a waiter in Paris before the war and could explain that they were now prisoners of war.

The news of the fort's fall spread quickly through the Continent. When the Kaiser heard about it, he immediately demanded to be taken to Verdun, whose fall he expected at any minute. Those few civilians still in the city were ordered to leave, as the French did not believe they could protect them any longer.

Although Joffre had, more than anyone else, been responsible for the parlous state of Verdun's defences, he recognized the danger that the German offensive there posed to French survival. The news of Fort Douaumont's fall, especially the circumstances behind

it, shocked him. From Chantilly, however, he could not get a full picture of what was happening. He remained calm, and agreed to Castelnau's requests to send Pétain's Second Army out of the French reserve and into Verdun on the heights of the left bank of the river. Castelnau raced to Verdun through the dark night of 24/25 February to see for himself what was happening there. He was charismatic, confident and from a legendary military family. He had already lost three sons in the war and, despite some conflicts with Joffre in 1914, had retained the commander's confidence.

Castelnau arrived at Verdun to find General Herr a broken man who began pleading for permission to destroy all French outposts on the right bank of the Meuse and set up his defences on the left bank of the river alone. Castelnau denied him that permission, saying that with or without Fort Douaumont, the French would fight for every inch of both banks of the Meuse. He then called Joffre's headquarters to inform the commander that Verdun could be saved, but not

The glory for capturing Fort Douaumont fell not upon lowly Sergeant Kunze, but a Lieutenant von Brandis (seen here centre, with his fellow officers and sergeants) who arrived after its capture. Brandis, of aristocratic Prussian stock, was awarded the *Pour le Merité* medal by a delighted Kaiser.

with Herr in charge. Castelnau informed Joffre that he had taken it upon himself to relieve Herr, whom many officers wanted put on trial for the loss of Verdun that virtually everyone believed was imminent. Joffre wanted no part of a public investigation of the defences of Verdun, so he agreed to *limogé* Herr, moving him far from the front as quietly as possible. In his place Castelnau promoted Pétain, regarded as one of France's best defensive warfare specialists.

PÉTAIN AND THE DEFENCE OF THE LEFT BANK

Pétain took a firm hold of the crisis at Verdun. Himself an artillerist, he stopped local, haphazard shelling of German positions and reorganized his guns. He personally oversaw the development of new artillery plans that directed fire where it was most needed. French artillery began a methodical attack on the German flanks and on the main roads where German reserves were assembling. The arrival of larger guns and plentiful ammunition allowed Pétain to direct a wider and fuller bombardment of German targets. He trained gunners in his methods and he removed those commanders unable to use the guns with maximum efficiency.

Although he had tense, even acrimonious relationships with fellow officers and most politicians, Pétain displayed a care and paternalism towards his men that helped build trust and restore morale at a time when both were badly needed. Unlike most generals, Pétain took an interest in details as small as the quality of food his men received and how often they received mail and rest. He was also one of the few senior commanders on either side to make appearances in the trenches, handing out medals, visiting the wounded and chastising officers who had performed poorly. Many of his trench visits were surprises, allowing him to see for himself the conditions at the front instead of relying on often-inaccurate reports from subordinates.

Pétain introduced a system called *noria*, named after the water wheels of Algeria. This method allowed the French Army to rotate men in and out of Verdun to keep fresh units in the sector and to give tired men rest and time away from the horrors of the combat at

Pétain's Promotion

First thing in the morning after being promoted, Pétain was expected to meet with Joffre at Chantilly then hurry to Verdun, but he was not at his Second Army headquarters as expected. No one seemed to know how to find him or tell him of his new command and responsibilities. Eventually, one of Pétain's staff officers was located who thought he knew where the commander was. The officer grabbed a car and sped to Paris's Hôtel Terminus near the Gare du Nord. He woke a protective hotel concierge in the middle of the night with a story of Germans advancing on Paris if she did not tell him which room the general had rented. He finally convinced her to give him the room number, and then he climbed the stairs as quickly as he could. Ignoring the pink slippers sitting alongside the general's boots in the hallway, he knocked on the door around 3.00am. The officer told a half-dressed Pétain of his promotion and his appointment with Joffre at Chantilly in the morning. Pétain returned to his female companion (whom he later married) and the officer left the hotel, his critical, if unusual, mission accomplished.

Verdun. Eventually 259 of France's 330 regiments fought there, making Verdun a shared experience of loss and sacrifice for a generation of young Frenchmen including Charles de Gaulle and André Maginot, the future war minister to whom a monument at Verdun is dedicated.

Pétain's greatest concern was his thin and exposed line of communications. The only reliable way to feed and equip an army of 500,000 men and tens of thousands of animals was over the small road from Bar le Duc. It was just barely wide enough to allow two vehicles to be on it side by side, but Pétain knew it was

Verdun's only link to the outside world. Pétain and his staff worked to make the road as efficient as possible, setting up hydraulic presses and workshops along the way, dedicating thousands of men (many from Senegal and Indochina) to work as repair crews and developing strict rules for drivers to follow to ensure that there would be no traffic tie ups. The French Army, which owned less than 200 motorized vehicles in 1914, found more than 3500 trucks and cars to transport more than 50,000 tons of *matériel* and 90,000 men along the road every week.

These actions helped to bolster wavering French lines. The battle now became more manageable and even soldiers at the front could see a difference on the battlefield as they finally received the weapons and equipment they needed. French units no longer conducted frivolous counteroffensives willy-nilly. Instead they planned careful defences against which German units took heavy losses. The clarion call of '*On ne passe pas*', 'they shall not pass', became the rallying cry of the French at Verdun. New French commanders were beginning to distinguish themselves, their defensive mindsets replacing the wild offensives of the war's preceding months. By 28 February, the German offensive began to slow thanks in large part to Pétain's deft handling of the crisis he had inherited.

From the German perspective, the stiffening French resistance presented a serious problem. For Falkenhayn, the new French methods, especially the intense artillery fire coming from the left bank of the Meuse, threatened to disrupt his plan to wear the French Army down by attrition. If the French began to inflict heavy casualties on the Germans, then Falkenhayn could not win the battle as he had planned. Crown Prince Wilhelm, his eyes fixed on the capture of Verdun, saw the French artillery fire

The Power of the German Barrage

One hundred and sixty kilometres (100 miles) away from Verdun, in the relative safety of the quiet Vosges Mountains sector, a French officer noted in his diary that even though he was underground in a solid shelter, he could hear 'an incessant rumble of drums, punctuated by the pounding of big basses'. Lucien Gissinger, a 21-year-old French soldier recently sent to Verdun, experienced the barrage in much less musical ways. With a shaky hand he wrote in his journal that 'everywhere the soil is upturned and broken by enormous shell holes. Everywhere there is the strong odour of poison gas and already there is a smell of decay'.

in equally dire terms, although he seems not to have shared Falkenhayn's vision of attrition.

MORT HOMME

Both men saw the need to eliminate the French artillery positions on the heights of the left bank, but an assault on such strong positions would require massive reinforcements. The high ground of the left bank of the Meuse comprised two critical ridges, Côte 304, and the appropriately named Mort Homme (Dead Man's) Ridge, whose two hills rose to 265 and 295m (869 and 968ft). Falkenhayn was reluctant to release additional units because he saw that an extension of the battle, hitherto restricted to the right bank, would bring massive German casualties. Surprise having been lost, dislodging the French from dominating positions on the high

A French corporal near Fort Vaux. French soldiers spent days, even weeks, at Verdun without rest. Pétain introduced a system of rotation that gave some men time away, but the stresses of the Verdun battlefield were unprecedented.

ground placed the Germans in a disadvantageous position. The crown prince recognized the dangers as well, but argued for an attack on the left bank with enough force to compel Falkenhayn to agree.

On 6 March, the Germans unleashed a bombardment on the left bank that was as powerful as the one they had fired at the right bank on day one of the battle. With this act, the Germans doubled the size of the battlefield at Verdun. The French had foreseen the German need to attack the Morte Homme and Côte 304; they had therefore moved five divisions on to the ridges, but many of these divisions were inexperienced. Several of them fell back in the face of the massive German artillery barrage, leaving openings for the German assault to exploit. German forces took

French supply columns along the 'sacred way' from Bar-le-Duc to Verdun. The single road was vital to the French effort; without it, men at the front could not be resupplied. In contrast, the Germans had eight railheads nearby to bring up the vast quantities of ammunition needed for the battle.

'Where we were there were hardly any trenches or communication trenches left. Every half-hour the appearance of the earth was changed by the unflagging shellfire. It was a perfect cataract of fire.'

Anonymous French officer, Mort Homme

most of the French first trench line and put several units on the northern slope of the Mort Homme. The French, however, held the southern slope, in large part thanks to accurate artillery fire.

Because they had held on to the ridges, the French could continue much of the flanking fire that had slowed down the German advance on Verdun. German assaults on the left bank therefore continued. On 14 March, the Germans launched six divisions at the Mort

German machine-gunners defending devastated terrain at Verdun. The featureless 'moonscape' that Verdun became removed cover and exposed men to enemy artillery fire. Poison gas' ability to seep deep into trenches and shell holes made digging in dangerous and contributed to the terrible conditions at Verdun.

Damage to the town of Verdun. Despite the shelling, French soldiers continued to sleep and eat there. The town's massive underground Citadelle served as Pétain's headquarters. Today, a memorial in the town's centre commemorates 'The walls that broke the wishes of Imperial Germany'.

Homme Ridge, but the French trench line held. Fighting on the ridges of the left bank became some of the most furious of the war, with much of it hand to hand. Combat at Verdun wore out men and units much faster than at any other point of the Western Front in the war thus far. The French lost a few small villages and woods, but their line held throughout March by sheer determination alone.

THE PILOTS OF VERDUN

Fighting continued into April. On 9 April, the Germans launched coordinated attacks on both banks of the Meuse. Pétain followed it all from his cavernous underground headquarters in the city's Citadelle. The French artillery broke up repeated German assaults. The gunners received critical assistance from the heroic efforts of French aviators, who began to offer a serious challenge to German dominance of the skies. The legendary *Cigognes* (storks) squadron, featuring one of France's best pilots, Georges Guynemer, arrived at Verdun, as did a volunteer squadron of American pilots known as the Lafayette Escadrille. Allied pilots had begun to fly in formations, providing a unity greater than the sum of individual parts. The pilots of Verdun soon became some of the battle's greatest heroes.

The German attacks of 9 April failed all along the line on both banks. French forces had even been able to retake parts of the northern slope of the Mort Homme Ridge. The next day, Pétain wrote his famous order of the day, destined to become one of the iconic moments of the battle, and the war. '9 April was a glorious day for our armies', he wrote. 'The furious attacks of the crown prince broke down everywhere. The infantry, artillery, sappers and aviators vied with one another for valour. Honour to all. No doubt the Germans will attack again. Let all work and watch, that yesterday's success be continued.' He ended with the words that would be associated with him for the remainder of the war: *'Courage. On les aura!'* 'Courage. We will get them.'

French courage was put to the test by renewed German attacks throughout April. Tens of thousands of men had already died in the fights for the two ridges. Combat on 4–7 May finally gave the Germans control of Côte 304, allowing them to begin to move

Artillery dominated the battlefield at Verdun. Thousands of men on both sides were killed without a trace by artillery shells, as is evidenced by the thousands of names of the missing and the piles of unidentified bones in Verdun's massive ossuary.

La Voie Sacrée

The road from Bar-le-Duc to Verdun, the N3, became so critical to French efforts at Verdun that Maurice Barrès named it *la voie sacrée*, the sacred way. Today, it is the only road on the Western Front with its own dedicated memorial. Drivers along the road will notice a series of white and red milestones, marking the distance between Bar-le-Duc and Verdun. Atop each sits a French infantryman's helmet, a fitting tribute to the road that kept French efforts at Verdun intact.

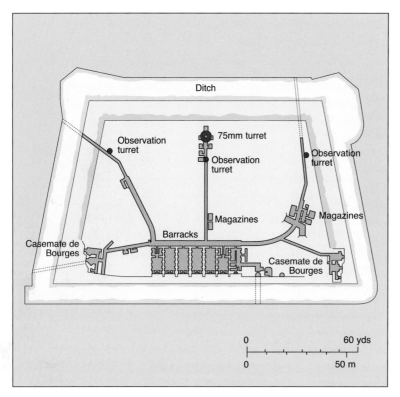

Constructed between 181 and 1884, and modernized in the early twentieth century, Fort Vaux was one of the stongest defensive works around Verdun. German forces surrounded the fort on 2 June and its commander, Major Raynal surrendered at 6.00am on 7 June.

on Mort Homme from the southwest. So many men had died on the ridges that German troops requested extra tobacco rations to cover the appalling smell of putrefaction. The Germans moved on Mort Homme anyway, making slow but steady progress until they held the entire ridge in their possession by the end of May.

The agony of Verdun had cut deeply into both armies. The lines had moved just a few thousand metres at tremendous cost. By the end of April, the Germans had already lost 89,000 men and the French had lost an estimated 133,000 men. Each side lost roughly 50,000 more men in the extremely violent fighting in May. Falkenhayn's murderous battle was indeed killing Frenchmen, but Germans were dying almost as quickly. The enormous costs of the offensive

thus far made many German officers question how many more men would have to die before the city itself fell. One senior German officer estimated that at the current rate of advance, the Germans would not take Verdun until 1920.

The crown prince had by this point concluded that the offensive had failed. The Germans would neither take Verdun nor succeed in attriting the French Army in any meaningful way. Falkenhayn began to look for alternatives, first in a possible offensive near Arras against the British, then in submarine warfare as a way to force the British to abandon their allies and come to the bargaining table. In March, a German submarine had in fact stepped up the pressure by sinking an unarmed civilian liner, the *Sussex*. The Americans protested vehemently, leading the Germans to pledge in May not to sink any more civilian liners without giving fair warning and taking measures to ensure the safety of passengers. By that point, Falkenhayn's fellow senior officers had already become more vocal in their criticism of him and by July at the latest the Kaiser also lost faith in him. As May turned to June, however, Falkenhayn kept up the offensive even if he was unsure about what it might accomplish.

Falkenhayn did get a piece of good news in early June when the French Fort Vaux fell. It had been cut off from resupply and constantly bombarded by both artillery and gas. Its commander had grown increasingly despondent as his repeated Morse code messages had gone unanswered, evidently because the French had given up the fort and thought the messages were a German ruse. The garrison held out until 4 June when the commander sent the fort's last carrier pigeon with a message about how desperate Fort Vaux's situation had become. The poor pigeon, suffering the effects of gas, made it to Verdun with its message intact, and promptly died. The French Army awarded it the

The Hindenburg–Ludendorff Team

General Paul von Hindenburg came out of retirement in August 1914 when events on the Eastern Front looked bleak. He went east with General Erich Ludendorff as his chief of staff. Ludendorff had made a name for himself as the conqueror of Liège. Together they designed a series of massive German victories over larger Russian armies. Based on this success, they consistently urged that more German resources be directed to the Eastern Front. Their demands caused great tensions among the 'westerners', who were convinced that victory in the war could only be achieved on the Western Front. These included the crown princes Wilhelm and Rupprecht, who believed that the Germans would only chase the Russians deeper and deeper into hostile territory, as Napoleon had done a century earlier.

When Falkenhayn's grand plans at Verdun fell apart, Hindenburg and Ludendorff assumed command of all operations on both fronts in late August 1916. They approached Verdun with an eye towards closing the battle down, but found they could not do so as easily as they had assumed. The pair would come to control most of the significant aspects of German decision-making until the war's end.

Legion of Honour and had it stuffed; it remains on display today as a symbol of French defiance. Nevertheless, the fort surrendered three days later, out of thirst as much as anything else; the gauge in the water cistern was faulty and therefore the fort's soldiers had gone days without any water at all.

Although the fall of Fort Vaux might have re-energized German efforts, the German offensive ground down in June. By the end of the month they had a tenuous hold on Côte 304 and the Mort Homme Ridge. They also held Forts Douaumont and Vaux, although French forces kept up a furious assault on the former, getting inside its galleries for a few days in May. French defences, however, had tightened, anchored around the forts of Souville and Tavannes on the right bank and two important ridges on the left bank. French infantry attacks, led by generals Robert Nivelle and Charles Mangin, had become more sophisticated and more aggressive. The chance to win a battle of any kind at Verdun had passed, but the killing continued. July would, however, bring important changes at Verdun, as the next great Western Front battle began along the slow, muddy French river known as the Somme.

Sitting at the edge of the Argonne Forest, Verdun once was a heavily forested area. Artillery bombardments uprooted whole trees and created the additional danger of falling debris. Parts of the Verdun region remained featureless for decades after the battle.

CHAPTER 6

The Somme

While Verdun was still raging, a second, equally murderous, campaign began. It involved eager, but untested men from the British Army attacking what Winston Churchill later called 'undoubtedly the strongest and most perfectly defended position in the world'.

W hile Pétain struggled to keep the situation at Verdun in hand, Joffre urged his alliance partners to meet their Chantilly obligations and attack the Germans and Austro-Hungarians as early as possible with as much strength as they could muster. In March, the Italians launched a half-hearted offensive in the Isonzo River valley, their fifth in a campaign that had thus far produced few tangible results. It failed to change the strategic situation at Verdun in any perceptible way. Austria-Hungary even launched its own offensive in the south Tyrol region, putting the Italians very much on the defensive. In June, the Russians launched their most successful offensive of the war, named after its commander

Members of Kitchener's New Army resting on their way to the Somme. The men of these battalions often joined together to form 'Pals' battalions' of men from the same occupation or neighbourhood.

Sir Henry Rawlinson (1864–1925)

An intelligent and capable officer with experience in Burma, Sudan and the Boer War, Rawlinson had been the head of recruiting in 1914 when the war broke out. He went to France with the BEF where he often clashed with Sir John French. He soon grew close to Haig, who promoted Rawlinson and gave him more important assignments. By the time of the Somme, Rawlinson was in command of the British Fourth Army, which had the primary responsibility for the 1 July attack. Although he had doubts about Haig's ambitious goals for the offensive, he did not challenge his commander.

General Alexei Brusilov. Although it frightened the Austro-Hungarian high command into halting their Tyrol offensive, it too had little impact on the Western Front.

Joffre knew that these offensives would be of only limited help, and that the best way to save the French position at Verdun was by launching the planned Franco-British offensive on the Somme as quickly as possible. The desperate situation at Verdun, however, meant that the French could no longer take the lead position in the attack, because most of its regiments near the Somme had been moved away to fight the Germans at Verdun. The Somme offensive therefore increasingly became a primarily British operation. Instead of 40 French divisions taking part in the attack as envisioned at Chantilly, the French would now

Kitchener inspects some of the men of the New Armies (also called the Kitchener Armies) that he helped to recruit. The idea of local recruiting provided Britain with the numbers of it needed, while also connecting regiments very closely to local communities.

contribute just 16. Rather than covering 40km (25 miles) of the Somme front, the French would now be responsible for covering just 13km (eight miles).

THE NEW ARMY

The new demands placed on the British Army meant that Haig had to find more divisions for the Somme offensive than he had agreed to at Chantilly. To augment his strength to 18 divisions, he decided to rely on 11 divisions of the so-called New Army. Also called Kitchener's Army, the new force was made up of 'Pals' battalions', and was a response to the sluggish recruiting numbers of late 1914 and 1915. As head of the War Office, the raising of troops was one of Kitchener's most important responsibilities. Lacking a tradition of conscription, Kitchener had to find a way to get Britons to volunteer for military service. He decided to build on an idea developed simultaneously by General Sir Henry Rawlinson and several civilian leaders in northern industrial cities. In August 1914, Rawlinson had raised a battalion of City of London employees by promising them that they could enlist together and remain together for the duration of the war. They became the 10th (Service) Battalion of the Royal Fusiliers Regiment, more than 1600 strong. As with many of these units they were more popularly known by a nickname that revealed something of their origins; in this case, the men of the City were known as 'The Stockbrokers Battalion'.

At about the same time in Liverpool, the wealthy British nobleman Edward Stanley, the Earl of Derby,

A British soldier and his kit. The rifle is the excellent Lee-Enfield Mark III, introduced in 1902. It held a 10-round magazine and featured a smooth and efficient bolt mechanism. In the hands of a good marksman it was deadly accurate.

had raised three battalions in five days through the 'Pals' method. Kitchener gladly encouraged local notables to raise men in this manner across Britain. Cities soon began competing with one another; to prove its patriotism, the city of Manchester raised four battalions in two weeks. By the end of September 1914 there were 50 Pals' battalions being formed. Eventually the Pals' system produced 145 battalions, with much of the expense for recruiting, housing and even feeding the men undertaken at a local level. The system was an enormous success in Kitchener's eyes, adding thousands of men to the army at relatively low cost. Raising sufficient numbers of men, however, proved to be the easy part. Training such men for the rigours of the Western Front proved to be a much more demanding task. Few of the new volunteers had much experience with soldiering; most of them had never fired a rifle, let alone an artillery piece or a machine gun. Finding men to conduct training also proved to be a challenge, as experienced officers and non-commissioned officers could not be spared from the fighting fronts.

By the time of the Somme, there were thousands of men from the New Armies on the Western Front. Some New Army battalions had fought at Loos, but Haig and others remained doubtful about how they would perform in the heat of a large battle. Their training had been rushed in order to dispatch them to the fighting fronts as quickly as possible. Untested and raw, the planners of the Somme offensive did not want to entrust them with any tasks they could not handle. As Haig himself noted, 'I have not got an army in France, really, but a collection of divisions untrained for the field'. In his instructions to his subordinates outlining his vision for the Somme offensive, he underscored this view reminding them that they 'would be working with New Army troops lacking the discipline, training, and tradition of the men they had led at the beginning of the war'.

The German defensive positions on the Somme were some of the strongest anywhere in the world. The Germans held a chalky ridge known as the Thiepval Ridge that afforded them excellent observation. The rolling nature of the terrain gave the Germans a number of places to situate machine guns and set up artillery observation posts. In addition, they had heavily fortified the buildings of several villages in the region including Serre, Beaumont Hamel and Fricourt, all of which would need to be cleared of resistance before the British could advance. The Germans also converted the region's many farms into small fortresses and had hidden defensive lines in two large woods, Delville Wood and High Wood.

But the real advantage of the Somme sector to a defender lay in the chalk itself. Unlike Flanders or the region around Loos, the chalk allowed the Germans to dig deep, nearly impregnable positions. By summer, 1916 these positions consisted of three trench lines, approximately 183m (200 yards) apart. Bunkers as far below the ground as 9m (30ft) provided safe

> ## La Boisselle
>
> Before the war, La Boisselle was a small village of just 35 buildings. As the Western Front solidified, La Boisselle became the centre of a minor German salient that the British would need to eliminate. Late in 1915 the British began to tunnel underneath the line at La Boisselle, moving quietly and deliberately. A daily advance of 46cm (18in) was considered good. The British eventually dug two tunnels 15–18m (50–60ft) below the German front line. They stuffed more than 45,359kg (100,000lb) of ammonal explosives into the tunnels and fired them on 1 July. The resulting crater, known today as the Lochnagar Crater, was 91m (100 yards) wide and 27m (30 yards) deep. It is still visible today.

> 'The object of that offensive was threefold
> i) To relieve the pressure on Verdun.
> ii) To assist our Allies in the other theatres of war by stopping any further transfer of German troops from the Western front.
> iii) To wear down the strength of the forces opposed to us.'
>
> Sir Douglas Haig

accommodations for 20–25 men and their equipment. By Western Front standards, the dugouts were exceptional, with excellent communications, storage facilities and even a few creature comforts like electric lights. The strongest trench defences were oval-shaped redoubts, the most important of which, the Schwaben Redoubt, sat on the crest of the ridge itself.

The Somme position would have been difficult for veteran troops to take. Haig believed that it was beyond the abilities of a novice army like the one he had on the Somme unless the men were given sufficient help. The British Fourth Army, led by the same Henry Rawlinson who had helped to bring about the Pals' battalions in 1914, would conduct most of the attack. Rawlinson agreed with Haig on the shortcomings of the men of the New Army and advocated limiting the goals of the offensive. He proposed that the British try to 'bite and hold', seizing the powerful German defences then converting them into solid defensive positions for the soldiers of the New Armies, who could then use them to fight off German counterattacks. Haig disagreed, insisting on a full-frontal attack designed to pierce the German lines and return mobile warfare to the Western Front. He expected to capture almost all of the German defences on day one of the infantry attack along a front of more than 26km (16 miles) from Serre to the Somme River itself.

The strong German position along the Somme had, Haig believed, two weaknesses that the British Army might exploit. First, German manpower shortages meant that the German Second Army had only six divisions in the line, although there were five more in reserve behind the lines. Thus if the Anglo-French attack could pierce the German front line, the Allies would have an overwhelming manpower superiority that they could bring to bear in open country. Consequently Haig wanted cavalry units brought as far forwards as possible to exploit gaps in the German line. Second, Haig believed that the Germans had packed the vast majority of their front-line men into their first and second trench lines. They therefore presented an inviting target for a massive application of artillery.

THE ARTILLERY PLAN

Haig's plan counted on annihilating German resistance with an enormous artillery barrage. Heavy pieces would destroy the German redoubts and trench defences while lighter field pieces would clear barbed wire and allow the infantry to go forward in safety. The inexperienced soldiers of the Pals' battalions would therefore only have to climb the ridge and exploit the gaps created by the artillery while the cavalry ranged deep behind German lines to strike targets of opportunity. Some of the Pals' units might have to dig in to defend against German counterattacks while being reorganized, but Haig did not expect them to bear the brunt of the fighting.

Like Champagne, then, this battle would be won or lost by the artillery. The artillery plan devoted five days to a preparatory bombardment stronger on paper than any yet fired. The first two days of the barrage would be devoted to cutting German barbed wire, while the last three would aim for the destruction of fortified places, trenches, redoubts and observation areas. German communications nodes and artillery batteries were also listed as priority targets. The

The artillery barrage used by the British at the Somme was among the most powerful ever fired. It nevertheless contained too many duds and too little high explosive. As a result, it did not provide the needed support to the infantry.

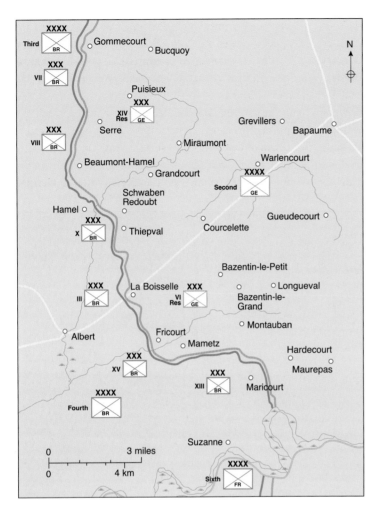

The arrow-straight Roman road from Albert to Bapaume was the central axis of the intended British advance on the Somme. South of the marshy river the French were to advance in order to threaten the German flanks and secure the British advance from German artillery fire.

still intact in most places. Worse still, German defenders were still firing from their machine guns in many parts of their trench networks, a bad omen for the infantry.

The German defenders had suffered terribly from the torrent of artillery the British had fired, but it had still not been strong enough. Haig's hope for a deep penetration of German lines on day one required the gunners to fire shells deep behind German lines, thus diluting the power of the shelling on the front line where it was most badly needed. Moreover, too many of the shells were shrapnel and therefore lacked the power to strike targets deep underground. The British shelling also suffered from a high percentage of duds and faulty fuses.

Final preparations on 30 June, the night before the infantry phase was to begin, revealed that in most sectors the German barbed wire was 'nearly intact and very thick'. Only a few gaps in the wire could be reliably observed, and German machine-gunners could easily cover these. This information, however, was not shared with the troops, most of whom were confident. German artillery had been weaker in the last few days, lulling many British soldiers into believing that their artillery had done its work. As daylight approach on 1 July, Haig remained confident that the tide was about to turn and that his men, their inexperience notwithstanding, were about to win a great victory.

THE FIRST OF JULY

On the night of 30 June/1 July, British troops began to move into their front-line positions. A dark, moonless night concealed their movements and most men were

number of shells available to the British had increased dramatically. Whereas at Loos the British 18-pdr guns (those most responsible for cutting the wire) had had 370,000 shells to fire, on the Somme they had been allotted 2,600,000 shells.

Although Haig would have preferred to wait until later in the summer to complete training before launching the offensive, the bloodletting at Verdun forced him to attack as early as possible. The massive preparatory artillery fire began on 24 June with shells being fired from 1500 guns. Over the five days of shelling the guns fired 1,500,000 shells. British observers reported 57 enemy artillery batteries destroyed, but at the same time, parties of men sent into no man's land reported that the German wire was in place by 5.15am on 1 July. Sappers moved into no man's land to cut the British wire in predetermined areas to allow the attacking troops easy and quick access into the battle area. At 6.30am on a cloudless, beautiful morning the British artillery barrage began to increase in intensity, aiming at known German barbed-wire positions still intact and presumed assembly points of German reserves. The latter were a special concern to British planners because after five days of endless artillery fire, surprise was out of the question. The British therefore needed to find a way to impede the arrival of German reserves. Once again they had turned to the artillery.

At 7.20am, with the British infantry still in their trenches, the British exploded one of the ten mines they had dug underneath German positions on the Somme. This one was under the Hawthorn Ridge near Beaumont Hamel. A British film crew was there to film it, and one of their cameramen left this impression:

'*The ground where I stood gave a mighty convulsion. It rocked and swayed. I gripped hold of my tripod to steady myself. Then for all the world like a gigantic sponge, the earth rose high in the air to the height of hundreds of feet. Higher and higher it rose, and with a horrible grinding roar the earth settles back upon itself, leaving in its place a mountain of smoke.*'

The mine had in fact been detonated eight minutes before the other nine on the insistence of the corps commander in the region. His reasons have never fully been explained. As the debris cleared, British and German troops

began a furious fight for the crater, with the Germans holding the eastern lip and the British the western lip. At 7.28am combat stopped momentarily as the noise and smoke of the other nine explosions rent the morning air.

The mines were expected to eliminate several key points of German resistance and stun surviving German defenders into surrendering. In many places they did so, but they also alerted the Germans to the most likely avenues of the British attack. German

One of the iconic British images of the war, this recruitment poster features the face of Kitchener. The British did not introduce conscription until 1916, preferring instead to rely on volunteerism.

gunners began to fire furiously into the direction of the clouds of white chalk dust thrown up by the mine explosions. Fully alert now to the imminence of the British attack, German soldiers began frantic movements to get their machine guns out from their underground bunkers and site them on the remnants of their parapets. German commanders also began to move reserves into the sectors most likely to be assaulted. A hurried race began between the Germans who were setting up their defences and the British who hoped to move through those defences with only light losses.

The Germans had every advantage in the race. They were holding solid defensive positions and, attacks of the previous days notwithstanding, still had possession of the high ground. British troops, on the other hand, advanced with full packs weighing as much as 32kg (70lb). Not expecting much active resistance, British officers had laden their men down with everything they could carry in the hopes that the extra equipment would help the inexperienced British soldiers withstand any German counterattacks. As a result, they carried with them too much ammunition (220 rounds in some cases), coils of barbed wire, entrenching tools and heavy weapons like machine guns. In some cases they advanced in close-order formations, offering irresistible targets to the surviving German machine-gunners.

Those Germans who had survived the British artillery and had managed to get into place began to fire mercilessly into the slow-moving British. The only protection the British could depend upon was a powerful rolling barrage. Theoretically, it would be an especially accurate barrage because of valuable aerial

A German machine-gun team. Well drilled, the gunner was supported by a spotter, a loader and several ammunition carriers. Teams like these caused significant casualties to the advancing Allied troops on 1 July 1916.

Wilfrid Nevill (1894–1916)

Captain Wilfrid Nevill was a company commander in the East Surrey Regiment on the Somme front. He was known as a daring, hard-charging officer who liked to stand on the parapet and shout insults at the Germans across no man's land. On 1 July he handed out a football to each of his four platoons, promising a prize to the platoon whose ball went the furthest. He himself kicked one of the balls as he left his trench at zero hour. He was killed within 18m (20 yards) and is today buried in Carnoy Military Cemetery not far from where he fell. Remarkably, one of the footballs survived and is in the regimental museum of the Queen's Royal Regiment (West Surrey).

reconnaissance photos taken by the Royal Flying Corps. The slow advance of the British soldiers, however, meant that the barrage rolled away too quickly, thus sacrificing much of its protective power. German soldiers had time to take shelter from the barrage in their deep dugouts, then emerge and position their guns before the British infantry could reach German lines.

The relative quiet of the German guns over the past few days had indeed been part of a German ruse to deceive the British into thinking that their artillery plan had been more effective than in fact it was. The German guns opened up a furious barrage on British soldiers as they crossed no man's land, which in some places was 732m (800 yards) wide. German gunners hit targets up and down the British front with shrapnel, breaking up the dense British formations and causing a great deal of confusion. Hundreds of British soldiers, if not thousands, died on their own parapets, a damning indictment of the failure of the artillery preparation to silence German positions. Many thousands more died without ever seeing an enemy soldier, let alone having the chance to shoot at one with the spare ammunition they carried. Only in a few isolated places did British troops have any success. Even where the British made temporary gains, they rarely had support on their flanks, thus leaving them exposed to deadly enfilading fire. Aware of the danger of his own line being pierced, Falkenhayn had ordered all ground lost to be retaken immediately at any cost. Fresh German reserves poured into threatened sectors, launching local counterattacks against now tired and confused British soldiers.

The tremendous size of the 26km-long (16-mile) battlefield complicated British responses. Unable to see much more than a fraction of the field in front of them, commanders (especially Haig) had to rely on the flurry of phone messages and runners coming at them to try to discern what was happening. These messages often came in too late or they contradicted one another. Commanders often preferred to place more emphasis on the good news, on the theory that much of the bad news was coming from inexperienced and panicky officers. Thus could Haig note in his diary 'Reports up to 8 am most satisfactory. Our troops had everywhere crossed the Enemy's front trenches'. The generals therefore ordered second and third waves to continue the attack, even though they had no chance of success. As late as 11.00am that morning Haig was still reporting that the situation was favourable and that he might be in a position to order the cavalry forward at any moment.

Efforts to reinforce also ran into the complete confusion existing everywhere along the British front. Wounded men in unanticipated numbers were pouring back through the communications trenches, impeding the efforts of reinforcements to get forwards. The sight of so many dead and wounded men (and so few German prisoners) must have been a demoralizing sight for men in their first battle. Thus the British soldiers who had bravely managed to get inside the Schwaben and Leipzig redoubts sat without help, almost entirely cut off from support and communication.

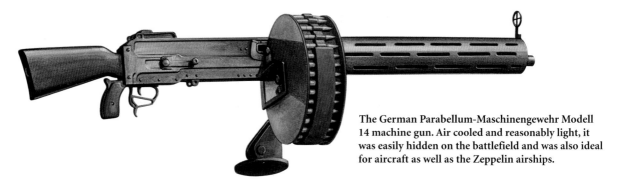

The German Parabellum-Maschinengewehr Modell 14 machine gun. Air cooled and reasonably light, it was easily hidden on the battlefield and was also ideal for aircraft as well as the Zeppelin airships.

The most promising area for the British was also one of the most disappointing. The villages of Fricourt and Mametz sat in a salient that jutted southwest into British lines. It therefore was exposed on three sides to intense British artillery fire. The British also had exceptional observation of German positions there, allowing them to fire an unusually heavy and accurate barrage. Underneath the German lines outside Fricourt the British had managed to tunnel three separate mines. Fricourt also sat close enough to

British troops advancing over a dugout in the Somme trench system. Judging by the leaves on the trees, this photograph was likely taken behind the lines and early on in the campaign.

French lines to allow the more experienced French gunners to add the weight of their shelling. Fricourt seemed to have all the pieces in places, and had therefore been designated as the place where the breakthrough was most likely to occur.

Indeed, British troops succeeded here better than at any other place on the line. They took both the area around Fricourt and the village of Mametz. Several of the divisions in this sector were veteran units, and their experience showed. War poet Siegfried Sassoon was one of the men who helped the British experience unusual success. Heavy casualties dampened the rare good news of British advances in the Fricourt Salient,

which was now a pile of rubble. Overall, British gains were far short of their day-one objectives, even around Fricourt.

The British official history noted with sadness that 'only bullet proof soldiers could have taken Thiepval on this day'. That morose judgment could well stand for the entire British effort on day one at the Somme. Some battalions hardly existed at all by the middle of the afternoon. The 2nd Battalion of the West Yorkshire Regiment and the Tyneside Irish Brigade each took 70 per cent casualties. The 2nd Battalion of the Middlesex Regiment took an astonishing 90 per cent casualties. Because of the tight links these battalions had with individual localities or businesses, the losses were concentrated and became all the more tragic. The British as a whole suffered 60,000 men killed, wounded and missing. More than one in three men listed as a casualty was dead.

South of the Somme, the French attacks had gone well, despite the doubts of the two men most responsible for leading them. Neither Ferdinand Foch nor Marie Emile Fayolle thought that the offensive had much of a chance to achieve the great breakthrough of the German lines that Haig had promised. Foch had even written on one of Joffre's memoranda about the Somme attack, 'An offensive to do what?' Fayolle argued that the offensive had 'no goal' and that even if the Allies did manage to break the line, they still lacked the logistics and manpower to achieve any meaningful exploitation. Still, the two men understood the need to support an ally and, more importantly, to do anything to help the French survive the slaughterhouse of Verdun. The fall of Fort Vaux on 7 June convinced the French high command that the attack had to go forward, no matter what the odds. 'We have', wrote Foch, 'completely succeeded in preventing disaster, but we have done nothing to achieve victory. What would Napoleon say if he saw us buried in our trenches without doing anything?'

Despite Foch's doubts, the French situation had much to recommend it. The German units opposite the French were estimated to be weaker and of lower quality than those opposite the British. Moreover, south of the river the terrain was more favourable; there were no ridges like the Thiepval Ridge and the curving of the line gave French gunners more opportunities for accurate fire. More experienced French soldiers used more sophisticated tactics, with infantry advancing in small groups carefully protected by machine guns. Grenadiers cleared trouble spots and commanders were urged not to take unnecessary risks. French soldiers took all of their day-one objectives, as well as 4000 German prisoners and advanced as far as two kilometres (one and a quarter miles) in many places. Joffre was thrilled, but the slow progress of the British north of the river meant that the French success could not be exploited.

THE JULY BATTLES

Haig ordered the British to continue attacking despite the disasters of the first day. There is some evidence that he did not have a complete picture of how bad British losses had been. He noted in his diary on 2 July that the day was one of 'downs and ups', even as British wounded from the day before still lay in agony in no man's land. The wounded men that Haig visited in field hospitals were, according to his own recollection, 'in wonderful good spirits'. This entry gives an indication that he had little idea of just how badly the offensive had failed thus far. The 2nd was a Sunday and Haig went to church with his staff officers. Afterwards, they attended a meeting with Rawlinson at which Haig ordered

This drawing depicts a seond lieutenant of the Artists' Rifles, a volunteer regiment founded in the 1860s from painters, sculptors, engravers, musicians, architects and actors. By the time of World War I it had become the 28th Battalion London Regiment (Artists' Rifles), and it deployed to France in October 1914, serving throughout the war on the Western Front.

him 'to devote all his energies' to the capture of key points like the village of Fricourt, then to press on to the German second line.

For his part, Joffre demanded that Haig continue the attacks. At a 3 July meeting, Joffre told Haig that he wanted the success of the French followed up and he also continued to argue that the perilous situation at Verdun afforded the Allies no time to rest. At one point, a furious Joffre insisted that Haig order British forces to attack the Thiepval Ridge with no delay. Haig

informed him that he thought the ridge too strong (an indication that he had finally come to realize the seriousness of the situation) and had already decided to shift the weight of the British attack to points south of Thiepval. Joffre exploded with anger telling Haig that he 'could not approve of it'. Haig, who remarked in his diary that Joffre 'cannot argue nor can he read a map', reminded Joffre that the French commander had no authority to direct British strategy. Joffre eventually calmed down and gave way to reality. A change in British strategy was under way.

Attacks in the two weeks following 1 July were largely local efforts, often conducted with inadequate artillery support. In some areas, like the wood near Mametz and the La Boisselle crater, the British made

The enormous mine explosion under the Hawthorn Ridge as captured by British photographers. The mine was fired eight minutes too early for reasons never fully explained. The premature firing of the mine disrupted the timing of the subsequent attack, with devastating results.

significant gains. By 13 July, the British had taken a total of 52 square kilometres (20 square miles) of territory on the Somme, albeit at enormous human cost. The French, too, had continued to advance. They had even broken the German line south of the river along an eight-kilometre (five-mile) front, but there were no reserves available to exploit the success, as most resources had been sent north of the river to help the faltering British. A frustrated Fayolle watched his opportunity slip away. Still, by 12 July the French had taken 12,000 German prisoners and seized more than 70 German artillery pieces. Ironically, the French attacks were working but lacked reserves to exploit them, while the British had the reserves, but had created no gaps through which they could advance. Relations between the British and French staffs improved, but it was increasingly obvious that they had different agendas and visions for the Somme offensive.

Allied gains caused a great deal of consternation among German commanders. Most German casualties in this period (and later in the campaign) occurred as a result of disjointed and unnecessary

> 'July 15th, one of the greatest days in the history of the Somme battles, the British troops broke the German second line at Longueval and the Bazentins, and inflicted great losses upon the enemy.'
>
> Official British war correspondent Philip Gibbs

counterattacks. Falkenhayn continued to insist on immediate counterattacks to regain any ground lost. He even removed the chief of staff of the German Second Army for his decision to straighten out the German line near Herbécourt opposite the French by retreating to more defensible ground. On 3 July, Second Army commander General Fritz von Below issued orders for lost ground 'to be attacked and

Newfoundland

In 1916, Newfoundland was not yet a part of Canada. It was still a formal part of the British Empire and thus its volunteer regiment went to war as part of the British Army's 29th Division, not the Canadian Expeditionary Force. On 1 July, it had the task of taking a position near the village of Beaumont Hamel. In trying to advance to a German position called the Y Ravine it took enormous casualties. After the war, the Newfoundlanders put up a statue of a caribou (because a caribou never leaves the herd) at Beaumont Hamel and another in Newfoundland itself to commemorate their losses at the Somme.

wrested back from the enemy … by means of counterattacks. I forbid the voluntary relinquishment of positions'. He concluded, 'the enemy must be made to pick his way forward over corpses'.

In one sense, the German policy was logically defensible. The loss of any one part of the line could cause a rupture of the entire line. But Falkenhayn's refusal to sanction tactical withdrawals to more defensible terrain cost thousands of German lives. Falkenhayn sent 15 divisions to the Somme out of the German reserve to ensure that the Allies did not break through. The men of these divisions were often hurried into counterattacks and hastily prepared defences that were vulnerable to British and French artillery. The Somme thus became a killing field for the Germans as much as it did for the British.

Under Haig's orders, Rawlinson had begun to prepare for the campaign's second phase. Recognizing the failures of the 1 July attacks, Rawlinson planned an assault that would begin in the last hours of darkness to give the troops protection. Rather than a massive artillery barrage, which the events of the past few days had shown to be wholly insufficient in any case, British gunners would fire only a quick five-minute 'hurricane barrage'. The brevity of the shelling, Rawlinson hoped, would prevent the Germans from

divining British intentions and stop them from moving reserves into threatened sectors. Haig thought the plan too complex for green troops; night operations are notoriously difficult to execute. Still, having no other alternatives and unwilling to pull the plug on the offensive, Haig gave his approval after forcing a few modifications to the original plan.

Rawlinson's plan focused on the area to the south of the arrow-straight road that ran northeast from Albert to Bapaume. Two British corps, XV and XIII, would attack together around the village of Longueval, the converging point of three roads in the region. Longueval also guarded the approaches to the thick forests of High Wood and Delville Wood. The terrain here was favourable to the defender, as the German front line ran along and behind a ridge just south of the village. An abandoned quarry known to the British as the Longueval Alley formed a natural defensive position that would need to be cleared.

On the night of 13/14 July, the British began to assemble more than 22,000 men within a few hundred metres of the German line. The British official history reported 'anxious moments' among brigade commanders as their inexperienced men tried to move in complete silence in order not to give away their attack. Diversionary artillery fire and smoke on other parts of the Somme front helped to disguise British intentions, although there were more anxious moments when British engineers discovered that the Germans had somehow managed to tap into the telephone lines of one of the brigades detailed to attack in the morning.

Still, the Germans seem not to have known and surprise was almost complete. The attack went forward in the dark morning of 14 July, Bastille Day. Artillery began a furious bombardment at 3.20am with the infantry going over the top at 3.25am. Rawlinson hoped to move quickly through the German first line, and then fight through the second as well. Aerial reconnaissance had reported to him the

German reinforcements advancing through a devastated town near the Somme. The Germans had to fight the Somme and Verdun simultaneously, placing tremendous stress on the German system.

existence of a third line of German defences being constructed and Rawlinson wanted to get through it before the Germans could complete it. The hurricane bombardment was astonishing in its intensity, with every foot of German trench being subjected to more than 136kg (300lb) of shelling. Surprise was thus maintained without sacrificing power.

Protected by the darkness and following closely on the heels of the artillery bombardment, several lead British units reached the German wire without even firing a shot. Confused Germans in the front lines surrendered or ran back through their communications trenches. German gunners began a belated counter barrage, but unable to coordinate with their front-line troops, the barrage missed its mark and did little damage to the waves of British troops moving into the German first and second lines.

A British soldier going 'over the top' on the Somme. He is wearing a gas mask to protect him from either enemy gas or his own side's. Gas masks allowed a man to survive, but they severely restricted both breathing and vision; wearing one while fighting was a fatiguing experience.

Marie Emile Fayolle (1852–1928)

Fayolle was on the retired list in 1914, but was soon returned to active duty and given command of a division. He was appalled at the profligate losses of the offensive tactics used in the war's early months. His careful, methodical approach to war led to promotion; by the time of the Somme, he was in command of the French Sixth Army. He argued for slow advances preceded by copious use of artillery. Deriding the British tactics on the Somme as 'infantile' he continued to press for the French to fight a war of *matériel*, not men. Popular with his troops because of his reputation for not sacrificing their lives unnecessarily, he remained one of France's most highly regarded commanders. The publication of his honest, emotional diary (*Cahiers Secrets de la Grande Guerre*) years after the war provided a rare insight into the mind of a general at war.

Organized German resistance collapsed in most places, although in a few key sectors such as the large sugar beet refinery at Waterlot Farm, the British were unable to make much progress. Still, in a few hours, they had captured two lines of enemy trenches and more than 1400 enemy soldiers. The French liaison officer, who had doubted that the New Armies could pull off a night attack, telephoned to the nearby French XX Corps headquarters with the simple message: '*Ils ont osé*; *ils ont réussi*', 'They have dared; they have succeeded'.

The attack was a major success, with Haig calling it 'the best day we have had this war'. Men from the 18th Division cleared a small wood known as Trônes Wood and the 7th Division captured all of its day-one objectives. The British took the tactically important ridge between Longueval and Bazentin and cleared the Longueval Alley of German resistance. The way seemed open for an exploitation of the gains to be conducted by British cavalry. The idea of using cavalry was not as backward as it might first appear. These men were not to charge their horses against German lines, but rather to move in behind German lines after they had been cleared, using their superior speed to attack vulnerable German positions. In many cases, the cavalrymen used their horses to get themselves into a position they could not have reached otherwise, then dismounted and fought as light infantry. In this regard, they have often been compared to paratroopers of later wars.

In this case, the 2nd Indian Cavalry Division was to advance to the German third-line positions in High Wood and patrol north to probe German positions for possible avenues of exploitation. The 1st Cavalry Division would press on to the German third-line positions around Morval, and both would hold until relieved by advancing British infantry. Before the cavalry could be sent forward, however, the British would need to know that German resistance had definitively collapsed. Otherwise, the cavalry would go in against intact German positions and be mown down.

Those opportunities never fully presented themselves. The German defences were stronger and deeper than Rawlinson had suspected. The collapse of several parts of the German second line around Longueval, itself a significant British achievement, did not lead to the collapse of German morale that Rawlinson and others had anticipated. Nevertheless, the British counted the events of 14 July as a great success. Rawlinson attributed the capture of the German first and second lines to the remarkable power and accuracy of the artillery. Unfortunately for Rawlinson and the British, the optimism did not last long. Contrary to all expectations, the Germans were not, as Haig believed, 'very much disorganized and rattled', but were rapidly recovering from the losses of 14 July and their quick reactions made exploitation of the gains of that day impossible.

Nevertheless, the strategic situation on the Somme front had changed in the favour of the Allies. The capture of the Bazentin–Longueval Ridge threatened the Thiepval Salient from its southern shoulder.

French troops advancing south of the Somme River. The French experienced some notable success early on in the campaign but ultimately proved no more able than the British to force the German lines.

British forces also stood poised to make an attack along the Albert–Bapaume Road, the most important in the region. The largest impediment to a further British advance was a square-shaped wood immediately northeast of Longueval called Delville Wood. The British official history described it as 'a thick tangle of trees, chiefly oak and birch, with dense hazel thickets intersected by grassy rides, covering about 156 acres'. From this position the Germans could, in the euphemism of the official history, 'embarrass' any British efforts to move forward. It would need to be eliminated as a German point of resistance before the campaign on the Somme could enter its next phase.

THE DEVIL'S WOOD

Mid-July brought rain and clouds that hampered aerial reconnaissance and artillery spotting. As the skies began to darken, so too did the mood at Haig's and Rawlinson's headquarters. The success of 14 July might have looked good compared to the disaster of 1 July, but much work remained to be done. The bad

The Vickers Mk I machine gun fired the same .303in round as the Lee-Enfield rifle and the lighter Lewis machine gun. The Vickers remained the backbone of the British Army's machine gun corps. It fired 500 rounds per minute and was accurate up to 550m (600 yards).

Schwaben Redoubt

An underground warren of trenches and fortified points on the Thiepval Ridge, the Schwaben Redoubt was one of the strongest German positions on the Western Front. Five hundred and fifty metres (600 yards) long by 183m (200 yards) deep, it was designed to offer fire in all directions. It was big enough to contain a field hospital and a telephone exchange. Ulstermen of the 36th Division temporarily took the redoubt on 1 July, marking one of the great Allied achievements of the day. They could not, however, hold it. Today the graceful Ulster Tower rises up from the area where the redoubt once sat.

weather meant mud and even more logistical problems. Nevertheless, on the morning of 15 July, Rawlinson ordered Delville Wood adjacent to Longueval taken 'at all costs'. The task fell to the South African Brigade, 9th (Scottish) Division, which attacked at 6.15 that morning. They moved through the thick woods, capturing half of it in a daring push that took less than two hours.

Tragically, they could not hold what soon came to be known as the Devil's Wood. The grassy pathways through the woods (called rides) became unusable owing to the heavy shelling that cratered them and sent tree trunks falling in all directions. Thus the South Africans could not easily move men and equipment to parts of the wood where they were most needed. Moreover, the thick groves of trees made it impossible for the men to dig in. Trees also created odd shadows and echoes that made the fighting here particularly eerie. Needless to say, neither the South

Africans nor the Germans opposite them had received any sustained training in fighting in forests.

The Germans counterattacked the wood in the afternoon from the north and east. Three German regiments kept up the pressure through the night and into the day of 16 July. Again and again the South Africans repelled German attacks, but their hold on the wood was becoming more precarious. The Germans crossed the central east-to-west ride of the wood, known to the South Africans as Princess Street, but the South Africans held. On the 17th, British reinforcements attacked along the main north-to-south ride, called The Strand on British maps. German machine guns hidden in the debris of the wood made all attacks futile. On 20 July, the South Africans finally left the Devil's Wood with only 750 men of the brigade's 3150 still in the ranks. Another month of bitter fighting was needed to finally clear the wood of all German resistance. The fighting in Delville Wood resembled another forest engagement at nearby High Wood, where casualties were equally as high.

Rawlinson and Haig kept the pressure up throughout July and into August, but the Germans were now fully on the alert. British artillery pieces were beginning to wear out and ammunition stocks were running low. The difficulty of supplying fresh water to so many soldiers in the full heat of summer also proved to be a limiting factor. A major attack on the night of 22/23 July failed owing to poor artillery preparation and poorer coordination. The offensive seemed to have run its course, but Haig insisted on its continuance.

He and his staff decided in late July to stop pressing around Longueval and try for the low ridge near

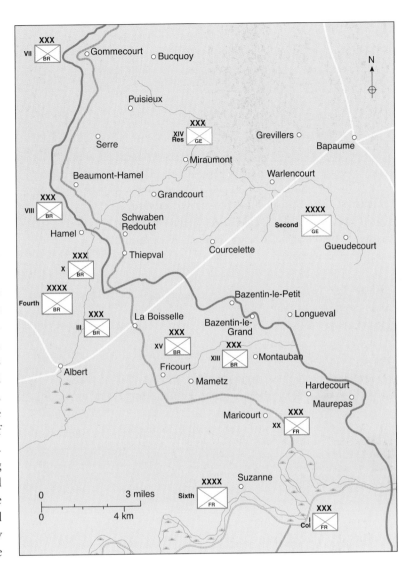

After three weeks of fighting, the British armies on the Somme had still failed to capture many day-one objectives, including the vital Thiepval Ridge. French forces had advanced further, but they, too, had been unable to threaten, let alone break, enemy lines.

Thiepval at the village of Pozières, adjacent to the Albert–Bapaume road. If the British could take Pozières, it might be possible to approach the dominating German positions on the Thiepval Ridge from the southeast, where the German defences were not quite as strong. Repeated attacks on Pozières since 1 July had yet to make much headway, and its

windmill on the top of the ridge (bits of the foundation of which are still visible) had already become an important symbol to men on both sides. In late July, the task of taking the sector fell to the 1st Australian Division, which had arrived on the Western Front after its bloody baptism of fire at Gallipoli.

The Australians developed a solid and detailed plan of attack, with massive artillery barrages hitting the ridge and the village cemetery whose crypts and stone walls offered protection to German machine-gunners. The Australians took much of the village, but had been unable to secure the German positions east of it. They therefore took heavy losses from the German enfilading fire on their right flank. Still, by nightfall on 26 July the Australians had taken almost the entire village except the windmill. The Australians had achieved another of the great feats for which they would justifiably become famous in this war. Haig called the Australian effort 'fine work', but Pozières had been a goal for 1 July. Thus the achievement was somewhat dimmed and its overall importance lessened. The ridges around the village stayed in German hands until 5 August, when the Australians finally secured them. Even then they still had to endure a furious German barrage and a vicious counterattack on 7 August. Having failed to dislodge the Australians, the Germans gave up on Pozières, but more than 23,000 British and Australian soldiers had been killed or wounded trying to take and defend it. In six weeks on the Somme the Australians took as many casualties as they did in eight months of brutal fighting on the Gallipoli Peninsula.

To support British operations, the French decided on another large push in the Somme region. Foch moved a second French corps to the north bank of the marshy river and tried a large-scale attack on 30 July. As had so often been the case, the attack began with some moderate success, as the French had learned to develop much more sophisticated rolling barrage techniques. Morning gains, however, soon led to

A famous image of British troops on the Somme. Soldiers found shelter wherever they could, and the chalky soil of the region allowed for the construction of deep dugouts.

afternoon disappointments, as the Germans counterattacked and the French had to give back the ground they had so bitterly won. They lost 3600 men in one day with very little to show for the suffering except a few top-secret German documents on defensive warfare techniques that later proved to be quite valuable after Joffre ordered them translated and distributed throughout the French Army.

After Pozières, the British staff finally realized that the German line was in no imminent danger of collapsing. Haig issued orders on 2 August refashioning the campaign as a 'wearing-out battle', designed to attrite the Germans to the point where another major push might be possible in the future. He advised commanders to 'practise such economy of men and materiel as will ensure us having the last reserves at our

A British 4.5in howitzer required a crew of ten men. It fired a 16kg (35lb) shell at ranges up to 7000m (7655 yards). They proved to be a reliable and dependable part of the British arsenal. Several thousand were produced.

disposal when the crisis of the fight is reached'. Haig noted that the next chance to win the Somme campaign would likely not occur until the end of September.

At the time Haig wrote his instructions, the British held Delville Wood, Longueval and Pozières, but the German position was still strong. Nevertheless, German general Erich Ludendorff noted that 'hardly a day passed without grave news' from the Somme front. It is thus important to understand that although the Somme badly bloodied the British Army, it also severely damaged the German Army, as encapsulated by the famous remark of a German officer that the Somme was the 'muddy grave' of the German Army on the Western Front. As long as casualties remained roughly equal, however, neither side would benefit unduly from the war of attrition that the campaign had become.

Throughout August the British kept up the pressure, but achieved little of note. Many of these operations were designed as 'line straightening' attacks

Germans receiving mail at the front. Creature comforts like news from home and dry socks were especially important to the morale of men in the trenches. Officers often used their own money or asked for help from home to provide warm clothes, better food, and other extras for their men. Parcels from home were to be shared with one's comrades.

to seize a particularly valuable piece of ground. Joffre and Haig argued about the causes of the failures on the Somme, as did Haig and Rawlinson. A joint Allied attack in mid-August underscored the difficulties of synchronizing the efforts of two armies with different languages, doctrines and military cultures. Both Joffre and Haig jealously guarded their independent command structures, further complicating planning.

The only successes of any meaningful sort in August and early September occurred on the Reserve Army front. Commanded by General Hubert Gough, an inexperienced protégé of Haig's who was quite out of his depth in modern war, the Reserve Army held the front between Thiepval and Pozières. In a month of grinding, slogging war, the men of the Reserve Army

captured the strategic Leipzig Salient at the south end of the Thiepval Ridge and much of the warren of German trenches around it. They also pushed out from Pozières, straightening their line and securing a German trench network known as the Elbow.

But the most important success occurred near a farm 1372m (1500 yards) due east of Thiepval village called Mouquet Farm. Inevitably known as Mucky Farm to the soldiers who had to fight there during the rainy days of August, it lay northeast of the main German lines of defence. Sitting almost equidistant from the villages of Thiepval and Pozières, it was an

The British 4.5in QF (quick firing). howitzer was introduced in 1910 and became one of the most efficient medium howitzers of World War I. They served with the field artillery batteries of the Royal Regiment of Artillery.

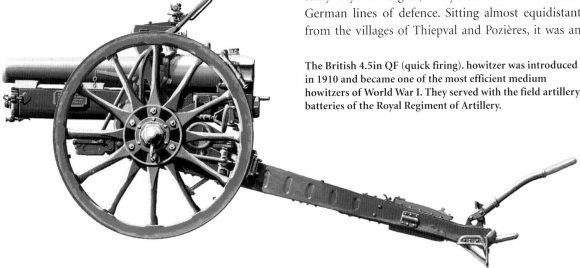

LEFT British troops in the remains of a German trench on the Somme. Entrances to dugouts and machine-gun nests are visible. The Germans made excellent use of even small holes to hide machine guns.

RIGHT A German *Flammenwerfer* or flamethrower team. The weapon was invented in 1901, but first used in 1915. They were primitive and could prove dangerous for their operators, but were effective if conditions were suitable.

enticing jumping-off point for an attack on Thiepval from the rear. Another 1 July objective, its smashed farm buildings still provided the Germans with enough protection to make it a mini fortress in its own right. Large dugouts and subterranean passageways increased its value, as did a trench line around it. By 22 August, the Australians had been able to approach it from the east and on 29 August they tried to take it again with few tangible results.

Gough accused the Australian officers of 'becoming less offensive in spirit', but the charge was manifestly unfair. Like most soldiers on the Somme front, they had begun to have their doubts about the wisdom of the offensive. Had they known that commanders on both sides were treating the battle as one of attrition, with they themselves acting as mere pawns, they would undoubtedly have been more frustrated. Many of them must have guessed it. The Somme was already becoming infamous as one of the most poorly

managed battles of the war. Frederic Manning's masterpiece *Her Privates We* (also called *The Middle Parts of Fortune*) gives an excellent account of what life was like for men on the Somme front.

Critics of Haig became more vocal. Winston Churchill (whom Haig wrote was 'openly very hostile to me') was one of them, as was David Lloyd George, who called Haig a 'dunce'. Critics of Joffre and Foch also began to speak of the need to make changes at the top of the French Army. Haig kept his job, partly because no obvious alternative was available, and partly because of his connections to the royal family, with whom he was invited to maintain a private correspondence. Still, to many observers, including many influential journalists, Allied strategy appeared to be going nowhere and doing so at an enormous human cost.

The Madonna of Albert

Albert was a small town of no particular importance just behind British lines on the Somme. Its main feature was the 70m-high (230ft) steeple of the Basilique Notre Dame de Brébières. Atop the steeple was a gold statue of the Virgin Mary holding the baby Jesus up to the heavens. In 1915 a shell struck the tower, tilting the statue 90 degrees. In its new position, the statue now appeared as if the Virgin were keeping the baby from falling to earth. The statue, visible to Germans, French and British alike, became one of the iconic symbols of the battle and the destruction it brought.

German prisoners being marched away from Thiepval. The ridge was one of the most important features of the Somme battlefield and is today the location of the campaign's largest memorial.

German strategy had its own problems. Falkenhayn's master plan at Verdun had collapsed in the first few days. The crown prince had been lobbying his father to put a stop to the Verdun offensive and reassign or remove Falkenhayn from command. Finally, in late August the Kaiser took his son's advice. He removed Falkenhayn from the Western Front and sent him east to deal with the Romanians, who had entered the war on the Allied side despite close links between the German and Romanian royal houses. The Kaiser wanted someone to make an example of Romania for its betrayal, and Falkenhayn gave him his wish. By the end of the year he had directed a massive, three-front offensive that reduced Romania to a German satellite. The Germans intended to bankrupt the vanquished nation to provide resources to continue the prosecution of a two-front war and to feed German civilians.

In Falkenhayn's place came the team of Paul von Hindenburg and Erich Ludendorff, whose dramatic successes on the Eastern Front seemed to be good omens for solving the frustrations on the Western Front. They were given responsibility for all German strategy and operations on the various fronts in which

Germany was engaged. They also oversaw unprecedented military control of the German economy. Their appointment marked yet another step down the road to total war. They ordered all units on the Somme front to assume a defensive posture and focus as much of their energy as possible on building new lines of trenches. They did not see the Somme as 'German' territory to be defended to the last man as Falkenhayn had. Instead, they wanted to save German lives by making the British attack strong German positions bristling with machine guns and artillery.

Haig was planning another major push on the Somme, with significant French support, to begin around 15 September. Although he must have been aware of how powerful the German defences were, he remained astonishingly optimistic. On 9 September, he told the commander of the British Cavalry Corps that the Germans were worn out and had exhausted their reserves. He advised the cavalry to be ready to exploit gains to be realized in the attack the following week. Although it does not appear that he shared all of his plans with the cavalry at that meeting, he had, he thought, good reason to be optimistic. On 15 September, he was going to unveil on the Somme front a secret weapon that he expected would help turn the tide of the campaign and restore mobility to the battlefield.

The devastation of a wood on the Somme serves as a silent testament to the ferocity of the combat in the region in 1916. The Somme woods were perfect for hiding strongpoints.

CHAPTER 7

The Debut of the Tank

The Somme will always be associated with the great tragedy of its first day, 1 July. But the campaign lasted for months and its last few engagements looked very different from those of July and August. Among the most important innovations was the first appearance of tanks on the battlefield.

The secret weapon Haig hoped to employ on the Somme had been in development for over a year. An engineering officer named Ernest Swinton developed the idea of putting an armoured platform on top of a caterpillar chassis similar to those used on tractors. Such chassis had been used on the Western Front in 1915 to reposition artillery pieces over open ground, but Swinton envisioned a much more aggressive use for them. The army initially showed scant interest in the idea, but Swinton convinced the well-connected Maurice Hankey, then secretary to the Committee on Imperial Defence and to Lloyd George's war cabinet, to pass the idea along to people in high places. Winston Churchill, First Lord of

The Somme featured a number of innovations designed to break the stalemate. The most famous of these was the tank, which first appeared on the Somme during the engagement at Flers-Courcelette in September 1916.

the Admiralty, warmed to the idea immediately and secretly diverted navy funds to enable the original research and development.

THE DEVELOPMENT OF THE LANDSHIP

Churchill hoped to call the new devices 'landships', but neither that naval-inspired name nor the more prosaic name of the first model, the Lincoln Machine No. 1, caught the imagination. Churchill, Swinton and others saw the new weapons as truly revolutionary, being able to cross quickly over open country, crush barbed wire and even move over thin trenches. Armed with machine guns, or in some designs a 15in howitzer, the machines could also provide fire support on the move. Ironically, the principal research on the new weapons was done by the navy, not the army which still showed reluctance. Partly, the navy's interest was a function of Churchill's early and sustained personal attention to the project, but it was

The Mark I tank remained in service, but efforts were soon underway to introduce improvements and modifications. The Mark II, III and IV tanks were all available by late 1917.

also a result of navy experiments in 1914 and 1915 with mobile armoured platforms to protect bases and amphibious landing areas.

By March 1916, a new committee, cryptically named the Tank Supply Committee to deceive any potential spies, had been formed. Although the devices they were to produce and test were still officially called armoured cars and were placed under the authority of the Heavy Branch of the Machine Gun Corps, the code name 'Tank' became the generic name of the new weapons. At first, the British were only willing to devote 28 officers, most of them from engineering units, and 255 enlisted men to training with the tanks. By August, as the campaign on the Somme had to all intents and purposes ground to a halt, the British had a tank prototype nicknamed 'Mother' ready to test in the field. The tanks had also matured into their own corps with a dedicated group of specialist officers and enlisted men.

Desperate for almost anything that could help turn the tide on the Western Front, Haig urged the tanks to be sent to France as soon as possible. The best way to employ them on the battlefield, however, remained a

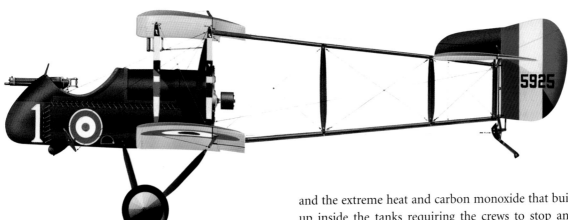

The Airco DH2 came into service in February 1916. It was a light and manoeuvrable plane that could deal effectively with the Fokker Eindecker but was soon outclassed by a new generation of German fighters.

point of debate. Like any new weapons system, the tank came with a lot of unknowns; the uncertainty of the tankers themselves about the field readiness of their weapons did not help to clarify matters. They had requested more time for the training of crews and for solving mechanical problems, but had been denied and sent to the front in late August. Rawlinson favoured introducing the tanks as part of another night operation, using them to blow open holes in the German lines, then withdraw at dawn in favour of the cavalry. Their secrecy could then be maintained, although under this scheme their role on the battlefield would also be limited.

Haig disagreed, arguing that the appearance of the tanks in broad daylight might be the factor that finally broke what he still believed was a wavering German morale. He wanted the tanks used 'on bolder lines' than those envisioned by Rawlinson and warned Rawlinson that the tankers themselves did not think that the new weapons would do well at night. Haig hoped to use the tanks as the central part of a battle plan to open holes for the infantry and cavalry to exploit in a massive daylight operation. Tanks themselves could not be used in an exploitation role, owing both to their slow speed (theoretically six kilometres per hour (3.7mph), but field tests had shown three kilometres per hour (two miles per hour) to be more realistic), steering problems

and the extreme heat and carbon monoxide that built up inside the tanks requiring the crews to stop and breathe fresh air. Many tankers passed out inside their machines from a combination of the heat, the noxious fumes and the rigours of trying to operate the clumsy machines in battle.

Rawlinson's revised plan for the tanks called for them to be used in place of a rolling barrage. He hoped that the tanks could advance with the infantry, correcting the accuracy of their fire as they moved. Advancing together, the tanks might also be able to hit targets of opportunity that a pre-planned rolling barrage could not. On the other hand, using tanks in

The Mark I Tank

The Mark I tank came in two versions, the male and the female. Both models required a crew of one officer and eight enlisted men. The male weighed 28 tonnes (31 tons) and was 10m (32ft) long. At more than two metres (seven feet) tall and carrying four Hotchkiss machine guns, it could shoot over parapets and into trenches. It boasted a six-cylinder, 105 horsepower engine that could achieve speeds in excess of a whopping six kilometres per hour (three and a half miles per hour). Its 174-litre (46-gallon) petrol tank, however, limited its range to just 37km (23 miles) before it needed to be refuelled. In addition to the machine guns, it carried two 6-pdr light artillery guns. The female version was one ton lighter and carried two extra machine guns instead of the light artillery pieces.

place of a rolling barrage meant sacrificing a known (if imperfect) method of protecting infantry for an entirely unknown method. Rawlinson watched a tank demonstration behind the lines on 2 September and came away decidedly unimpressed with both the machines and the skill level of their crews, an impression he shared with both Haig and Lloyd George, who was then visiting the Western Front.

Haig, working from bad intelligence given to him by over-eager staff officers, continued to believe that the Germans were ready to break. His chief of intelligence, Brigadier-General John Charteris, was far too young for the job (he was 38, and one of the army's youngest generals) and even Haig's wife had her doubts about him. Charteris regularly gave Haig the numbers and advice he knew his commander wanted to hear. These figures often clashed with the more cautious numbers provided by the War Office in London. Haig always gave Charteris the benefit of the doubt, in part because he deeply mistrusted the judgment of the War Office's Director of Military Intelligence, the shy and intelligent George Macdonogh, because he had converted to Roman Catholicism. On the Somme front in early September, Charteris told Haig that all indications suggested an imminent collapse of German morale. This belief informed every decision Haig made in the crucial weeks of late August and early September. These decisions included amassing the largest number of horses ever on the Western Front to exploit the anticipated German collapse with the utmost vigour.

The tanks were, in Haig's eyes, a modern way to start a traditional battle. Artillery having largely failed so far in the campaign to do the job of clearing the first line of German trenches, the tanks would do it. Rolling barrages would only be used in areas where there were no tanks available. Haig, often criticized as a Luddite, was more optimistic about the value of the tanks than was Rawlinson, and was reluctant to agree

British infantry pose with a Mark I tank. Troops were grateful for the fire support and protection tanks provided, but coordinating armour with infantry, artillery and aviation proved to be quite a challenge in the chaotic conditions of battle.

Ernest Swinton (1868–1951)

Born in India and a veteran of the Boer War, Swinton had been an observer at the 1904–05 Russo-Japanese War where he saw the stasis of trench warfare at first hand. Kitchener sent him and several other officers to France in 1914 to act as his eyes and ears on the Western Front. He came back to London in 1915 to serve as secretary to the Dardanelles Committee, where he floated his ideas about armoured warfare to several influential figures. He dreamed big and wanted to spring the new weapons on the Germans after they had been perfected and amassed in large numbers with new tactics developed to support them. In February 1916, he became commander of the Tank Detachment and urged Haig in vain not to use tanks on the Somme because he did not think they were yet ready to be a war-winning weapon.

Swinton's post-war career included a stint as a director at Citroën and a time as Chichele Professor of Military History at Oxford.

even to the rolling barrages in the non-tank sectors. He therefore urged that tanks be used on the Somme as a fundamental part of the plan (primarily for their psychological value) even over the objections of most of his senior advisers.

Haig was under pressure to turn the Somme fiasco into a major success before winter. He had convinced himself that the French had given up on their commitments to fight a meaningful battle on the Somme. 'The fact is', he wrote, 'that the French infantry is very poor now and lacks the offensive spirit.' He was certain that the French had only made their gains against second-rate German soldiers 'very much inferior in physique' and poorly supported by the weakest German artillery pieces. Haig concluded from such evidence that it was up to the British to win the war. His offensive on the Somme was the best chance to achieve victory, breaking through the German lines and turning north to attack the Germans near Ypres.

Rawlinson's final plan called for 59 tanks to be assembled in 'penny packets' with two British corps getting 18 tanks each, one corps receiving 12 tanks,

and the Canadian Corps receiving just six. As a result, some divisions were allotted as few as two tanks. The plan spread armour support widely (and thinly) in order to give the most number of British troops possible some protection. In doing so, though, the plan also sacrificed the full striking power of the tanks that might have been realized by massing them together at some critical point. It also left no tank reserves to replace those that experienced mechanical failure or were put out of action by enemy fire. The former was a real concern, as ten tanks could not even be brought to the battlefront owing to breakdowns before the battle, but the British largely dismissed the latter, expecting German troops to flee in fear at the mere sight of the tanks.

The attack targeted the region east of the Albert–Bapaume road from Pozières to Ginchy. The final objectives were the village of Courcelette, which sat on the road itself, as well as the villages of Martinpuich and Flers. Past this line, the Germans only had rudimentary trench systems and the ground flattened, becoming more favourable to the employment of cavalry. Martinpuich was especially well defended by some of the strongest German trenches in the region. The offensive was also expected to achieve the final clearing of High Wood between Martinpuich and Flers.

FLERS-COURCELETTE

From the air, the British attack on 15 September would have had a zebra-stripe pattern against the background of the now completely devastated farmland of the region. Where rolling barrages were used, powerful artillery shells threw up big clouds of white dust from the chalky soil of the Somme. British gunners fired more than 800,000 shells at German positions, making the barrage less intense than the artillery fire that preceded the attack of 14 July, but impressive all the same. In those areas where the tanks advanced, appropriately called 'dark lanes', black smoke from the exhaust of the tank engines would have been clearly visible from the air.

The performance of the tanks on 15 September was uneven at best. Only nine of the 48 that saw action on that day remained in service for the entire day. The rest experienced mechanical failures or were disabled

by German gunners, several of whom quickly learned how to use field artillery pieces against their exposed tracks. In most cases, the tanks failed to provide the kind of fire support expected of them. In a few places, they might have been of great utility. The British broke

> 'It is impossible to revive the extraordinary thrill and amazement, the hilarious exultation with which these things [tanks] were first seen on the fields of the Somme. It had been a secret, marvellously hidden.'
>
> Philip Gibbs, a British reporter

open a hole in the defences of Martinpuich even though none of their tanks were able to come forward and provide fire support. The tanks might have made an important contribution in exploiting the success by suppressing fire on the flanks of the advance.

In a few places, the tanks did perform as expected. Most famously, a British tank advanced right down the main street of Flers while three others advanced to the east of the village. German forces ran from the village in the direction of Gueudecourt. One German machine gun in the town held up a battalion of East Surreys, but a tank came up and destroyed it. British soldiers enjoyed the rare treat of walking into a Somme village at a leisurely pace without significant opposition. A later news report boasted, 'a tank is walking up the High Street of Flers with the British Army cheering behind'. In another case, a tank nicknamed 'Crème de Menthe' supported a Canadian advance by destroying German positions near Courcelette's sugar beet refinery.

Tanks provided an illusion of security, but they were very dangerous. This tanker's helmet is designed to protect the wearer from shell debris, although it must surely have exacerbated the heat inside a tank. Toxic fumes were a special danger for tankers.

For the most part, though, the tanks had been unable to keep up with the infantry. They had steering problems in broken country, especially when moving over the heavily cratered no man's land of the Somme. Owing to the hasty testing and relentless driving, many tanks were in need of spare parts even before the offensive began. Fuel and oil for these large monsters had to be brought forward by the infantry, often on foot, as no adequate supply arrangements had been made. Thus when they ran out of petrol, they often stopped for good. They could still be used as stationary fire platforms, but they were sitting ducks for German field gunners.

The attack of 15 September offered evidence for both optimists and pessimists. Using armoured support in some areas, the British had gained a 4115 by 2286m (4500 by 2500 yard) patch of territory, including many German third-line positions. Most of the day's objectives had been taken, including the strong German positions inside High Wood. The tanks had been of no use in the woods, but infantry

supported by trench mortars had advanced and captured a position that had been a goal of British officers since the start of the campaign. In all the British had taken twice the territory that they had seized on 1 July at about half the human cost.

The most obvious piece of bad news was that Haig's assessment of German morale had been wrong. Despite the loss of their last line of defences in many places, the Germans did not panic and their lines did not collapse. Even where they had to evacuate in a hurry, as in Flers, they recovered and established new lines of defence. Because of what Haig called 'the disorder and mixing up of units' typical of all armies, but endemic to the inexperienced British, attacks for the next morning had to be cancelled. Local success therefore could not be pursued. He was disappointed at the failure of a supporting French offensive, but thought that the events of 15 September showed that the Germans were weakening. He ordered the offensive renewed as quickly as possible, but the moment to exploit the surprise of the tanks had been lost. The Germans had bent but had not broken.

The French offensive had been designed as a diversion to give the British relief from German reinforcements. It was only to go forward with 'la plus grande activité' if German lines actually broke. When they did not, the French continued their diversions as they reorganized for another attack later in the month. On 18 September, French forces attacked without artillery support, surprising the German defenders and taking the village of Bouchavesnes north of Péronne, cutting off a main German supply route in the process. It was the easternmost advance of Allied forces during the entire campaign, but it was designed solely to support British efforts further north, not as a breakthrough of its own.

Its obvious limitations notwithstanding, Haig was a convert to the potential of the tank. He wanted larger models, as big as 69 tonnes (68 tons), with stronger

Oswald Boelcke, author of the *Dikta Boelcke*, the first rules for air combat. During the Somme offensive the British had control of the air, allowing aircraft to spot for their artillery. Boelcke was killed after colliding with one of his squadron's Albatros D.IIs during a dogfight on 28 October 1916.

armour to withstand German field artillery fire. He called Swinton to his headquarters on 17 September and told him that the tanks had 'fully justified themselves' and had saved British lives. Swinton, however, was thinking that the British Army needed larger numbers of smaller and more mobile tanks capable of keeping pace with the infantry, not the monsters Haig proposed. Two days later, Haig sent a staff officer to London to demand the production of 1000 more tanks. Rawlinson was less optimistic, arguing that the tanks were not yet reliable enough to depend on them in battle or to modify British doctrine around them.

Thus, a glimpse of the future of warfare had been seen on the Somme. In September 1916, however, it remained far from clear how the new way of war would help the British win the campaign. As the days grew shorter, moreover, the need to win the Somme campaign became more acute. The pressure on Haig kept mounting when Lloyd George appeared at Foch's headquarters to ask why French forces had advanced further at lower costs than had British forces. He also asked Foch for his opinion of the senior British generals. Foch, who had a healthy distrust of politicians of all nationalities, refused to give him a straight answer, but did report the conversation to a furious Haig. Whether the news provided him with additional motivation or not, Haig planned another attack on the Somme against an enemy that he still believed to be worn out and ready to crack.

THE FRENCH COUNTERATTACKS AT VERDUN

As the successful French capture of Bouchavesnes demonstrates, the French had not given up on the Somme. They had, however, definitely subordinated it

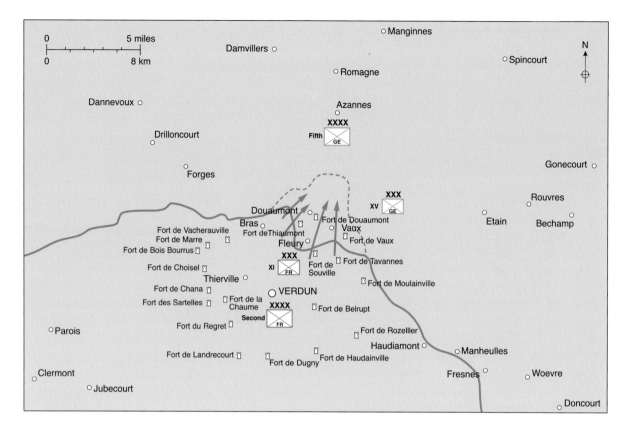

to the situation at Verdun. After taking Fort Vaux, the Germans aimed for the French line of defences from Thiaumont to Souville. The latter fort served as the forward tactical command post for the French at Verdun and its loss would greatly impair the communications the French so desperately needed. In between the two strongpoints sat the village of Fleury, which had been pounded into rubble by the incessant shelling of both sides. Running southeast from Souville to the Fort of Tavannes sat a 1400m (1531-yard) tunnel that the French used to store munitions and protect men from German artillery fire. Control of the line from Thiaumont to Tavannes would give the Germans the last solid defensive line before the city of Verdun and allow their gunners to target the bridges over the Meuse. Without those lines of support, Verdun would have little choice but to surrender at long last.

On 22 June, just days before the massive British shelling on the Somme began, the Germans saturated the Thiaumont–Souville line with artillery. The next

French counterattacks focused on the recovery of high ground and fortifications previously lost to the Germans. At the end of the battle, the lines were almost exactly where they had been 10 months earlier.

day they attacked with infantry and introduced a newer, more powerful form of phosgene gas called Green Cross that contained cloropircin, a powerful and sometimes lethal form of tear gas. It had been specifically designed to pass through the gas masks taken from French prisoners early in the campaign. The gas killed rats and flies (for which many German and even French infantrymen were grateful), and turned leaves black. Horses suffered especially badly. Green Cross was designed to incapacitate French gunners on the right bank of the Meuse, especially the heavy gunners in Fort Moulainville hidden in the woods southeast of Tavannes.

German forces overran Thiaumont and reached an unusual underground command bunker at Froidterre known as the Four Chimneys after its four ventilation pipes. The complex contained an underground hospital and a munitions storage dump. Unable to get inside, German soldiers threw grenades down the chimney pipes and ordered more Green Cross gas fired at the vicinity. The heavy gas seeped down into the bunker and the French soldiers underground who had no gas masks died horrid deaths. Just when it seemed as though the French would have to give up the position, the Germans withdrew late in the day. Although they seemed on the verge of a breakthrough, the Germans had called off the attack.

The decision to stop the 23 June offensive came as a great relief to the French, who were beginning to fear that they would lose Verdun. Pétain had informed Castelnau that it might become necessary to evacuate

the right bank of the Meuse if the Germans kept up the pressure for much longer. A quick evacuation would yield to the Germans one-third of the French artillery pieces in the Verdun sector, a calamity whose seriousness did not escape either Pétain or Castelnau. Pétain was considering the very evacuation of the right bank that he had been brought in to avoid during the battle's first days in February.

The Germans had come close to success, but had ultimately failed. German gas had actually done its job too well, sinking so deep that most French soldiers

Using new artillery methods and aggressive infantry tactics, the French Army began to counterattack at Verdun in June. These attacks helps to keep pressure on the Germans throughout the simultaneous Somme campaign.

could climb out of ravines or on to their fire steps until it dissipated. The gas sank deep into the forts and *ouvrages*, but left the gunners in the upper turrets unharmed. Men like the poor unfortunates caught at Froidterre with no masks and no high ground suffered terribly, but most Frenchmen survived the gas attack. The French reported 1500 gas casualties that day, most of whom eventually returned to battle.

More importantly, as had so often been the case in the war thus far, the Germans had too few reserves on hand to exploit success. Those men that did attack suffered terribly from thirst in the summer heat, as no water could be brought forward to them. German losses in June were as high as French losses. The start

French troops getting a welcome ride to work. By the middle of the war, Allied developments in industry and mechanization had begun to give Allied armies important advantages. Control of sea lanes gave them relatively unhindered supplies of oil as well.

of the Somme offensive on 1 July put further pressure on German reserves, as did the collapse of the Austro-Hungarian front in the face of the Brusilov Offensive. Soon the Germans were down to just one fresh reserve division on the Western Front.

The Germans felt confident enough in their repulse of the 1 July attack on the Somme to try once more at Verdun. On 11 July, German troops attacked in the direction of the eastern end of the Tavannes Tunnel and made another rush on Fort Souville. The crown prince's headquarters tried to halt the attack at the last minute because of inadequate artillery support, but it was too late. The attack went ahead with only minimal gains and enormous casualties. The Germans reached a crossroads near the ruins of the Chapelle de Sainte-Fine near Fleury. That village changed hands 15 times in three weeks of combat; evidence of the ferocity of the combat there is still visible today in the ruins and the chewed-up earth of Fleury's remains. Although no

one knew it at the time, these small gains marked the closest that the Germans came to Verdun. Today the emotional Wounded Lion of Souville monument commemorates the spot of their high-water mark.

THE RISE OF NIVELLE
The battle might have cooled off at this point, but the French determined to counterattack and recover their losses. The weakness of the German 11 July attacks, combined with the major accomplishments the French anticipated on the Somme, led a new generation of officers to develop battle plans for the recapture of forts Douaumont and Vaux. By then, Pétain had been promoted to commander of Army Group Centre, allowing him to exert even greater control over the Verdun flanks and the management of resources in the sector. At the same time, however, the promotion reduced his influence over the tactics and operations around Verdun itself, in part because

A German soldier takes aim in a posed photograph in a rudimentary trench. Even exposing oneself as this soldier has would have been nearly suicidal in an active combat sector. Note also that his steel helmet is on the ground and he is wearing his soft cap only.

Joffre thought that Pétain had been too cautious in his counterattacks.

In Pétain's place as commander of the French Second Army came Robert Nivelle, a general no one could accuse of being too cautious in counterattacks. Nivelle was a rarity in the French Army in 1916. He was a Protestant with a half-Italian father and an English mother. He held firmly to the prewar French belief in the offensive at all costs, and had retained an optimism that many politicians found refreshing. Many of his fellow officers doubted his intellect and his understanding of all of the intricacies of modern warfare, but even his critics recognized him as one of the best artillerists in the army. He had been at the forefront in the development of the rolling barrage and several sophisticated techniques for neutralizing German artillery batteries.

On 9 August, Nivelle appealed to Pétain for more reinforcements. He planned to give many of them to the 5th and 37th infantry divisions under the command of another disciple of the offensive, Charles Mangin. Nicknamed 'the Butcher', Mangin had been a member of the 1898 Fashoda expedition under Marchand. After a tour in Tonkin, he went back to West Africa where he developed the idea of using Senegalese troops to form a *force noire* that could compensate for France's small population relative to Germany. He had risen to high rank by 1916 by conducting costly, but often-successful offensives that he sometimes led himself. The Butcher lost a lot of men, but his offensives were always daring and always carefully prepared. Churchill called him 'the anvil of Verdun' and 'the fiercest fighter in France'.

The Lafayette Escadrille

In March 1915 two American pilots who had being serving as volunteers with the French Air Service formed the Lafayette Escadrille. With money from wealthy donors and the enthusiastic support of famous Americans like former president Theodore Roosevelt, the squadron became celebrated both for its playboy lifestyle and its impressive combat record. The men of the Lafayette Escadrille volunteered to fight on the Verdun front, where they helped the French maintain air superiority in the late summer and autumn. Three of its members were killed in action at Verdun. On American entry into the war, its members were distributed across the United States Army Air Service to help train new pilots.

Hindenburg and Ludendorff's decision to halt offensive operations at Verdun in early September gave Nivelle and Mangin time to organize their line and find replacements for the men and guns they had lost. In the middle of the month Joffre came to Verdun and approved their plan to resume the offensive as soon as the attack could be organized. He had already lost faith in the British attempt to break the lines at the Somme and was willing to reinforce the Verdun sector with his few remaining artillery pieces and fresh divisions if he thought they could be used in an offensive manner. Nivelle and Mangin hardly needed to be encouraged any further. Both men were itching for the chance that Joffre had just given them.

The plan Nivelle and Mangin had developed was minute in its preparation and in many ways quite novel. The Germans having been forced to stretch their resources to defend the Somme, French

Raoul Lufbrey was one of the most celebrated members of the famed Lafayette Escadrille, a group of volunteer pilots who flew for France. Unlike Lufbrey, most of them were Americans who had enlisted in the French Foreign Legion. Upon America's entry into the war, the squadron was broken up and its pilots sent to help train arriving American aviators.

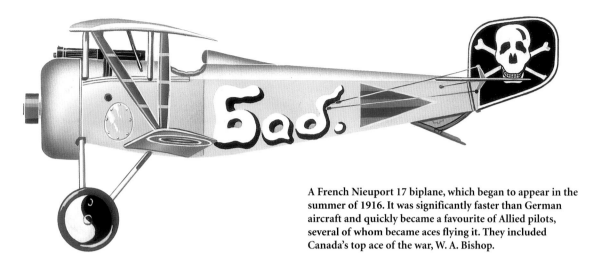

A French Nieuport 17 biplane, which began to appear in the summer of 1916. It was significantly faster than German aircraft and quickly became a favourite of Allied pilots, several of whom became aces flying it. They included Canada's top ace of the war, W. A. Bishop.

commanders knew that they would have their first real superiority in artillery and aviation of the entire campaign. French aviators, flying in formations, cleared the skies of German planes, giving the French the badly needed ability to move men and supplies unobserved. At the same time, French aviators tried to minutely photograph every square metre of the German line, locating German artillery batteries and scouting new lines of German defences.

On 22 October, the French began a standard preparatory barrage. They then fired the rolling barrage that the Germans had come to expect as the signal of the start of an infantry assault. When the French guns began to fire, German soldiers fired flares to indicate the anticipated avenues of French approach. When they did, German artillery batteries began to fire a barrage into no man's land to do as much damage as possible to the French attack. Thus far it was all a more or less typical battle of this war, but the German barrage did not kill a single Frenchman in no man's land, because the French had never left their trenches.

The Germans had fallen for an ingenious trap Nivelle had set for them. Instead of sending French troops into a curtain of German fire, he had sent his aviators aloft to spot the flashes of the hidden German guns, which were now firing furiously and in vain. French pilots then reported the positions of 158 German batteries to French heavy gunners who used

their 155mm guns to fire thick and powerful barrages of their own. In two days, French gunners destroyed 68 German batteries and did significant damage to dozens more. Many other German gunners saved their equipment by moving it out of range of the French guns, which effectively rendered the batteries useless. Consequently, when French soldiers went over the top for real on 24 October, they did so against much lighter German artillery resistance. When surviving

'Douaumont is ours. The formidable Douaumont, which dominates with its mass, its observation points, the two shores of the Meuse, is again French.'

An anonymous French staff officer

German pieces did fire, French aviators were often able to report their locations for the 155mm batteries to target and destroy.

Nivelle then began the next phase of his artillery plan, aimed at ending all German resistance in forts Douaumont and Vaux. Against the former alone France had concentrated dozens of guns, including two 270mm guns, two 280mm guns, one 370mm gun and two 400mm pieces. The latter were the most powerful guns the French fired in the entire course of the war and were so heavy that they could only be moved by rail. They fired one-tonne (one-ton) shells that travelled 8000m (8749 yards) in the air before descending at a speed of more than 120kph (75mph). This astonishing artillery park would be trained on Fort Douaumont, once designed to withstand a powerful German artillery barrage, but ironically now to be the victim of the most powerful French barrage ever fired. In all the French fired 855,000 shells between 20 and 27 October, a remarkable industrial achievement for a nation that had lost its most valuable iron and coal fields to the German invasion.

From 21 to 23 October, 73 heavy artillery shells and 170 370mm mortar rounds hit Fort Douaumont, tearing through the concrete roof of the fort and killing dozens of its German defenders. Hundreds of shells hit the German trenches around the fort, and gas shells fired around the fort's perimeter inflicted

André Maginot (1877–1932)

Emile Driant was not the only veteran of Verdun who had been a member of the Chamber of Deputies. André Maginot was a representative from the Verdun area who passed up a chance to be an officer and instead enlisted, being wounded in action in 1914. Unable to return to the front, he went back to his seat in Parliament. He came away impressed by how well the French fortifications around Verdun had withstood the year of artillery pounding they had taken. After the war, he supported the construction of a modern line of forts designed to buy France time to mobilize its allies and resources. A memorial to him near Souville strikes the modern visitor as odd, but stands as a tribute to him and his service to France.

German soldiers conduct a local counterattack at Verdun. Small uncoordinated attacks proved to be very costly in terms of casualties but often served to keep enemy operations off balance.

greater casualties on the fleeing defenders. The barrage also prevented the Germans from sending reinforcements into the fort. French pilots lost 20 airplanes that day, but they took photographs of the damage to the fort and the nearby trenches, which were quickly developed at darkrooms near the airfields and rushed forward with such efficiency that Mangin was able to hold the photos in his hands at his command post inside Fort Souville when he gave his men their final orders before they went over the top.

Mangin's infantry had been specially prepared for this attack. They included his beloved Senegalese and a contingent of Moroccans. On 24 October, they began their attack, moving behind a deft rolling barrage that took account of the contours of the ground and the training of the infantry. Regiments and companies also featured the new system of organization Nivelle had introduced to his Second Army. French units now featured a mix of riflemen, grenadiers and light machine-gunners to provide a variety of options to the attackers.

In a rare example of a battle that went to plan, French infantry actually moved through holes torn open by the artillery. The artillery had in fact conquered. Now the infantry had only to occupy. By the end of the day, they had redeemed the loss of Douaumont, entering the fort and taking control of it. Even in its dilapidated and beaten state, it was a powerful position and a moving symbol. The French had moved the line three kilometres (two miles), retaking the majority of the terrain the Germans had seized since February in a single afternoon. Every single objective sat in French hands. French troops walked back into the *ouvrage* at Thiaumont without even firing a shot. On 2 November, the French intercepted a German radio message indicating that the garrison at Fort Vaux intended to leave because it could no longer withstand the power of French artillery. French infantry retook the fort the next day, also without firing a shot.

Key
- Neutral countries
- Entente Powers
- Central Powers
- Annexed to Germany
- German controlled economic zone

The unbounded ambitions of the Kreuznach Programme to strengthen Germany's frontiers forced German strategists to think only in terms of a total victory. They therefore ruled out any discussions of offering the Allies a compromise peace based on the return of some occupied territory.

Colonel Driant and his men had met the first wave of the German attack on Verdun.

The recapture of the forts was the most dramatic French accomplishment since the victory at the Marne more than two years earlier. Nivelle received the lion's share of the credit for the dramatic success and became an instant hero across France. He seemed to have found a winning formula to overcome the bloody challenges of the Western Front. In contrast to Joffre, moreover, he was cheerful and charming. Whereas Joffre had tense relations with politicians, Nivelle welcomed them to his headquarters where he happily answered their questions and showed them generous hospitality. Also in contrast to Joffre, he understood British culture and spoke perfect English, legacies from his mother. Even though Pétain, Foch and others continued to have serious doubts about him, he was clearly the rising star of the French Army.

In mid-December, the French Government decided that it had had enough of Joffre. They soothed his firing by promoting him to marshal of France (the first such promotion since the days of Napoleon III) and in the spring sent him off to the United States on a triumphal speaking tour. There he met with senior American military officials to give them his sense of the Western Front and what the Americans needed to do to prepare to fight there. The French Government

The French steeled themselves for German counterattacks, but they did not materialize. With the weather starting to turn colder and cloudier, the Germans had decided to lay low until winter and then regroup. The French took advantage of German inactivity, conducting a series of careful attacks, all limited in their goals and supported by masses of artillery. By 15 December, the line had extended to an arc around the towns of Louvemont and Bezonvaux, only a few hundred metres south of the Bois des Caures where, ten months earlier, Lieutenant-

passed over Pétain and Foch and named Nivelle as the new commander of the French Army. Foch, too, was a victim of the command shake-up, being sent off on a series of meaningless assignments before being dispatched to Italy. France would turn to a new team and new ideas in 1917.

THE FINAL PUSH ON THE SOMME

French politicians were not the only ones who were impressed with Nivelle. Many British politicians, including Lloyd George, began to look quite favourably on him as well. His attacks at Verdun had produced real results at acceptable costs while Haig's on the Somme continued to grind away with many first-week objectives still in German hands. The failure of the tanks to make a difference on 15 September only seemed to underscore in the minds of critics the

The ossuary and cemetery at Verdun. Built from 1920 to 1932 on the former site of the town of Douaumont, the 46m (150-foot) tower stands over the scattered remains of 130,000 Germans and Frenchmen with no known grave.

Memorials at Verdun

Among the many notable memorials at Verdun is the ossuary at Douaumont, completed in 1932. Through the dark glass on the ground level, one can see the scattered bones of more than 130,000 French and German soldiers who died on the battlefields of Verdun but were never identified. Outside the ossuary sit the crosses, Stars of David and Muslim headstones of 15,000 French dead. Legend has it that Pétain was to have been buried where the flagpole now stands, but plans were changed after the ignominy of the Vichy years. Inside the monument is a long gallery with 18 alcoves representing the parts of the battlefield from which bones were recovered. Atop the 46m (150-foot) tower sit a lantern and a bell. Remnants of several *ouvrages* remain within easy walking distance of the ossuary.

bankruptcy of British strategy and operations on the Somme. So, too, did the introduction of new aircraft by the Germans in early September that were clearly superior to British models. Experienced pilots like Oswald Boelcke and the 'Red Baron', Manfred von Richthofen, used their new planes to reassert German mastery over the skies of the Somme.

Haig still remained convinced that 'the German reserves were now almost exhausted' and that 'the time was approaching' for another hard strike. As he wrote in his diary on 24 September, 'The enemy has no reserves now, so the situation is different as to what it was at the beginning of the battle.' He ordered the capture of the Thiepval Ridge, from which the British could advance to the east using the Albert–Bapaume road, ideally with support from tanks. He also ordered a number of local supporting actions to capture ground of significant tactical value and to prepare the British line for the next stage of operations.

A small-scale attack by elements of the British Fourth Army in conjunction with the French on 25 September produced some limited gains and gave Haig some reasons for optimism. Unable to count on the tanks, the British went back to a standard artillery preparation with the tanks in reserve. The artillery barrage was unusually heavy and was followed by one of the British Army's best rolling barrages of the war. Working in conjunction with the French to their right, the Allies took the villages of Gueudecourt, Lesboeufs, Morval and Combles. It was an impressive tactical achievement, with a British cavalry patrol taking Gueudecourt in a daring raid as the Germans were beginning to pull out. Still, the British had been unable

to pursue and the local gains failed to result in anything more meaningful. The tanks never joined the fight because of mechanical problems.

At the same time, the British made a new effort against the Thiepval Ridge from the direction of Mouquet Farm. The task fell to the confident and careful General Ivor Maxse and his 18th (Eastern) Division, a New Army formation that he had raised and trained. It had been one of the few large units to advance to all of its objectives on 1 July and it had quickly developed a reputation for excellence. Its task on 26 September was formidable. From Courcelette and Mouquet Farm the ground rose gently but significantly. The Germans had defended this area as well as any in the region, with a series of strong trenches and three solid redoubts. The most important of them, the Schwaben Redoubt, sat at the

Inter-allied planning proved a great challenge. Here British Field Marshal Douglas Haig and French politician Aristide Briand confer over a map. They symbolize the differences between men of different nations as well as the differences between the 'frocks' (politicians) and 'brass hats' (generals) that often transcended national borders.

German prisoners from the Battle of Beaumont Hamel. The Newfoundland Regiment had failed to capture the position on the first day of the offensive. In November, Scotsmen of the 51st (Highland) Division took it, as commemorated by the famous 'Jock on a Rock' memorial.

highest point just north of the smashed ruins of what had once been the village of Thiepval. These German positions were too numerous and solid to be eliminated by either a preparatory barrage or a rolling barrage. The fight for them would be difficult.

The British assaulted the village of Thiepval, a day-one objective, from the south, clearing it in bitter combat. Instead of charging forwards to the Schwaben Redoubt, Maxse stopped to reorganize his scattered units and bring up supporting artillery. The division also had the use of four tanks, which cleared German positions in the ruins of Thiepval's château. British

forces attacked the redoubt again on 28 September and captured parts of it in hand-to-hand fighting, although they did not completely clear its northern sections of German resistance until mid-October. The so-called Battle of the Thiepval Ridge had lasted four days and had finally resulted in British control of the crest of the ridge.

It did not, however, lead to the pursuit Haig had envisioned. Although the British had captured more than 13 square kilometres (five square miles) of territory in four days (equal to all of their gains from 1 July to 14 September), the Germans still controlled important trenches on the reverse slope of the ridge. More than 12,000 British soldiers had been wounded or killed to take the ridge, although by most estimates German losses were as high, if not higher. Haig concluded that the British were figuring out the right

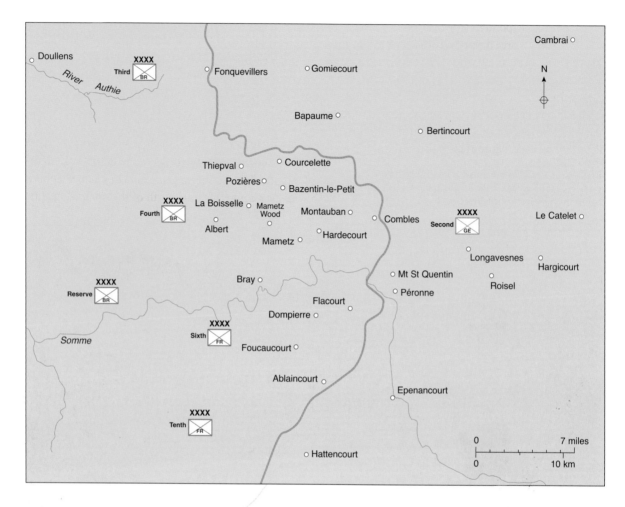

Map showing the minimal Allied gains on the Somme. The battle, which was supposed to rupture German lines, instead became a 'wearing out' battle of attrition that wore out both sides at tremendous human cost. Casualties were higher on both sides than they were at Verdun.

methods for fighting large battles and that the Germans would crack if he kept up the pressure. He ordered further offensives for October that would advance northeast along the axis of the Albert–Bapaume road, then turn east, crossing the Canal du Nord and moving into the flatter area around Cambrai, where he still hoped to employ cavalry and armour.

These were ambitious goals, to say the least. German troops were surely tired, but so were British troops. Aerial reconnaissance reported that the Germans had built as many as three more solid lines of defence on small ridges that would afford them good observation. They had also developed an armour-piercing bullet capable of firing through the skins of British tanks. Finally, the generally clear and cool weather of September (which had only two days of significant rainfall) gave way to much colder and wetter weather in October. The rains turned the roads and fields into muddy bogs, which both hindered supply and reduced the power of artillery. Rain also made it extremely difficult to employ tanks or use aircraft for observation. The poor weather did, however, give the British some much needed respite from German aircraft.

These problems notwithstanding, Haig went ahead with his plans. He knew that he had to work quickly, as all indications pointed to much more wet weather ahead. The first three days of October were reasonably dry and resulted in what Haig considered 'highly satisfactory' results, notably the capture of another fortified village, Eaucourt L'Abbaye, and pressure on the next line of German trenches. But the following days saw heavy rainfall and diminishing British accomplishments. More rain meant that the chances

British troops atop the strategic Thiepval Ridge. Although it was a goal for day one of the attack, it did not fall into British hands in its entirety until October.

for a breakthrough led by the cavalry were growing smaller every day. The rain became so bad that the delivery of ammunition, food and potable water became a serious problem. As a result, British attacks became smaller and more piecemeal, producing ever smaller gains at heavy costs.

THE BATTLE OF THE ANCRE
The Somme drama had one more act, known as the Battle of the Ancre. Haig and Gough planned another major assault, this time north of the Albert–Bapaume

road. The region had seen little fighting since 1 July, when the British had detonated the Hawthorn mine and the Newfoundlanders had charged at Beaumont Hamel with heavy losses. The shift to this sector was occasioned in part by the better road network, which could more easily supply British units across the muddy terrain. British forces here looked directly at a

British soldiers moving ammunition near the end of the Somme campaign. Much of the heavy labour of war fighting had to be done at night in order to avoid being targeted by enemy aircraft and snipers.

number of positions that were supposed to have fallen on 1 July, but remained in German possession. In November they would try to redeem their failures of four months earlier. Heavy artillery began on 10 November during a brief respite from the rain. There is some evidence to suggest that British commanders were unenthusiastic about the attack, but had been pushed by Haig to achieve a major success before a high-level Allied conference at Chantilly, scheduled to start on 15 November. Even Haig himself showed some doubts, telling Gough that 'nothing was so costly

Sir Julian Byng (pointing with whip) commanded the Canadian Corps at the Somme. He is shown here pointing out features of the battlefield from the Thiepval Ridge to King George V.

as a failure', but he also told Gough that a significant British victory (defined as an advance of 914m (1000 yards) and the capture of 3000 German prisoners) would strengthen his hand at the conference vis-à-vis the French.

The infantry went over the top on 13 November, just two days before the conference was to start. The mud and rain rendered the rolling barrage ineffective, even though there were more guns on the Ancre front on this day than there had been in the entire Somme sector on 1 July. In some places the British registered notable gains. The Scots of the 51st (Highland) Division achieved the goal of taking Beaumont Hamel

by 10.45am. Gough also filled Haig's order for prisoners and even exceeded it, as British forces captured more than 7000 Germans. But British casualties had been high as well and British forces stopped well short of their objectives. Several officers began openly to question the wisdom of the attacks.

Haig at first suggested that the battle could continue throughout the winter, when colder weather would freeze the ground and thereby ease the transportation problem. But the weather continued to be wet and it was increasingly obvious that the British Army was exhausted. The Germans were as well, with Ludendorff particularly concerned by the British ability to catch the defenders of Beaumont Hamel by surprise. The Germans had lost 45,000 men on the Somme front in November, on top of their heavy losses at Verdun in October. They therefore welcomed the poor weather and the chance to use the winter of 1916–17 to recover and lay out a new strategy.

Casualty figures for these two campaigns remain a subject of intense debate. Even Haig thought that Charteris's estimate of 680,000 German casualties on the Somme was too high, although some historians still accept Haig's revised estimate of German losses

At Joffre's Chantilly headquarters in December 1915 the Allied commanders agreed to attack the Central Powers with simultaneous offensives in the summer 1916. Germany's massive offensive at Verdun disrupted that planning.

Key
- Neutral countries
- Entente Powers
- Central Powers

on the Somme of 600,000 men. A recent analysis of German sources sets German casualties for the Somme in the period 1 July to 31 October 1916 at 82,000 men killed, 109,000 missing and 347,000 wounded in action. The high number of missing is a function of the power of artillery, which often obliterated bodies so badly that identification was impossible. If one accepts these figures, the German losses at the Somme amount to 538,000 men. The most reliable studies of British casualties estimate that the British lost 150,000 men killed (including the missing), and 100,000 too badly wounded to return to action. Total casualties are estimated in the British official history at 419,654. Add to that figure the estimated 204,253 French casualties on the Somme, and total Allied losses amount to 623,907.

Two conclusions can be reached from these figures. First, more than one million men were killed, wounded or captured to move the lines a few largely insignificant miles. By the end of 1916 the Allies held no decisive ground that would justify the high losses of the year. Second, because Allied casualties had been higher than German casualties, the strategy of attrition had manifestly failed to work. The Somme had surely worn down the Germans, but it had been a brutal campaign for the British and the French as well. To be sure, the British Army learned many valuable lessons in how to fight modern battles, but these lessons came at a staggering price.

The losses at Verdun need to be added to the losses of the Somme in order to gain a full picture of how bloody 1916 had been on the Western Front. German losses at

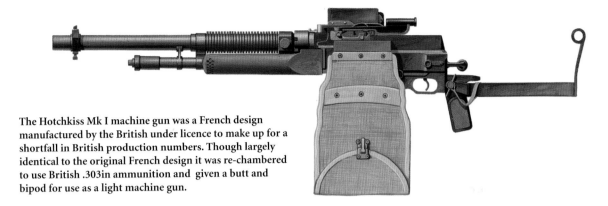

The Hotchkiss Mk I machine gun was a French design manufactured by the British under licence to make up for a shortfall in British production numbers. Though largely identical to the original French design it was re-chambered to use British .303in ammunition and given a butt and bipod for use as a light machine gun.

Verdun are estimated at 73,000 men killed, 50,000 missing or prisoners and 305,000 wounded, for a total of 428,000 casualties. French losses are estimated at 186,000 dead (including the missing), 31,000 prisoners and 318,000 wounded, for a total of 535,000 casualties. The prisoners of war included a young French officer named Charles de Gaulle, who was left for dead on the battlefield but later entered a German prisoner of war camp, from which he made five unsuccessful escape attempts.

Verdun and the Somme had been longer, nastier and bloodier than any other campaigns in European history. They also offered men little rest from the horrors of the battlefield. The battlefields of 1916 had presented an unprecedented array of new weapons and new dangers. Aeroplanes strafed men from above while tanks advanced against them on the ground and mines blew up underneath them. Little wonder, then, that men began to show signs of the psychological malady soon to become known as shell shock. These two battlefields had been unlike any others in history.

Verdun and the Somme had both been designed as major campaigns to win the war in 1916. Both had failed to achieve their aims. The Germans responded by using the winter to build a line of super trenches called the Siegfried or Hindenburg Line. They featured steel and concrete pillboxes, interlocking fields of fire, miles of barbed wire and prepared positions for reserves who could move in to fill gaps or conduct counterattacks. The line ran more or less straight from Vimy Ridge to Reims, taking advantage of the terrain and in the process yielding the very

Somme territory that had been so bitterly contested for four gruelling months. Thus could the British Army safely walk into the remains of positions that had so defied their earlier efforts.

For their part, the Allies knew that they had no choice but to attack in 1917. The reality of the German occupation of France remained, as did the need to help out a staggering Russia. With Joffre gone and Haig under increased pressure, the strategic direction of those offensives would come from the 'man of the hour', Robert Nivelle. It would be up to him to take the methods he had seemingly perfected at Verdun and apply them across the Western Front to bring victory to the Allies.

Memorials at the Somme

There are 11 British cemeteries and more than 30 official memorials on the Somme. The largest and most famous is the giant Thiepval Memorial, designed by Sir Edward Lutyens and inaugurated in 1932. It contains the names of the 75,000 citizens of the British Empire who died here with no known grave. They are the 'Missing of the Somme'. The largest British war memorial in the world, its open design is supposed to evoke the sense of loss and emptiness that the tragedy of 1 July created. Adjacent is an Anglo-French cemetery that symbolizes the Allied nature of the battle here, while the largest German cemetery is at Fricourt.

FURTHER READING

Blond, G., *The Marne: the Battle that Saved Paris and Changed the Course of the First World War* (London, Prion, 2002)

Chickering, R., *Imperial Germany and the Great War, 1914–1918* (second edition, Cambridge, Cambridge University Press, 2005)

Doughty, R., *Pyrrhic Victory: French Strategy and Operations in the Great War* (Cambridge, MA, Harvard University Press, 2005)

Ellis, J., *Eye Deep in Hell: Trench Warfare in World War I* (Baltimore, John Hopkins University Press, 1989)

Foley, R.T., *German Strategy and the Path to Verdun: Erich von Falkenhayn and the Development of Attrition, 1870–1916* (Cambridge, Cambridge University Press, 2005)

Herwig, H., *The First World War: Germany and Austria-Hungary* (London, Edward Arnold, 1997)

Hull, I.V., *Absolute Destruction: Military Culture and the Practices of War in Imperial Germany* (Ithaca, Cornell University Press, 2005)

Mombauer, A., *Helmuth von Moltke and the Origins of the First World War* (Cambridge, Cambridge University Press, 2001)

Neiberg, M.S., *Fighting the Great War: a Global History* (Cambridge, MA, Harvard University Press, 2005)
—— *Foch: Supreme Allied Commander in the Great War* (Dulles, Potomac Books, 2003)

Sheffield, G., *Leadership in the Trenches: Officer–Man Relations, Morale, and Discipline in the British Army in the Era of the First World War* (New York, St Martin's Press, 2000)
—— *The Somme* (London, Cassell, 2003)

Simkins, P., *Kitchener's Army: the Raising of the New Armies, 1914–1916* (Manchester, Manchester University Press, 1988)

Smith, L.V., Stéphane Audoin-Rouzeau, and Annette Becker, *France and the Great War* (Cambridge, Cambridge University Press, 2003)

Wiest, A., *Haig: Evolution of a Commander* (Dulles, Potomac Books, 2005)

INDEX

Subheadings are arranged in alphabetical order. Page numbers in *italic* denote illustrations. Page numbers in **bold** denote information boxes.

PICTURE CREDITS

Art-Tech/Aerospace: 29, 30, 42(bottom), 47, 53, 84, 105, 188, 190, 194, 216

Art-Tech/MARS: 22, 24, 41, 88, 89, 143, 152, 163, 192

Cody Images: 12, 33, 44, 56, 57, 62(top), 65, 69, 74, 96, 97, 101, 102, 106, 107, 112, 117, 134(bottom), 138, 145, 155, 160(bottom), 164, 166(bottom), 169, 171, 176, 180(top), 186, 191, 196, 215

Corbis: 144

Mary Evans Picture Library: 1, 6, 10, 14, 21, 23, 35, 51(top), 66, 67, 70, 80, 85, 86, 104, 111, 123, 147(bottom), 184

E. W. W. Fowler: 28, 79, 93, 131, 217

Getty Images: 73, 198, 199

Getty Images/Popperfoto: 18, 173, 213

Greatwardifferent.com: 132

Library of Congress: 16, 36, 61, 124, 157, 180(bottom), 206

Bertil Olofsson/Krigsarkivet: 20, 31, 37, 77, 120, 121, 172, 187(top), 189, 205

Photos 12: 64, 76, 108, 151, 159, 201, 203, 204, 208, 211

Photos.com: 15, 17, 32, 42(top), 87, 134(top), 166(top)

Suddeutsche Zeitung: 26, 48, 52, 54, 59, 60, 72, 95, 98, 100, 129, 136, 140, 141, 146, 148, 156, 160(top), 161, 174(bottom), 178, 181, 200, 209, 212

TopFoto: 113, 114, 116, 119, 125, 128

US Department of Defense: 8

Artworks

Art-Tech/Aerospace: 38, 62(bottom), 71, 83, 91, 115, 127, 139, 147(top) 187(bottom) 195, 207

Art-Tech/John Batchelor: 110, 133, 174(top), 175, 182, 219

Art-Tech/De Agostini: 51(bottom), 58, 99, 158, 167

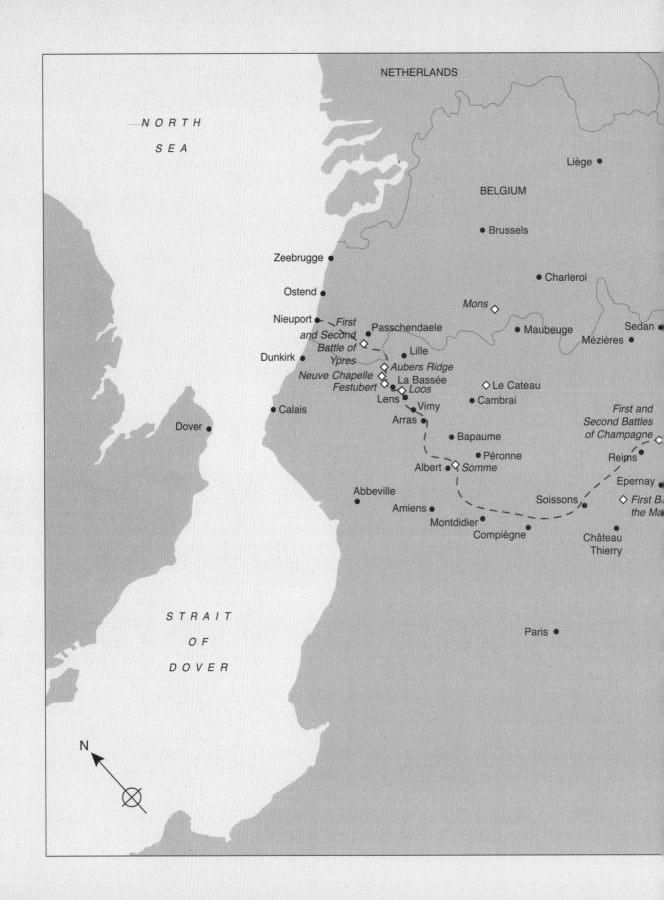